Providence and the Problem of Evil

Richard Swinburne

CLARENDON PRESS · OXFORD

1998

OXFORD
UNIVERSITY PRESS

Great Clarendon Street, Oxford OX2 6DP

Oxford University Press is a department of the University of Oxford.
It furthers the University's objective of excellence in research, scholarship,
and education by publishing worldwide in

Oxford New York

Auckland Cape Town Dar es Salaam Hong Kong Karachi
Kuala Lumpur Madrid Melbourne Mexico City Nairobi
New Delhi Shanghai Taipei Toronto
With offices in
Argentina Austria Brazil Chile Czech Republic France Greece
Guatemala Hungary Italy Japan South Korea Poland Portugal
Singapore Switzerland Thailand Turkey Ukraine Vietnam

ISBN 978-0-19-823798-3

Printed in the United Kingdom by
Lightning Source UK Ltd., Milton Keynes

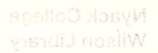

Acknowledgements

I have discussed the topic of this book in many lectures and classes in many universities over many years, and I am very grateful to all those whose comments have forced me to abandon certain lines of argument and encouraged me to develop others. I have given several graduate classes at Oxford in which I have used earlier versions of all this material; and most recently I have had the benefit of reactions to it of a graduate class at St Louis University. I am especially grateful to Eleonore Stump, to Sarah Coakley, and to two referees for the Oxford University Press, both for detailed criticisms and for very general reactions to some of my moral assumptions. I owe very considerable thanks also to various secretaries who have typed and retyped versions of this book over the years, and among them especially to Mrs Fiona Snyckers and Mrs Rosemary Clayton.

Some of my material has been published in various earlier forms. Two and a half chapters of *The Existence of God* (Clarendon Press, 1979; rev. edn. 1991) were concerned with theodicy, and I am grateful to the Oxford University Press for permission to reuse some of that (in a much changed form). I am grateful to the editors and publishers of four more recent papers for permission to reprint material which has some recognizable connection with chapters of this book: 'Knowledge from Experience and the Problem of Evil', in W. J. Abraham and S. Holtzer (eds.), *The Rationality of Religious Belief* (Clarendon Press, 1987); 'Does Theism Need a Theodicy?', *Canadian Journal of Philosophy*, 18 (1988), 287–312; 'Theodicy, our Well-Being, and God's Rights', *International Journal for the Philosophy of Religion* (Kluwer Academic Publishers), 38 (1995), 77–93; and 'Some Major Strands of Theodicy', in D. Howard-Snyder (ed.), *The Evidential Argument from Evil* (Indiana University Press, 1996).

Contents

Introduction

The Universe with its billions of galaxies, each with billions of stars, many of them probably orbited by the smaller and colder bodies which we call 'planets', has been expanding rapidly for the last fifteen billion years. The 'Big Bang', which began this period of the Universe's history, may have been the beginning of the Universe itself, or the Universe may have had an earlier history—possibly one without beginning. For the last three billion or so years there have been animals on the planet Earth, and more recently humans. Maybe there are animate beings on other planets too, but of them we have as yet no knowledge. The traditional theist, who believes that there is a God who is all-powerful and perfectly good, believes that God created and sustains all this, for supremely good purposes. Some of these good purposes, he believes, have already been realized or are now being realized. But most traditional theists, and among them Christian theists, believe that other good purposes are yet to be realized in this Universe or in another one; and that what is happening in the Universe now is a necessary step towards the realization of these other purposes. These good purposes include the perfecting of this Universe in all its aspects and the worship of God in the life of Heaven by those humans who have freely chosen that sort of life. The world is thus, according to Christian theism, the object of God's providential care—he foresees and meets the needs of his creatures. Some of the good purposes of God concern all creatures or all humans, and these are the concern of what is called his general providence; others concern particular individuals—he has a certain good purpose for me and another one for you—and these are the concern of what is called his special providence.

Such is the Christian doctrine (and that of many other forms of theism). But if God has these supremely good purposes for the future, why the delay? Why cannot we have their benefits now? And notoriously the world contains much suffering and other evil which it would seem that God would (in virtue of his perfect goodness) have sought to prevent, and (in virtue of being all-powerful) would have been able to prevent. The theist maintains that God (who can do anything logically possible, that is anything the description of which does not involve a contradiction) could not achieve some of his good purposes except by means of a delay before they are achieved, and these and other good purposes except by means of allowing evil to occur. In this book I shall expound and justify this view, especially in the form which it has taken in Christian theology.

I begin by arguing in Part I that, at any rate in the West in our modern world, most theists need a theodicy, an account of reasons why God might allow evil to occur. Without a theodicy, evil counts against the existence of God. I shall then consider in Part II what are some of the purposes which an all-good God might have for the Universe; and point out that Christian doctrines (of varying degrees of centrality to the Christian tradition) teach that many of them (and especially the most important ones) are indeed God's purposes. I shall point out that so many of these good purposes have been, or—if the Christian revelation is true—will be realized in the world. I shall go on, however, to list the various evils which the Universe contains. I shall then argue in Part III that some of the good states cannot be achieved without delay and suffering, and that the evil of this world is indeed necessary for the achievement of these good purposes. I go on to argue in Part IV that God has the right to allow such evils to occur, so long as the goods are facilitated and the evils are limited and compensated in the way that various other Christian doctrines (of human free will, life after death, the end of the world, etc.) affirm. And I shall conclude by claiming that the good states which (according to Christian doctrine) God seeks are so good that they outweigh the accompanying evils.

Theodicy, the defensive element of this book, is territory on which I have ventured before—two and a half chapters of *The Existence of God*[1] were concerned with it. But, while continuing to endorse the general approach of that book, I have come to believe subsequently that theodicy is a considerably more difficult enterprise than I represented it there. This is because there are so many diverse goods and evils, and they have intricate logical connections with each other: you cannot have certain goods without certain evils, unless you bring about other goods as well which would bring

---

[1] Rev. edn. (Clarendon Press, 1991).

about certain evils, which could be avoided but only at the cost of other evils, etc. I assumed in that book that theodicy does not need to bring in doctrines peculiar to different religions (such as rein-carnation in Eastern religions; or life after death in a new world etc. in Christianity), in order to show that the occurrence of evil does not count against the existence of God. I am not fully convinced about that any more. In any case most other contemporary humans are a lot more likely to be convinced if theodicy does bring in such doctrines. So this book invokes relevant Christian doctrines, such as those mentioned above, which make claims about what God has done and will do.

I seek to show how the whole Christian doctrinal package taken together—the claim that there is a God together with the claim that he has done and will do certain things for his creatures—faces the difficulty of delay and suffering on the way to the good things God plans for us. I shall not be producing positive arguments for the truth of these other Christian doctrines; although I shall occasion-ally point out with respect to some of them that they are compatible with our secular knowledge of how the world works and of what is morally good or bad. Positive argument must come largely from revelation. In so far as there is evidence that God through Christ founded a church as the vehicle of revelation, and that church has taught these other doctrines, that is the positive evidence that these doctrines are true. Some of these doctrines are very central to the Christian tradition, such that if you believe that there are any doctrines revealed by God through Christ's church, you will have to believe these ones. Others, I shall note, are more peripheral: you could believe that God gave the church the authority to teach doctrines, without believing that these doctrines are included; more consideration of how to determine what are the exact boundaries of revelation would be needed. So evidence that God through Christ founded a church as the vehicle of revelation is less strong evidence for these doctrines. There is no space to discuss the evidence for revelation here;[2] I seek only to explore the conse-quences of supposing certain doctrines to be true, for the central doctrine which is the concern of this book—the doctrine of Providence.[3]

[2] For discussion of what would be evidence for a Christian revelation, see my *Revelation* (Clarendon Press, 1992), esp. pts. 2 and 3.
[3] Any evidence (received by a revelation or in any other way) of the truth of some

Of course a particularly Christian doctrine of Providence is itself a central Christian doctrine, and any evidence for the revelation through Christ is evidence in its favour. But in view of the obvious initial objections to it, I seek to explore how with the aid of other Christian doctrines (not subject to initial objections of the same kind) the doctrine of Providence can be defended against those objections, when given its specifically Christian form. *Providence and the Problem of Evil* is the last of four books in which I have been examining the philosophical issues involved in certain Christian doctrines.

If the only goods in the world were thrills of pleasure and the only bad things stabs of pain, then it would be easy for God to make a good world with nothing bad in it. And if there was any pain at all—if just one human felt the slightest toothache—that would be conclusive evidence against the existence of God. But in fact, I shall be claiming, the good of individual humans (and in so far as they are capable thereof, the good of animals) consists (as well as in their having thrills of pleasure) in their having free will to choose between good and evil, the ability to develop their own characters and those of their fellows, to show courage and loyalty, to love, to be of use, to contemplate beauty and discover truth—and if there is a God it consists above all in voluntary service and adoration of him in the company of one's fellows, for ever and ever. All that, I shall be arguing, cannot be achieved without quite a bit of suffering on the way.

This book will only convince fully those readers who come to accept many of the moral views advocated in Part II about which actions and states of affairs are good, and the views about just how good are such actions and states of affairs advocated in the final chapter of Part IV. I hope that many readers, if they do not already

specific doctrines of some religion rival to Christianity could also be evidence in favour of a doctrine of Providence (though not the Christian doctrine) enabling it to rebut an atheistic objection from the fact of evil. One doctrine which is denied by Christianity but affirmed by Hinduism and Buddhism, and would be of assistance in this connection, is the doctrine of Pre-existence. Hinduism and Buddhism teach that souls become reincarnate in different bodies in the next life, according to their behaviour in this—good behaviour leads to a higher life, bad behaviour to a lower one. Present-day humans are supposed to have had a long series of previous lives. Hence their suffering in this life could be explained as a punishment for misdeeds in the last one. This defence is not now open to orthodox Christianity—though a few early theologians, including one of the greatest, Origen, held it—see Origen, *De Principiis* 1. 8. 4.

share those views, will come to accept them in the light of my arguments. But I am very well aware that some of them are views very different from those taken for granted in the moral climate prevalent today in the Western world; and many readers may react instinctively against them, sometimes with hostility. I understand that reaction—part of me shares it. But I believe that the views which I have expressed are true, and are implicit in many of the moral judgements which even today's Westerners make; and I have tried to draw out the implications. I am well aware, however, that a radical change of moral stance often requires much reflection on what is good and bad about many situations, real and imaginary, more than there is space to set out here; and often some harsh experiences as well. But I hope that readers who do not yet come to share those moral views will come to recognize that a satisfactory theodicy can be constructed, if those moral views are accepted— and that the grounds for accepting those moral views are very largely independent of theology.

I can easily understand many deeply sensitive people reacting with horror at the very attempt to show that a loving God could allow humans and animals to suffer, let alone suffer some of the horrible things that happen on Earth. But this book constitutes a plea to such people, whose sensitivities I deeply respect, to ask themselves just what in detail love might amount to in an all-powerful being who brings all creatures into being out of nothing, concerned to be generous—not just to already existing humans for the short space of an earthly life, but to many possible kinds of creatures for unending time—and generous with the best and deepest of gifts. I suggest that long reflection on this will make it less and less obvious that some significant suffering for the very short period of an earthly life is ruled out.

I
The Problem of Evil

I

The Need for Theodicy

My soul is weary of my life; I will give free course to my complaint; I will speak in the bitterness of my soul. I will say unto God, Do not condemn me; Show me wherefore thou contendest with me. Is it good unto thee that thou shouldest oppress, that thou shouldest despise the work of thine hands, And shine upon the counsel of the wicked?

(Job 10: 1–3)

The Problem of Evil

I understand by 'God' a being who is essentially eternal, omnipotent, omniscient, creator and sustainer of the Universe, and perfectly good.[1] An omnipotent being is one who can do anything logically possible, anything, that is, the description of which does not involve a contradiction: such a being could not make me exist and not exist at the same instant, but he could eliminate the stars or cover the Earth with water just like that. An omniscient being is one who knows everything logically possible for him to know, anything the description of his knowing which does not involve a contradiction. He would know everything that has happened, everything that is happening or could happen. But, in my view (to be explored more fully in Chapter 7) he will not necessarily know everything that will happen unless it is already predetermined that it will happen. For there is a logical inconsistency in supposing that any being knows necessarily what is yet to happen when that has yet to be determined (i.e. when it is not already fixed by its causes). But if the omniscient being is God and so also omnipotent, it will be through

[1] See Additional Note 1.

his own choice that there is anything not already predetermined and so that there is any limit to his knowledge.

I shall henceforward normally contrast the 'good' with the 'bad' rather than with the 'evil', both when talking about the actions of agents and their characters, and also when talking more generally about states of affairs—though an agent of very bad actions and character is appropriately called evil. 'States of affairs' is a term which I use in the widest sense to include the things that happen to people as well as the intentional actions they perform. Pains and other suffering are bad states of affairs, but it is odd to call them evil (as I did in the Introduction), even if some agent causing them or allowing them to occur would be doing an evil act. Although the problem with which we are concerned is called 'the problem of evil' (and so those words form part of the title of this book) it is really the problem of the existence of bad states of affairs, such that (it is claimed) it would be bad for an agent who could prevent them to allow them to occur. But though I shall contrast good states with bad states as such, in deference to the terminology in which our concerns are discussed, I shall, when I come to discuss bad states in detail in Part III and need to distinguish them into two groups, subdivide them in the traditional way into 'moral evils' and 'natural evils' (using the term 'evil' only when preceded implicitly or explicitly by the relevant adjective).

I understand 'moral evil' as including all bad states caused deliberately by humans doing what they believe to be bad, and especially wrong (or allowed to occur by humans negligently failing to do what they believe to be good, and especially what they believe to be obligatory) *and* also the bad states constituted by such deliberate actions or negligent failure. It includes the pain I deliberately inflict on you, the pain of the disease which I negligently allow you to contract by allowing you to come into contact with an animal of mine who suffers from it, and the bad state of my deliberate infliction or negligent omission. There is also moral evil constituted by humans doing what they believe to be bad where no suffering results, e.g. telling a lie, breaking a promise, or attempting to inflict suffering without success. (Doing something bad which the agent does not believe to be bad counts, on my definition, as natural evil.) I understand by 'natural evil' all bad states not thus deliberately produced by human beings, or through negligence allowed by human beings to occur. Natural evil thus includes all the trail of suffering which disease and accidents unpreventable by man bring in their train. It also includes the bad desires with which we find ourselves: the temptations to take more than our fair share of the world's goods, to lie and deceive for the sake of our reputation. Among natural and moral evils are the sufferings of non-human sentient beings, of which the only ones known to us are the higher animals.

While the adjective 'moral' in front of the word 'evil' thus distinguishes a certain kind of bad state from others, there is a wider sense in which all the 'good' and 'bad' states with which we are concerned in this book are ones which are morally good or bad. In this wider sense (which will always be the one used, except where the adjective 'moral' precedes the word 'evil') the 'moral' is the 'overall' or 'overriding'. A morally good act is one which is overall a good act. It might be bad from the point of view of aesthetics or etiquette that I should support a project for building cheap housing or speak to someone to whom I had not been introduced, but if it is overall a good act, then it is morally good. The morally best act for me to do is the one which is overall the best act, the one whose goodness overrides that of the goodness of other acts. Among (morally) good acts are obligations—to keep promises or not to wound someone; but there are good acts which go beyond obligation—to give money needed to feed me at a proper level, in order to feed someone else at a proper level, for example. A morally bad act is one which is overall bad; and among such acts are ones which are wrong, i.e. obligatory not to do. A wrong act which wrongs God is a sin. I shall use a 'right action' in the same sense as a 'good action'. (I contrast a 'right action' with someone having 'a right' to do some action, which is to be understood as saying that it is morally justified or permissible, i.e. not wrong, to do the action.) I shall mean by saying of some state of affairs that it is morally good, that it is good (on balance, overall) that it occur; and by saying that it is morally bad, that it is bad overall that it occur. Natural evils are thus morally bad states. I apologize for this double usage of 'moral': it is alas current in the philosophical literature, and it will, I think, be less confusing to the reader to stick with it (having made clear when 'moral' is being used in one sense rather than another) than to introduce totally new terminology.

When I write (as in the last paragraph) of 'good', 'bad', etc. acts, my concern—unless I specify otherwise—is with objectively good,

bad, etc. acts. An act is objectively good (bad) if it is good (bad) in
its nature or consequences, apart from what the agent believes
about it. But an act may have a nature or consequence of which the
agent is ignorant. An act is subjectively good (bad) if its agent
believes that it is good (bad) in nature or consequences. The subjective goodness of an agent is a matter of the subjective character
of his actions. A subjectively perfectly good agent will do many
subjectively good acts and no subjectively bad acts. Such an agent
notoriously may do many acts with many bad consequences,
unforeseen by him but foreseeable by more knowledgeable agents.
However, if the agent is also omniscient, he will know all the consequences of his actions which it is logically possible for him to
know. But unless it is already predetermined what consequences
some action will have, he will still not (in my view—to be explored
more fully in Chapter 7) know incorrigibly what consequences that
action will have. He will, however, know what consequences that
action is naturally likely to have, the extent of the (indeterministic)
bias in nature towards certain consequences rather than others.[2] I
shall in future understand the objective goodness of an action more
precisely than on my previous definition: as the goodness it has in
virtue of the objective features of the world at the time it is performed. Its goodness in respect of its consequences is a matter only
of its objectively likely consequences, not of its actual consequences. And not every act which has some predetermined bad
consequences is objectively a bad act; its other consequences or
aspects of its nature may make it overall a good act. An objectively
perfectly good and omniscient agent will do many objectively good
acts and no bad acts. (Unless stated otherwise, my concern henceforward is with the objective goodness of actions and agents.)

I believe that Western religion (i.e. Christianity, Judaism, and
Islam) has understood by God roughly a being of the kind which I
have described; and it is that understanding of 'God' which gives
rise to the 'problem of evil', initially in the form of an apparently

[2] To the extent to which there is a bias in nature, we say that the earlier state or
action makes a later state naturally or physically probable or likely. Probability of
this kind is to be contrasted with evidential probability, which is a measure of the
extent to which certain evidence makes it likely that some event occurred; and with
statistical probability, which is a measure of the proportion of certain kinds of events
in wider classes (e.g. of tosses of heads among tosses of a coin). On all this, see e.g.
my *An Introduction to Confirmation Theory* (Methuen, 1973), chs. 1 and 2.

conclusive argument against the existence of God. For, the atheist's argument goes:

1. If there is a God, he is omnipotent and perfectly good.
2. A perfectly good being will never allow any morally bad state to occur if he can prevent it.
3. An omnipotent being can prevent the occurrence of all morally bad states.
4. There is at least one morally bad state.

So (conclusion): There is no God.

The argument purports to be—and fairly obviously is—a valid deductive argument, i.e. one in which the conclusion simply draws out what is implicit in the premisses; one in which if you admit the premisses but deny the conclusion, you contradict yourself. This is to be contrasted with a correct inductive argument, which I shall understand for present purposes as one in which the premisses make the conclusion probable. A sound deductive argument is one which is valid and in which all the premisses are true. I understand by a sound inductive argument one which is correct and in which all the premisses are true.

The first premiss of the above argument simply states some of what is involved in the Western understanding of God, as I have spelled it out. If God's goodness were supposed to be other than moral goodness, then it might be no objection to his existence that there is pain and other suffering. But, despite the fact that some philosophical theologians[3] have attempted to expound God's goodness in non-moral ways, it seems to me deeply central to the whole tradition of the Christian (and other Western) religion that God is loving towards his creation and that involves his behaving in morally good ways towards it. There is no doubt more to loving someone than not kicking them in the teeth. But it does (barring special considerations) seem to involve at least not kicking them in the teeth. Western religion has always held that there is a deep problem about why there is pain and other suffering—which there would not be if God were not supposed to be morally good. Again, God is supposed to be in some way personal, and a personal being who was not morally good would not be the great being God is

[3] Thus Brian Davies claims that 'Theologians have taught that God is good without holding that his goodness is that of a morally good agent' (An Introduction to the Philosophy of Religion, 2nd edn. (Oxford University Press, 1993), 48).

supposed to be. Hence, in view of the fact that my concern in this chapter is with the existence (or not) of the sort of God with which Western religion is concerned, this understanding of the definition of God must stand.

Premiss 4 is obviously true. Theists have sometimes challenged premiss 3 on the ground that to be omnipotent a being has only to be able to do the logically possible, and to prevent the occurrence of all morally bad states of affairs is not logically possible; maybe he could prevent the occurrence of any particular bad state, but not of them all taken together. This challenge does not look very plausible: it does look as if it is logically possible to make a beautiful world in which the only conscious beings are predetermined to live lives of unalloyed pleasure; and then surely there would be no bad states. It might be that in such a situation, without the existence of contrasting bad states, the world's inhabitants would not realize that their world contained nothing bad—but it would be true all the same. Anyway I see no reason to suppose that the inhabitants could not realize that their world contained nothing bad; they could have the concept of bad (they could be born with an ability to recognize bad states, if they were to occur) without there actually being any instances of bad states. Again, if the world's badness were supposed to be other than moral badness, it might not be logically possible for God to prevent it. That might be so, for example, if the bad were understood in one old-established way of dealing with the problem of evil as *privatio boni*, taken simply as the absence of some good. For then it would not be logically possible for God to prevent the occurrence of all bad, since whatever world God makes, he can always make a better one.[4] However many persons God made, for example (even if it were an infinite number), he could always add another one (at sufficient distance from others so as not to crowd them out) and then there would be a better world. It follows that the objection from the existence of bad states of affairs to the existence of God is not that he did not create the 'best of all possible worlds', for to do that is not logically possible: there is no best of all possible worlds.[5] The objection to God's existence is

---

[4] The rejection of the third premiss on these grounds is in effect the solution to the problem of evil given by G. Schlesinger, *Religion and Scientific Method* (D. Reidel, 1977), pt. I.

[5] Leibniz classically claimed that God would make 'the best of all possible worlds', and indeed had done so. 'If there were not the best among all possible worlds, God would not have produced any' (G. W. Leibniz, *Theodicy*, trans.

rather that there are some actual morally bad eliminable states; moral badness is not just the absence of moral goodness. So premiss 3 must stand.

The normal challenge to the atheist's argument and surely by far the most plausible challenge is to premiss 2, and I shall be concerned with that alone in the main argument of this book. I suggested earlier that a perfectly good being will do many (morally) good actions and no bad ones. The reader might have thought that this was too modest an account to constitute a definition of perfect goodness. Surely a perfectly good being, it might be thought, will, in any situation, always do the best action; or, at any rate, if there are a number of equal best actions, do one of them. I agree that the definition should be made more precise by adding to it that a perfectly good being will always do the best or an equal-best action—where there is one. But the point made above that there is no best of all possible worlds has the consequence that for an omnipotent being, there is sometimes no best or equal-best action. For an agent of limited power, a human being for example, will have available to him only a limited range of actions; and one of them may indeed be the best, or some of them be equal best. It may, for example, be the best action for me to do to give a lot of money to some charity for the relief of famine, but equally best to give it to the Red Cross, or to give it to Oxfam or Christian Aid. We could understand the perfect goodness of such a being as its doing always the best or an equal-best action. But we cannot understand perfect goodness generally in this way; and we cannot understand the perfect goodness of a God who is omnipotent in this way. For he will so often have available to him an infinite range of actions, each of which is less good than some other action he could do. Thus for any world of conscious agents which God could create there is, I suggested, a better one, for example one obtained by adding one more conscious agent. And so among the actions of creating conscious agents there is no best (or equal best). What goes for creating conscious agents goes also for creating inanimate things. And no doubt, though I do

E. M. Huggard (Routledge & Kegan Paul, 1951), §8). But, alas, in Leibniz's sense of 'possible world' God cannot fail to make actual some possible world. For not to create any creatures is to make a world empty of all things except God. And that too, on my argument, would be to make a world less good than some other world. Aquinas, by contrast, rightly claimed: 'God could make other things, or add other things to those he has made, and there would be another and better universe' (*Summa Theologiae*, Ia. 25. 6 ad 3).

not need to argue this here, for much else too, for the kinds of plea-sure and opportunities of service he gives to beings. For such a sit-uation we cannot say anything more positive about what a perfectly good God will do.

Note, however, that although God may not always be able to do a best act, he will always be able to fulfil his obligations. For obli-gations arise either from commitments entered into voluntarily (e.g. one's obligations to one's children) or from benefits received (e.g. one's obligations to parents). The only benefits which God receives are ones which he chooses to receive. Hence all God's obligations are ones voluntarily entered into. And God can ensure that they form a limited set such that he can fulfil all of them; and since failing to fulfil one's obligations would be a morally bad act (of omission), God will always fulfil his obligations.[6]

Now what is wrong with premiss 2 is that it is not always a bad act to bring about or to allow to occur a bad state of affairs. For it may be that the only way in which an agent can bring about some good state is by bringing about first (or simultaneously) some bad state, or by allowing such a state to occur. Thus the only way in which a human parent can get his child's teeth repaired may be by taking him to the dentist and allowing pain to be inflicted upon him; and sometimes the only way in which he can reform the child may be to punish him by deliberately inflicting suffering upon him. But the human parent is none the less good for taking the child to the dentist, or for punishing him. So premiss 2 is false.

The atheist is able, however, to put forward a more sophisticated version of premiss 2. He may claim, plausibly, that it is always a bad act to bring about a bad state of affairs, or, more generally, allow one to occur, where the agent can prevent it, unless thereby the agent makes possible a good state of affairs which would not other-wise be possible. And even so, it is only under restricted conditions that a perfectly good being will allow a bad state of affairs for the sake of the good that it makes possible. We need to qualify premiss 2 in various further ways. First, for some bad states, even if that bad state is a necessary condition of some good, agents would have no

---

[6] Obligations are, I suggest, always obligations to someone else. They are debts, what one owes; and the notion of a debt to oneself makes no sense. So one cannot wrong oneself, only someone else. One may of course harm oneself, do something bad to oneself—but it only constitutes a wrong, if it is a wrong to someone else—e.g. to my parents, who have lavished care on me, or to God. On this, see my *Responsibility and Atonement* (Clarendon Press, 1989), various pages up to p. 77.

right ever to bring it about or even to allow it to occur for the sake of some good. (That is, it would never be morally permissible for them to bring it about or allow it; they would never be morally justified in so doing.) A beating may do some child much good, and that amount of suffering might even be logically necessary to effect that particular good; but, unless I am the child's parent or teacher, I do not have the right to beat the child for the sake of that good. And there are other bad states which I do not have the right to allow to occur (if I can easily prevent them), e.g. some stranger strangling my baby in order to use its organs to save the life of some other baby. Since one is obliged not to do that which one does not have the right to do and God always fulfils his obligations, the bad states which he allows to occur must be ones which he has the right to allow to occur. Take, for example, the traditional free-will defence which we will consider in detail later in the book. This claims that many of the bad states which God allows to occur are ones which humans freely choose to inflict on each other, that it is a good thing that humans have such freedom, and the bad states—e.g. the pains and other sufferings which humans inflict on each other—are the price which is paid for that freedom. If this defence is to work, God must have the right to allow the human victims to suffer in the circumstances in which they do suffer.

Secondly, the atheist must acknowledge that the logically necessary condition of the good may not be the actual occurrence of the bad, but some agent P having the power to cause the bad state to occur without being caused to exercise that power or being caused to refrain from exercising that power. Consider again the free-will defence. This claims that humans have the power, which I shall call libertarian free will, of choosing whether or not to bring about effects without being subject to causes which determine how they will exercise that power; and that among the effects which they can choose whether or not to bring about are happiness or suffering for others. This good of their having this choice *and* their choice making a difference (free will *plus* efficacy, which I shall call efficacious free will) has as its necessary condition that their actions are not predetermined and that if they choose to bring about suffering, suffering will result. But the actual occurrence of the suffering is not a necessary condition of the good. (Humans might simply always choose the good—but they would not have efficacious free will if God ensured that only their good choices were efficacious.)

Note that the necessary condition of the good might not be allowing the particular bad state in question but allowing some state of affairs just as bad or worse. It is no objection to theism that God allowed something bad to occur, in order to achieve some good, when he could have achieved the good by allowing a different but equally bad state to occur instead. Thus allowing you to suffer is not a necessary condition of my having efficacious free will to choose whether or not to cause suffering, but allowing someone to suffer is such a condition.

Thirdly, it must be the case that the perfectly good agent does all else that he can (compatible with allowing no further bad state to occur) to bring about the good. If allowing some bad to occur makes possible some good, but God does not do all else that he can to bring about the good, then he should not have allowed the bad state to occur. Thus if God would be justified in allowing you to suffer in order that I may exercise efficacious free will in choosing to respond to it with sympathy, but God does not in fact give me such free will, then clearly the defence does not work. Or if God would be justified in allowing a certain amount of suffering on Earth, if it is compensated by happiness in the afterlife, but God does not give us an afterlife, then again the justification does not work.

And finally, we need some sort of comparative condition. It cannot be as strong as the condition that the good aimed at, G, be more of a good state than the bad means, E, is bad. For obviously we are often justified, in order to ensure the occurrence of a substantial good, in risking the occurrence of a worse state. To save one life, we are often justified in embarking on a course of action where there is a small risk of two lives being lost but quite a good chance of no lives being lost. But it must be that if the perfectly good agent intentionally brings about E for the sake of G, G must be at least a bit more of a good state than E is a bad state. And if he allows E to occur but does not bring it about (e.g. brings it about that chance or some other free agent determines whether E occurs), then the more probable it is in these circumstances that E will occur, the closer E must be to being a less bad state than G is good. A formal way of capturing this condition, if we measure good consequences by positive units and bad consequences by negative units, is that the action must overall have a positive expected value.[7]

---

[7] The expected value of some action is the sum of the values (positive or negative) of its possible consequences, each multiplied by the probability of its occurrence if

So given these amplifications, the atheist should agree to abandon premiss 2, 'A perfectly good being will never allow any morally bad state to occur if he can prevent it', and replace it by the more careful premiss 2*, 'A perfectly good being will never allow any morally bad state E to occur if he can prevent it, unless (i) allowing E to occur is something which he has the right to do, (ii) allowing E (or a state of affairs as bad or worse) to occur is the only morally permissible way in which he can make possible the occurrence of a good state of affairs G, (iii) he does all else that he can to bring about G, and (iv) the expected value of allowing E, given (iii), is positive.' I shall in future sometimes summarize premiss 2* as 'A perfectly good being will never allow any morally bad state to occur if he can prevent it—except for the sake of a greater good', but understand by this the careful spelling out which I have just provided.

The atheist will now claim that the earlier argument can be reconstructed, using premiss 2* instead of 2, as a valid deductive argument from the existence of many a particular evil E to the nonexistence of God, as follows:

1. If there is a God, he is omnipotent and perfectly good.
2*. A perfectly good being will never allow any morally bad state E to occur if he can prevent it, unless (i) allowing E to occur is something which he has the right to do, (ii) allowing E (or a state of affairs as bad or worse) to occur is the only morally permissible way in which he can make possible the occurrence of a good state of affairs G, (iii) he does all else that he can to bring about G, and (iv) the expected value of allowing E, given (iii), is positive.
3. An omnipotent being can prevent the occurrence of all morally bad states.
4*. There is at least one morally bad state ϵ which is such that *either* God does not have the right to allow ϵ to occur, *or* there is no good state γ, such that allowing ϵ (or a state at

the action is done. Anyone who thinks that there are no limits to God's knowledge of the (to us) future actions of free agents (or consequences of chance processes), can clearly operate with the simpler formula, that the positive value of G must exceed the negative value of E. (Some may reasonably hold that all that is required is a non-negative, i.e. positive or zero, expected value. But I am putting the requirement in the simpler form, since the difference between zero and a very tiny positive balance is so small that virtually nothing will turn on this.)

least equally bad) to occur is the only morally permissible way in which God can make possible the occurrence of γ, that God does all else that he can to bring about γ, and that, given the latter, the expected value of allowing ϵ is positive.

So: There is no God.

While accepting the new second premiss, the theist now denies the new fourth premiss. He claims that there are no morally bad states of the kind specified there.

Since all things are possible for an omnipotent being, except the logically impossible, the theist's defence is then that, compatibly with his perfect goodness, God may allow a bad state E to occur, caused either by himself or some other agent, if (and only if):

(a) God has the right to allow E to occur.
(b) Allowing E (or a state as bad or worse) to occur is the only morally permissible way in which God can bring about a logically necessary condition of a good G.
(c) God does everything else logically possible to bring about G.
(d) The expected value of allowing E, given (c), is positive.

The theist claims that all these criteria are satisfied with respect to each bad state which there is in the world. The atheist denies this, and certainly it is not obvious to an impartial inquirer that the new premiss 4* is false. Some of this world's horrors seem at first sight to be such that God does not have the right ever (or in existing circumstances) to allow them to occur, or that there is no comparable good which they make possible.

Does the Theist Need to Prove his Case?

Having thus clarified on what the dispute turns, I now seek to investigate whether the theist is entitled to hold that all the morally bad states of affairs are such that (by our four criteria) God could, compatibly with his perfect goodness, have allowed them to occur, without having any view about how those criteria are satisfied. Can he just say: God must have some good reason for allowing bad states to occur, though we cannot see what they are? Or does the theist, in order justifiably to maintain his belief, need to be able to show (to his own satisfaction) how, if there is a God, our four criteria (*a*, *b*, *c*, and *d*) are probably satisfied in respect of all the world's morally bad states (namely, that probably they are such that a perfectly good God could allow them to occur)? I shall understand by an attempt to show the latter, the construction of a theodicy (*theou-dikē*, 'a justification of God') for that state. I thus understand by a 'theodicy' not an account of God's actual reasons for allowing a bad state to occur, but an account of his possible reasons (i.e. reasons which God has for allowing the bad state to occur, whether or not those are the ones which motivate him).[8] The world's morally bad states fall into kinds (e.g. pain deliberately caused by humans, pain allowed to occur through human negligence, pain caused by natural processes uncontrollable by humans, malevolent desires, grief, etc.). If the theist can provide for states of each kind a reason why God could justifiably allow a state of that kind to occur—e.g. pain deliberately caused by humans being justified in terms of the good of humans having a free choice of whether or not to cause pain deliberately to others—he will have provided an adequate total theodicy. But does the theist need to have available a theodicy which shows to his satisfaction (and so in the face of those objections from the atheist of which he is aware) how the four criteria are satisfied in respect of each kind of morally bad state?

Talk of the theist being 'entitled' or 'rational' to hold, or 'justifiably' (i.e. epistemically, not morally) maintain, this or that belief can be understood in many different ways. There are internalist senses in which the justification of a belief is a matter of its right relation to other internal states of the subject (or something in the nature of the belief itself); and 'externalist' senses in which justification of a belief is a matter of its being produced in the right way,

---

[8] I believe this to be the traditional use of the term 'theodicy'. Alvin Plantinga has confined the use of 'theodicy' to a doctrine about what are God's actual reasons for allowing evil to occur. (See his *The Nature of Necessity* (Clarendon Press, 1974), 192.) This use has been adopted by many other writers. What I call a 'theodicy' is closer to what Plantinga calls a 'defence'. The difference is that a Plantinga-type 'defence' is required merely to show that the existence of the bad state is compatible with the goodness and power of God—in effect that there is a *G* for which clauses (*a*), (*b*), and (*d*) are satisfied. I require also that it be shown that (*c*) is probably satisfied for such a *G*. This is vital if the atheist's argument is to be resisted. In those cases where the claim of (*c*) is a central claim of Christian revelation (e.g. that there is life after death), I am assuming in this book that arguments for the probable truth of this revelation (e.g. those adumbrated in my *Revelation* (Clarendon Press, 1992)) are successful.

e.g. by a process which normally produces true beliefs. My concern here is solely with that (subjective) internalist sense in which a belief is justified (the subject is 'entitled' to hold it, is rational in holding it) if and only if either (by the subject's own standards of probability) it is rendered probable by the subject's other justified beliefs[9] or it is properly basic. A belief is properly basic if it is probably true without deriving this probability from any other belief. For an internalist this latter probability will not come from anything external to the subject; rather, a properly basic belief is one which is probably true because of its content alone, e.g. because it is a belief about what the subject is now perceiving.[10] (I shall have more to say about this notion shortly.) Loosely, people are justified

---

[9] This first clause would need to be stated rather more precisely in a work of epistemology. My precise statement would involve claiming that for a subject to believe a proposition p is to believe p more probable than one or more incompatible propositions—normally (but not always) the negation, not-p. But since it is not always clear, when someone is said to believe some proposition, what is the contrasting proposition, it is not always clear what is meant by the claim that he or she believes. To believe p is normally to believe p more probable than not-p, but not always. To believe an explicit conjunction (q and r), for example, may be only to believe (q and r) to be more probable than (q and not-r), and more probable than (not-q and r), and more probable than (not-q and not-r). For the belief to be justified is then for the believed relations actually (by the subject's own standards of probability) to hold. Since the normal contrasting proposition is the negation, not-p, it then follows that normally for a belief to be justified is for it to be more probable than not, i.e. probable. Where the probability is derived from the subject's other beliefs rather than from its properly basic status, we then get the statement in the text. The sense of 'rational', 'justified', etc. with which I am concerned here is the one which I called 'rationality$_1$' in my *Faith and Reason* (Clarendon Press, 1981), 45.

[10] The notion of 'properly basic' beliefs came into philosophical discussion through the work of Alvin Plantinga (see his use of it in his essay 'Reason and Belief in God', in A. Plantinga and N. Wolterstorff (eds.), *Faith and Rationality* (University of Notre Dame Press, 1983)). For Plantinga a 'properly basic belief' is merely one which the subject is justified in holding quite apart from any support which it might gain from other beliefs. (Plantinga usually talks of the subject being 'rational' in holding the belief; or the belief being 'acceptable'. 'Justified' is my word.) On this definition it might still be required (by an internalist theory) that for some belief to be properly basic, the subject should have certain other appropriate internal states, such as sensations (e.g. for him to have a properly basic belief that he is seeing a desk, it might be necessary that there be a certain pattern of colour in his visual field). However, it seems to me that for an internalist, whether a subject is justified in holding a belief (and so not at fault epistemically) can depend on what sensations he has only in so far as he is aware of them, i.e. has beliefs about them. And so for simplicity's sake (in a work not primarily concerned with epistemology) I shall assume here and subsequently that, for an internalist, whether a basic belief is properly basic depends only on its content and not on any other internal states. And then the issue is whether all basic beliefs are properly basic, or only ones with certain sorts of content.

in holding their beliefs to the extent to which they fit with their other beliefs or are forced upon them by their beliefs about what they are experiencing. People whose beliefs do not fit together are epistemically at fault, because sorting out our beliefs so as to make them fit together better is something we can do something about. It is desirable that we should sort out our beliefs in this way because they are more likely to be true if they are rendered probable by our evidence (i.e. our properly basic beliefs); and our standards of what makes what probable are the ones which we believe to be the correct ones. But we have access to no reason for conforming our beliefs to some external standards of justification unless it follows from beliefs which we have or acquire that those standards are correct.[11] We cannot be criticized for failing to conform our beliefs to standards and facts to which we have no access; and our concern here with a subject's entitlement to a belief is a concern with whether he is at fault in holding it.

It follows that whether a theist needs a theodicy for every known bad state in order justifiably to believe that there is a God, despite the 'argument from evil', depends on what else he believes and how strongly he believes it. There may indeed be theists who need no theodicy, but I shall be claiming that most of us do need a theodicy, and for the rest of the book I shall be endeavouring to provide one.

An atheist's claim with respect to some bad state that the criteria are not satisfied may turn on a purely moral issue, or it may turn on an issue of non-moral contingent fact. Thus if he claims that a child's suffering can never satisfy criterion (*a*), since God does not have the right to allow a child to suffer for the sake of some good however great, the issue turns on a purely moral issue. But if he claims that the 'free-will defence' does not work because, although God would be justified in allowing one human to cause another to suffer if humans had libertarian free will, as a matter of fact they do

---

[11] Theories of a subject being justified in holding some belief *B* often add a condition to the effect that whatever grounds provide the justification for *B* must be causally operative in sustaining that belief. The belief must be 'based' on those grounds. But whether the justifying grounds (i.e. the other beliefs which make *B* probable) are causally operative in sustaining *B* can only be something of which the subject can take account if he has a belief *C* about it. If he does, then that belief *C* can play its role in raising or lowering the probability of *B*. Otherwise the 'basing' condition must be ignored by a purely internalist theory of justification which is concerned only with a justification which is accessible to the subject. We shall see the need for a 'basing' clause when developing a largely internalist theory of knowledge (as opposed to justification) in Ch. 4.

not have libertarian free will, then the issue turns on whether criterion (*c*) is satisfied in such cases—whether God has provided
what would justify him in allowing the bad state in question, a matter of contingent non-moral fact.

In order to distinguish between the two kinds of challenge, it is
important for me to establish at this stage a position on the status of
moral judgements. I hold that they have truth-value: some are true
and some are false. I do not need to argue for that aspect of my position in this context, since anyone who thinks that the occurrence of
bad states raises for theism the 'problem' which I have described
must think this; or must, in order to show that theism is at odds
with some evident fact, have temporarily assumed it. For there
could only arise an issue whether certain bad states were *compatible*
with the existence of a good God if goodness and badness were
properties which belonged to persons, actions, and states of affairs,
and judgements which affirmed or denied their possession had a
truth-value. If moral judgements were mere expressions of emotion, they could not be incompatible with any factual claims.

Now the moral goodness (or otherwise) of particular actions is
supervenient on non-moral features of those actions. That is,
judgements such as 'You ought to fight for France', 'It is good to
give money to Oxfam', derive their truth-value (whether true or
false) from contingent states of affairs describable in non-moral
terms, i.e. (in Moorean terminology[12]) 'natural' states. If the first
were true, what would make it true would be such things as you
being a French citizen, and France being attacked by an enemy who
seeks to rule her; what would make the second true would be such
things as that Oxfam feeds the starving in Africa but does not have
enough money for this purpose. But once all the natural circumstances which make the moral judgements true are set out, that in
those circumstances (fully described) you ought to fight for France,
or it is good to give to Oxfam, if the moral judgements are true, they
could not but be true; they would be necessary truths (i.e. ones
which held in any logically possible world). There could not be a
world identical with the actual world in all natural respects but in

---

[12] In *Principia Ethica* (Cambridge University Press, 1903) G. E. Moore distinguished non-natural 'objects' and 'properties' (the goodness, rightness, ought-to-
be-doneness of things) from natural objects and properties (almost all other
properties of things, including whether they are wanted, desired, commanded, or
will make people happy).

which different moral judgements were true (e.g. a world identical with our world in all natural respects but in which murder and torture—in our world morally bad actions—were morally good actions). No doubt particular necessary moral truths, such as 'In circumstances C you ought to fight for France', derive their truth from more general moral truths such as 'Everyone ought to fight for his country when it is attacked by enemies who wish to rule over it', but my argument does not depend on such derivability. My only point is that, if moral judgements are ever true, and those which are contingently true depend for their truth on natural facts, then the judgements that they hold when those natural facts hold must be necessary. Hence contingent moral truths derive their truth from contingent natural truths and necessary moral truths. The basic moral truths are necessary truths.

It might be that among the necessary moral truths are truths to the effect that whatever God commands humans to do, humans ought to do—within such-and-such limits, or without limits. But even if whatever God commands becomes a human obligation, that will be so in virtue of a necessary truth connecting the natural fact of God commanding and the non-natural fact of an obligation to obey.

Now premiss 2* would seem (if, as I have argued, it is true) to be a necessary truth. Its truth does not depend on whether or not there is a God, or apparently on anything else. (Note too that its truth is unaffected by whether or not you suppose God's rights to command to be unlimited.) Premiss 3 is also a necessary truth—deriving from the nature of omnipotence (as defined on p. 3) and moral badness; it holds whether or not there are any omnipotent beings or bad states of affairs. Premiss 1 is also a necessary truth; it just says what is involved in there being a God, of the sort I defined. Premiss 4*, affirming the existence of bad states of a certain sort, is not, however, a necessary truth; it is a contingent matter whether there are such bad states. But if an argument from a contingent truth and general necessary truths to some conclusion is valid, so is the argument without the necessary truths explicitly stated—necessary truths being entailed by all other propositions and so already entailed by the other premisses. (I am using 'p entails q' in the wide sense that q holds in every possible world in which p holds.) Hence whether the atheist has a sound argument from his premisses to the non-existence of God turns solely on whether premiss 4* is true.

So when an atheist claims that there is some bad state E which does not satisfy the four criteria, his objection may turn solely on necessary truths of morality. If he claims that criterion (*a*) could never be satisfied with respect to E (that God never under any conditions has the right to allow E to occur), or that (*b*) is not satisfied because there is no good which E makes possible, he claims that there is an E which a perfectly good God would never bring about. Once E is described (e.g. a child suffering), then the issue of the truth of premiss 4* turns solely on whether certain proposed moral principles are necessary moral truths or not.[13] Alternatively, as we have seen, the atheist may admit that God would be justified in allowing E to occur under certain contingent conditions F, but claim that F do not in fact hold. The truth of premiss 4* then turns on both necessary and contingent issues.

Either way, the question remains what is the rational response to the suggestion that there is a bad state E with respect to which premiss 4* is true (i.e. such that either for moral or contingent reasons, criteria (*a*), (*b*), (*c*), or (*d*), which would justify God in allowing E to occur, are not all satisfied).

A supreme principle which covers the justification of belief (in our present internalist sense) is surely the principle which has been called the Principle of Credulity[14]—that, other things being equal, it is probable and so rational to believe that things are as they seem to be (and the stronger the inclination, the more rational the belief). By 'seem' (or 'appear') I mean 'seem epistemically'; the way things seem epistemically is the way we are initially inclined to believe that

[13] If the atheist is right in his views about the necessary moral truths, and nothing turns on anything contingent, he will then have a valid deductive argument from true premisses (including one reporting the occurrence of E) to the non-existence of God. It seems to be generally agreed by atheists as well as theists that what is called 'the logical problem of evil' has been eliminated, and all that remains is 'the evidential problem'. See e.g. Paul Draper, who writes that he 'agrees with most philosophers of religion that theists face no serious logical problem of evil' ('Pain and Pleasure: An Evidential Problem for Theists', *Nous*, 23 (1989), 331–50: 349). But whether that is so depends on what we understand by 'the logical problem'. It has not been shown to the satisfaction of atheists that there is no valid deductive argument from the existence of certain evident bad states E (via some necessary moral truths) to the non-existence of God. It has been shown merely that there is no such valid deductive argument evident to theists, who dispute the validity of any such argument by disputing the necessity of the relevant purported necessary moral truths.

[14] For a much fuller and so more adequate discussion of the Principle of Credulity, as it applies to apparent perceptual experiences, see my *The Existence of God*, rev. edn. (Clarendon Press, 1991), ch. 13.

they are.[15] We find ourselves with involuntary inclinations to belief; in the absence of reasons against going along with such an inclination the rational person will do so. This must be the starting-point for all justified belief; if all beliefs needed to be justified by other beliefs before they could be believed with justification, no belief could ever be justified. All and only beliefs forced upon us by such inclinations are properly basic.[16] The reasons against going along with such inclinations will come from other inclinations leading to contrary beliefs, which may be stronger inclinations and/or more numerous inclinations.

If it seems to me that I am seeing a table or hearing my friend's voice, I ought to believe this until evidence appears that I have been deceived. If you say the contrary—never trust appearances until it is proved that they are reliable—you will never have any beliefs at all.

[15] Note the two very different uses of such verbs as 'seems', 'appears', and 'looks'. When I look at a round coin from an angle I may say that 'it looks round' or I may say that 'it looks elliptical', but I mean very different things by the 'looks' in the two cases. By 'it looks round' in this context I mean that, on the basis of the way it looks, I am inclined to believe that it is round. By 'it looks elliptical' in this context I mean that it looks the way elliptical things normally (that is, when viewed from above) look. The former sense in philosophical terminology is the epistemic sense; the latter the comparative sense. The epistemic sense of such verbs describes how we are inclined to believe that things are; the comparative sense describes the way things seem by comparing them with the way things normally seem. My statement of the Principle of Credulity utilizes the epistemic sense.

[16] That is, all basic beliefs are properly basic. Many philosophers have sought to develop more restricted principles governing the proper starting-points for rational belief, the foundations on which a person's corpus of belief ought to be based. There is, for example, the principle which Plantinga has described and criticized so fully, called 'classical foundationalism', that 'a proposition *p* is properly basic for a person *S* if and only if *p* is either self-evident to *S* or incorrigible for *S* or evident to the senses for *S*'. (See A. Plantinga, 'Reason and Belief in God', in A. Plantinga and N. Wolterstorff, *Faith and Rationality* (University of Notre Dame Press, 1983), 59.) But, as Plantinga has argued at length, this is not a priori obvious: ought not beliefs about the mental which are not incorrigible and the deliverances of memory to be included? There is indeed a kind of justification in which beliefs are not justified unless they start from (in some sense) objectively correct starting-points; and a system such as Classical Foundationalism might tell us what these are. I shall come to discuss the notion of objective justification in Ch. 4. But our only grounds for adopting such a system must be that it follows from other things which we believe, and that means ultimately from beliefs which are properly basic on my internalist understanding. We have to start from where we find ourselves, in respect of our beliefs as well as all else. It is because we cannot be faulted for where we start from that all basic beliefs are on this understanding properly basic. But we can be epistemically at fault if (through not applying our own standards properly) we found the wrong beliefs on those starting-points—or do not eliminate some of them because they are rendered improbable by others.

For what would show that appearances were reliable, except more appearances? And if you cannot trust appearances as such, you cannot trust these new ones either. But appearances may give grounds for believing some general view, a consequence of which is that a particular 'seeming' should not be taken as showing how things are. If it seems to me that I am seeing a table, but when I put my hand out it seemed to pass through where the table seemed to be, and so did the hands of other people and so did other material bodies, then I ought to conclude that the initial 'seeming' was delusory: perhaps what seemed to be a table was really a hologram. The Principle of Credulity applies not merely to the deliverances of sense but to the way things seem morally, mathematically, or logically. If some inference seems to be valid, I ought to believe that it is, until someone gives me good reason to believe otherwise. And it must apply also (in the absence of reasons to make an exception in this case) to apparent experiences of God—if it seems to you that you are aware of the presence of God, you ought so to believe (until someone produces reasons why you should be more cautious in such a case).

It follows that, if it seems to someone that there is some bad state incompatible with the existence of God, he ought so to believe, and so believe that there is no God—in the absence of counter-reasons. The incompatibility might involve no further factual assumptions; namely, the inquirer may conclude that, whatever further factual assumptions you make, the state is such that (*a*) or (*b*) or (*d*) are not satisfied. It might seem to him that the horror is so great that under no circumstances would God have any right to let it occur, or that there is no sufficiently great good which it could conceivably make possible which a God could not bring about in some better way. Alternatively, the inquirer might believe that a God would have the right to bring about the bad state, and that it is necessary for a great good, but that if there is a God, he (probably) does not do what else is needed to bring about that good. The inquirer might accept that a God would be justified in bringing about certain bad states if he compensated the sufferer with life after death, but claim that it is most unlikely that there is life after death. So again probably one of the justifying conditions—in this case (*c*)—is not satisfied with respect to the bad state. So, he must conclude, probably there is no God. All this, unless he has evidence that seems to him to tell against that conclusion. The onus of proof has passed to the theist; he needs reason for resisting the conclusion.

Many of us are surely often in this situation, and there would be something wrong with us morally if we were not. Our understanding of an agent being good would be gravely deficient unless we thought that, other things being equal, a good agent will stop pain and other suffering, if he can do so easily. And if our understanding of possible reasons why anyone might allow suffering to occur provides us with no reason for supposing that a good God might allow certain suffering, we ought to believe that there is no God—unless we have contrary reason. Just reflect on some of the horrors that we read about in our newspapers and history books: the prolonged cruelty of parents to lonely children, the torture of the innocent, the long-drawn-out acute physical pain of some disease, and so on. If we cannot see all that as a reason for believing that there is no all-good and all-powerful being, when we cannot think of any reason why such a being should allow it all to happen, there really is something deeply wrong with *us*. We have lost our sensitivity to the good.

We may, however, have a contrary reason for not going along with this argument as far as to reach the conclusion that there is no God. This contrary reason may be of three kinds. It may consist of other reasons for affirming that there is a God; or general reasons for doubting the force of this sort of inference to his non-existence; or reasons for supposing that criteria (*a*), (*b*), (*c*), and (*d*) are satisfied (a 'greater good' defence works) in respect of the particular bad state which seemed initially to show the non-existence of God; in other words, a theodicy.

Let us begin with the first reason. No argument for denying a true conclusion can be a sound deductive argument. Either it is invalid, or it has one or more false premisses; and if it seems to a subject strongly enough (as a necessary truth or a deliverance of experience) that some proposition is true, then any inference to its falsity must be judged unsound. If it seems to a subject strongly enough that there is an external world or that $2 + 2 = 4$, powerful philosophical arguments to the contrary must be judged by the subject to be unsound, even if she cannot put her finger on where they go wrong. Likewise, if it seems to a subject strongly enough (as a basic belief, delivered either by experience or reason) that there is a God, then she is entitled to the belief, whatever else she is initially inclined to believe. In that case, the subject must conclude that any purportedly valid deductive inference from some bad state E to the non-existence of God begins from a false premiss (E did not occur) or is not in fact a valid argument. If the argument requires a further contingent premiss—e.g. that the conditions F under which God would be justified in allowing E do not occur—and there is a purportedly strong inductive argument to this (i.e. an argument showing F to be improbable), then (however improbable) either F holds, or E did not occur, or again the argument must be invalid. So much is, I hope, undeniable.

But the basic belief will have to be overwhelmingly powerful if it is not to be overcome by an apparently simple deductive inference, relying on apparently incontrovertible moral principles, from a very evident bad state. The less sure the thinker is about the moral principles, the less strong the basic belief needs to be. Again, the less confident the thinker is about the inferential principles, the less strong the basic belief in the existence of God needs to be in order to overcome it. And finally, the weaker any inductive inference to not-F, the less strong the basic belief that there is a God needs to be in order to outweigh it.

Even if the belief that there is a God is not a basic belief, as long as it seems to the subject to be supported by evident basic beliefs on the basis of evidently cogent inferential principles,[17] it may be strong enough for the subject rationally not to abandon it in the light of counter-argument. Again, it will depend on how evident are the basic beliefs and inferential principles involved in the counter-argument and how probable it seems to the subject that they make the existence of God.

However, in the absence of positive evidence of sufficient strength for the existence of God, we need some reason for doubting the strength of the original atheistic inference in order to continue justifiably to believe. One kind of reason will simply be a theodicy, grounds for supposing it is probable that the bad state in question is such that the four criteria (a) to (d) are all satisfied in respect of it. The rest of this book will be concerned with developing a theodicy for the various kinds of bad state which we find around us. As stated in the Introduction, that theodicy will assume that God has done and will do for us the things which Christian revelation claims, e.g. that he will provide a life after death. It will assume, that is, that any contingent justifying conditions required

---

[17] For full discussion of the strength of arguments for the existence of God, see my *The Existence of God, passim.*

to satisfy (*c*), which are centrally affirmed by Christian revelation, are in fact satisfied. It will then proceed to argue that the other conditions stated there are satisfied for each kind of bad state.

There exists, however, the possibility of a more general argument against the kind of inference involved in the atheist's argument. I shall consider two such arguments. One is a very old argument to the effect that if there is a God, he will be so much greater than us in his understanding of which states are good and which are bad that we should expect there to be bad states for which we do not see how criteria (*a*) to (*d*) are satisfied in respect of them, i.e. in summary we do not see what greater good they would serve. We do not know all the greater goods there are, and so we are not entitled to say what a perfectly good God would allow to occur. This argument has recently been deployed in a version which has received quite a bit of attention, by Stephen Wykstra.[18]

Wykstra recommends an amendment to my Principle of Credulity to obtain a principle which he calls CORNEA or 'Condition of Reasonable Epistemic Access':

> On the basis of cognized situation *s*, human *H* is entitled to claim 'It appears that *p*' only if it is reasonable for *H* to believe that, given her cognitive faculties and the use she has made of them, if *p* were not the case, *s* would likely be different than it is in some way discernible by her.

That is, we can only justifiably assert 'It appears that *p*' if we have reason to believe that, if not-*p*, the observed situation would be different in respect of those features which lead us to assert 'It appears that *p*'. For example, we can only justifiably say of some object 'It appears that it is red' if we have reason to believe that if it were not red, our experience of it would be different. In general, if we are not colour-blind, we shall have such reason. But if we know that we are in a room illumined only by a red light, we are not entitled to our claim. For we know that if the object were not red, our experience of it would still be the same. Wykstra then uses this principle to claim that we cannot claim that it appears that there are bad states which serve no 'God-justifying purpose', i.e. that it appears that there are states 'such that God (if he exists) would not allow them

[18] Stephen J. Wykstra, 'The Humean Obstacle to Evidential Arguments from Suffering: On Avoiding the Evils of "Appearance" ', *International Journal for the Philosophy of Religion*, 16 (1984), 73–93.

to occur'. Wykstra claims that we cannot make this latter claim because we have no reason to think that if there were no bad states such that God would not allow them to occur, we would recognize this fact; our moral beliefs being so much shallower than those of God, if there is a God, we are likely to think some states of affairs to be bad states serving no greater good, although in fact they do serve a greater good.

Wykstra's claim in his CORNEA is that we can only assert 'It appears that p' if we have positive reason to think that if p were not so, our experience would be different. But that is too bold a claim. The most Wykstra is entitled to by way of amending my Principle of Credulity is to hold that we can only assert 'It appears that p' if we have no reason to think that if p were not so, our experience would be the same.[19] For if Wykstra's stronger claim were correct, what will constitute a positive reason to think that if p were not so, our experience would be different? We may think that it appears that we have such a reason (r). But before asserting 'It appears that r', we must have reason to think that if r were not so, our experience would be different. And so *ad infinitum*. If before asserting 'It appears that it is red' we needed positive reason to think that if an object were not red, our experience would be different, we would indeed be in a hopeless situation for making any justified assertions about the colour of the object. If we are ever to be justified in making claims of the kind 'It appears that p', it must be the case that our inclinations to believe them suffice—in the absence of counter-reasons. These latter will include any reason we have to suppose that if not-p, we would not notice any difference. If we actually have a positive reason for supposing the room is illuminated by red light, then maybe we are not entitled to the assertion 'It appears red'; but only a positive reason could bar the justification. Given the basic point that a positive reason for supposing that if p, we would not have any different experience, defeats any justification we might have for concluding p on the basis of experience, the point is made more simply (and more fairly to ordinary language) by say-

[19] Wykstra defends this stronger interpretation against the weaker version in his follow-up paper, 'Rowe's Noseeum Arguments from Evil', in D. Howard-Snyder (ed.), *The Evidential Argument from Evil* (Indiana University Press, 1996). He accuses Rowe of misunderstanding CORNEA by interpreting it in the weaker way. See W. L. Rowe, 'The Empirical Argument from Evil', in R. Audi and W. J. Wainwright (eds.), *Rationality, Religious Belief and Moral Commitment* (Cornell University Press, 1986); note his p. 237.

ing that the defeat occurs not by our no longer being entitled to say 'It appears that p' but rather by our no longer being entitled to infer from 'It appears that p' to p. If we have reason to suppose that the room is illuminated by red light, we may still say that the object 'appears red', but we are not justified in inferring that it is red. That is, I can maintain my Principle of Credulity in its original form, while allowing that among the reasons which make the inference no longer correct (i.e. the conclusion no longer probable) is that things would appear the same to the subject even if they were in fact quite different.

The only way to put the kind of point which Wykstra is trying to make in terms of my original Principle of Credulity is to say that while it appears that there are bad states which serve no God-justifying purpose, i.e. 'states such that God (if he exists) would not allow them to occur', we cannot infer that there are such states. This is because, Wykstra claims, we have reason to suppose that if there is a God, his understanding of moral goodness will be so much deeper than ours that it is to be expected that we should think that there are bad states which serve no greater good, when in fact they do serve a greater good. But the trouble with this version of the argument is that while our moral beliefs (and factual beliefs, we must add) may indeed be in error in relevant respects, we need some further argument to show that they are more likely to be biased in the direction of failing to understand that some apparent bad states really serve greater goods, rather than in the direction of failing to understand that some apparent good states really serve greater bad states. Why should our inadequacies of moral belief lead us to suppose that the world is worse rather than better than it really is? And if it is equally probable that the world is worse rather than better than it appears, it follows that it is probably at least as bad as it appears; and very probable indeed (since there are very many apparently bad states which apparently do not satisfy my criteria) that it contains at least one bad state which does not satisfy one of my criteria $(a) \ldots (d)$. True, if there is a God, then there will not be any apparent good states which really subserve greater bad states. But we cannot assume at this stage without positive argument that there is a God and so that there are no such states; for that would be to beg the question against the atheist who has produced the argument under discussion in order to show that there is no God.

Wykstra's version of the argument, that we cannot be expected to know all the greater goods for the sake of which a God would allow bad states to occur, is only one of many slightly different versions put forward recently by theistic philosophers.[20] Alston correctly points out that God (if he exists) might allow some bad state of affairs for the sake of some greater good, when we suppose falsely that he would not, either because the good state for which the bad state was necessary was one of the nature and goodness of which we have no inkling; or because although we are aware of the good state in question, we falsely suppose that it is logically[21] possible for an omnipotent God to bring about the good without the bad. Both our moral intuitions and our logical intuitions may be in error. All that is indeed so. But unless we have reason to suppose that our error is more likely to lie in the one direction rather than in the other, Alston's point is worthless. What the Principle of Credulity tells us is that we must be guided by the way things seem to us, in the absence of positive argument for supposing that certain appearances rather than others are misleading. And if that positive argument depends on what God would do, it requires to be supported by argument to show that there is a God, strong enough to oppose this argument from apparent bad states.

There is available to some inquirers, however, a more general argument against accepting the kind of inference involved in the atheist's argument, which meets the problems involved in Wykstra's argument. It is an argument from a premiss which, if true of the particular inquirer, would lead him reasonably to suppose that improvement in his moral understanding would be in the direction of seeing all present puzzling bad states to be such as God would permit for the sake of a greater good. This is that when initially it seemed to this inquirer that many kinds of bad states were incompatible with the existence of God (directly, or given further contingent states of affairs which seemed to the inquirer to be highly probable), subsequent reflection, argument, and experience led him to see, one by one, with respect to a number of such kinds

---

[20] See e.g. the two papers by Peter van Inwagen, the two papers by William Alston, and the paper by Daniel Howard-Snyder in Howard-Snyder (ed.), *The Evidential Argument from Evil*.

[21] Alston talks of 'metaphysical' rather than 'logical' possibility (ibid. 116–18). Whether or not we accept the distinction between 'logical' and 'metaphysical' possibility does not affect the present issues, and so I phrase his point in terms of logical necessity.

of bad state, with apparent clarity, that they were not incompatible with the existence of God; a greater-good defence apparently worked in respect of them. But the reverse did *not* happen: the inquirer did not come to see states of affairs which he regarded initially as good as apparently incompatible with the existence of God (although he gave time to considering whether there were any such states). It is satisfaction of the clause that 'the reverse did not happen' which would provide an asymmetry of a kind not present in Wykstra's argument (without begging the question), necessary to generate a conclusion favourable to theism. If what is hypostasized were true of some inquirer, that would give him good grounds for supposing that eventually he would come to see with respect to all bad states for which initially a greater-good defence could not be provided that such a defence could be provided.

Whether a given inquirer has this kind of evidence of finding more and more kinds of bad states explicable in terms of a greater-good defence is an empirical matter. Certainly some inquirers have a record of such progressive understanding; and an inquirer with such a record must rationally be much more doubtful about the moral principles involved in his judging the remaining puzzling bad states to be incompatible with the existence of God than he would otherwise be. Depending on the strength of his initial conviction, this evidence of his past record may tip the balance in favour of God.

I conclude that it follows from the Principle of Credulity that bad states for which no greater-good defence can apparently be provided must count against the existence of God. In order rationally to believe that there is a God, despite this counter-evidence, we need *either* strong positive evidence for the existence of God, *or* a record of discovering with respect to many apparent bad states that a theodicy works with respect to them, *or* a theodicy for each kind of bad state which seems to count against the existence of God. The rest of this book (after the next chapter) seeks, in the course of discussing the good purposes God might have for creating the world, to provide such a theodicy. But first, in the next chapter, I need briefly to consider to what extent there are already in place in the Christian tradition a number of strands of theodicy.

2

Theodicy in Christian Tradition

And unto Adam God said, Because thou hast hearkened unto the voice of thy wife, and hast eaten of the tree, of which I commanded thee, saying, Thou shalt not eat of it: cursed is the ground for thy sake; in toil shalt thou eat of it all the days of thy life; thorns also and thistles shall it bring forth to thee; and thou shalt eat the herb of the field; in the sweat of thy face shalt thou eat bread, till thou return unto the ground; for out of it wast thou taken; for dust thou art, and unto dust shalt thou return.

(Genesis 3: 17–19)

The 'problem of evil' does not arise if one denies either the omnipotence or the perfect goodness of God (in the senses of these terms delineated in the last chapter). Very occasional writers at different periods have denied the perfect goodness of God, in the sense of his moral goodness—and we noted one modern example in the last chapter. But no writer who could plausibly be called a Christian has denied the omnipotence of God until this century. In the early centuries AD Manichaeism, a rival religion to Christianity, did hold that the reason why the bad occurs is that God is not strong enough to prevent it; Good (God) and Evil were two powers equally strong in the world. In our century many Christian theologians have talked in a vague way about the 'weakness' of God and seen this exemplified in the crucifixion of Christ. But I do not think that many of them have really meant to claim that God (either the Father or the Son, God incarnate) was too weak to prevent the crucifixion. Rather I suspect that talk about God being 'weak' was, for most of them, a somewhat misleading way of putting the point that God humbled himself in his incarnation in Christ and did not exercise the power he possessed. However, one group of modern Christian writers who have clearly and seriously expressed the view that God is not omnipotent and that the occurrence of the bad is explained by his inability to eliminate it are Process Theologians. It is a feature of the system of theology that Charles Hartshorne, John Cobb, Schubert Ogden, and many others developed from the philosophy of A. N. Whitehead, that God is limited in his power.[1]

From time to time, Christian writers have expressed the view, mentioned earlier, that it would be logically impossible for God to prevent the occurrence of all bad states. This view has usually derived from a view that the bad is simply imperfection, the absence of some sort of good (*privatio boni*); and since any world is bound to lack some sort of perfection, there will always be bad. But then the bad is not something real; it is, in some sense, nothing. This view reached Christian thought from the Neoplatonism which exercised a powerful influence on it from the third to the thirteenth century. Plato claimed that all the Forms and so all beings participate to some degree in the Form of the Good. It follows that τὸ κακόν/*malum* (the bad, normally translated 'evil') is just inadequate participation, and so the absence of some good. Pseudo-Dionysius wrote that 'evil is contrary to progress, purpose, nature, cause, source, goal, definition, will and substance. It is a defect, a deficiency, a weakness, a disproportion, a sin. It is purposeless, ugly, lifeless, mindless, unreasonable, imperfect, unfounded, uncaused, indeterminate, unborn, inert, powerless, disordered. It is errant, indefinite, dark, insubstantial, never in itself possessed of any existence.'[2] But presumably the bad is not just the absence of any good, but the absence of a good which in some sense ought to have been present. Writers in this tradition clearly had in their mind the view that each thing belongs to a kind (participates in a Form essential to it) and the bad consists in not being a perfect specimen of the kind. Thus Aquinas: 'nothing that exists is called bad in so far as it is an entity, but rather in so far as it lacks some being. Thus a man is called bad in so far as he lacks a virtue, and an eye is said to be bad in so far as it lacks the power of sight.'[3] This idea of the bad as in some way a lack of being surfaces

---

[1] See e.g. D. R. Griffin, 'Creation out of Chaos and the Problem of Evil', in S. T. Davis (ed.), *Encountering Evil* (T. & T. Clark, 1981), where Griffin spells out how God's non-omnipotence explains the existence of the world's ills.

[2] *De Divinis Nominibus*, §32, trans. C. Luibheid (Paulist Press, 1987).

[3] St Thomas Aquinas, *Summa Theologiae*, Ia. 5. 3 ad 2.

again in Hegelian thought, and in modern continental theologians influenced by Hegel or Heidegger. For Barth, evil is *das Nichtige*, the 'nothingness' which inevitably accompanies the creation of creatures.[4]

It does, however, seem very implausible to claim that pain and other suffering, bad desires, and wicked acts are just an absence of some good—pain is not just an absence of pleasure, and wicked acts are not just the non-occurrence of good acts.[5] It looks as if we can describe a world without pain or wickedness (even if it may lack certain other good states). I suspect that most writers in the *privatio boni* tradition were half-aware of this, because they have usually combined expression of this view with some view to the effect that God brought about the bad for the sake of some good which could not otherwise be realized.

Most Christian thinkers have held (either with or more normally without the *privatio boni* view hovering in the background) that God has allowed the bad to occur for some good purpose—whether or not we know what that purpose is. That involves, given the later category of the logically impossible, the view that allowing the bad to occur is *logically* necessary for the attainment of good. The view that some bad makes possible 'greater good' (as the point is usually put) has been expounded by various analogies, especially aesthetic ones—a picture as a whole being more beautiful in virtue of containing an ugly part, for example. 'What horrifies us in a part by itself, may please us much when we consider it as part of a whole,' wrote Augustine. And 'As the beauty of a picture is increased by well-managed shadows, so, to the eye that has the skill to discern it, the universe is beautified even by sinners, though, considered by themselves, their deformity is a sad blemish.'[6] And, a millennium later, Leibniz also wrote 'shadows enhance colours'.[7]

---

[4] For references to Barth and analysis thereof, see Nicholas Wolterstorff, 'Barth on Evil', *Faith and Philosophy*, 13 (1996), 584–608.

[5] One of the last of the Scholastics, the 16th-century Spanish Jesuit Francisco Suárez, saw this clearly and tried to develop his own theory of the bad within the Scholastic framework. See J. J. A. Gracia, 'Evil and the Transcendentality of Goodness: Suárez's Solution to the Problem of Positive Evils', in S. MacDonald (ed.), *Being and Goodness* (Cornell University Press, 1991).

[6] Augustine, *On True Religion*, 40. 76; and *City of God*, 11. 23.

[7] *Theodicy*, §12.

The Free-Will Defence

Many Christian theologians have claimed not merely that God has some good purposes for the sake of which he allows the bad to occur, but that such-and-such were God's actual purposes; or at any rate that such-and-such were possible purposes to realize which God (omnipotent and perfectly good) could have allowed the bad to occur. In other words, they have provided a theodicy for many of the world's bad states. And central to the view of almost all of them has been the 'free-will' defence in respect of moral evil— that the bad states caused (or negligently allowed to occur) by human beings result from their own free choice; and that it is such a good thing that humans should have free will that it is worth the risk that they will abuse it in various ways. Almost all Christian theologians have affirmed that humans have 'free will'—the only exceptions are a few of the classical Protestant theologians.[8] But there is reason to suppose that some Christian theologians who affirmed 'free will' were affirming free will only in the compatibilist sense, and not in the libertarian sense. By an agent having free will in the libertarian sense, to repeat, I mean that which intentional action he does is not fully caused—either through some process of natural causation (i.e. in virtue of laws of nature) or in some other way (e.g. by an agent such as God acting from outside the natural order). In that case whatever the current state of the Universe (including the agent's beliefs and desires) and the causes at work in the Universe (including those whose operation is codified in laws of nature), it remains possible either that the agent will do the action in question, or that he will refrain from doing it. The compatibilist sense of 'free will' has been expounded in various subtly different ways, but the basic idea is that someone has free will in this sense if they do what they want and value (and do not act in consequence of psychological or physical pressure), even if they are fully caused to want and value what they do.[9] The crucial difference for our

[8] Luther wrote in his *Disputation against Scholastic Theology* (10): 'The will is not free to strive toward whatever is declared good. This is in opposition to Scotus and Gabriel [Biel]' (in *Works*, trans. H. J. Grimm, xxxi (Muhlenberg Press, 1957)). For Luther, free will was confined to morally indifferent matters.

[9] For some variants of compatibilist free will, see the papers of Frankfurt and Watson in G. Watson (ed.), *Free Will* (Oxford University Press, 1982); W. Neely, 'Freedom and Desire', *Philosophical Review*, 83 (1974), 32–54; and D. Dennett,

purposes is that an agent may have compatibilist free will even if God (or any other cause) causes him (via causing him to want and value what he does) inevitably to make the choices he does, while he cannot have libertarian free will if God (or any other cause) causes him inevitably to make the choices he does.

If the only free will humans have is compatibilist free will, there will be no distinction to be made between God allowing some human to do a bad act, and causing him to do it. For then humans will inevitably do the acts they do because of the way they are made. And if there is a God, it is God who made them that way. If they do bad acts, that will be because God causes them to do bad acts. So if a compatibilist free-will defence is to work, what has to be shown is that the actual occurrence of a bad choice when the agent wants and values what he chooses (not merely the agent having the power to make a bad choice without being caused to do so) is a necessary condition of some good state satisfying the demands stated earlier. And that is a more demanding requirement. The free-will defence clearly becomes more plausible if 'free will' means libertarian free will.

Just what various theologians meant by the 'free will' they ascribed to humans is not always clear; although I think that the context does often make it clear. But it seems to me that the natural primitive understanding of 'free will' is as libertarian free will. Our movements are not free if someone causes us to make them—my movement of my hand is not free if someone else moves it for me. But if someone else (or something else) causes those movements, they are not intentional actions of ours, i.e. caused by our wills. Analogously, our will is not free if someone or something else causes us to will as we do—whatever the way that cause operates (e.g. whether via causing us to will what we value, or to will what we do not value). To understand 'free will' in a compatibilist sense seems to give the term a more sophisticated, less natural sense. Hence, I suggest, the assumption must be (even if the context does not positively suggest it), unless the context positively suggests otherwise, that when an ancient theologian ascribes to humans 'free will' and thereby seeks to excuse God from responsibility for our bad actions, he is ascribing libertarian free will.

Elbow Room (Clarendon Press, 1984). Of course libertarian free will belongs only to an agent choosing intentionally between alternatives; it does not belong to any non-mental events, such as the random swervings of atoms, which are not fully caused.

Bearing this point in mind, my assessment of the Christian theological tradition is that all Christian theologians of the first four centuries believed in human free will in the libertarian sense, as did all subsequent Eastern Orthodox theologians, and most Western Catholic theologians from Duns Scotus (in the fourteenth century) onwards. The main Catholic declaration on this issue is that of the Council of Trent in the sixteenth century, which is firmly in favour of human free will, and in my view the context of that declaration positively implies libertarian free will. St Augustine in the fourth century seems to me, at any rate in his later writing, to believe that humans have only compatibilist free will. Whether Western theologians subsequent to Augustine and before Duns Scotus did in general believe in libertarian free will I am unclear; though I am clear that the greatest one, St Thomas Aquinas, was ambivalent on the issue.[10]

In my view most of those who deployed the 'free will' defence as part of their theodicy, to the extent to which they were clear about what they were doing, were deploying a defence in terms of libertarian free will. The free-will defence in this form is also a central plank of my own theodicy, and I shall be defending it at length over the course of later chapters. I shall in future understand by 'free will' free will in the libertarian sense, unless I state otherwise.

The Fall

The other strand central to many but by no means all theodicies has been the 'Fall' of the first human being, Adam; and (less

[10] For references to authors, in support of my assessment of the history, see my *Responsibility and Atonement* (Clarendon Press, 1989), 138–9. The authors referred to whom I cite as believers in libertarian free will (e.g. theologians before the 4th century) often do not explain what they mean by 'free will', but since they are normally putting forward the view that humans have 'free will' in contexts where they are seeking to show that God is not responsible for our bad choices or their consequences (e.g. the bad suffering in Hell), this, together with my point about the natural primitive understanding of free will, means that we must understand them as advocating libertarian free will.

Rowan Greer has argued that St Augustine initially accepted the traditional view that humans have significant free will, but that in his later theology he regards only Adam and the angels at the moment of their creation as having had this free will. (See Rowan A. Greer, 'Augustine's Transformation of the Free Will Defence', *Faith and Philosophy*, 13 (1996), 471–86.) I gloss this transformation as one from a belief in libertarian free will to a belief merely in compatibilist free will (for all humans other than Adam).

prominently) the Fall, before Adam, of angels, rational beings created by God with great powers, some of whom (their leader often
being called Satan or the Devil) chose the bad. Those theologians
who, like Augustine in his later period, came to believe that all later
humans had at most compatibilist free will were prepared to ascribe
to Adam and the angels (before their respective falls) libertarian
free will, and regarded much, if not all, of the later moral and natural evil in the world as due entirely to their (libertarianly) free bad
choices. The more numerous theologians who held that all humans
have some free will (and in my view that means libertarian free will)
saw the choices of Adam and the bad angels as having a significant
(though limited) role in causing natural evils, and in bolstering the
bad desires of later humans (though not predetermining whether or
not they would yield to those desires).

Bad angels and in particular Satan are mentioned occasionally in
the Old and New Testaments, and both the Book of Job and the
Revelation of St John picture them as having significant influence
in the world for bad. Later theologians developed the theory that
the angels at the beginning had just one free choice, which would
fix their subsequent character for ever. If an angel chose a good
character, that was fixed for ever; and if the angel chose a bad character, that too was fixed for ever. Angels, good and bad, were given
temporary influence over the world. Church tradition saw Satan as
the serpent of Genesis 3: 1, who tempted Eve, who in turn tempted
Adam to commit the first human sin.[11]

But theology has given much greater prominence to Adam, the
first human, as the source of much of the world's bad states. This
is because of the explicit statement in the opening book of the
Bible, that human suffering and death were due to the sentence
passed by God on Adam and Eve for their sins.[12] Later theology
did not take the details of this passage (the temptation being to
take a fruit etc.) very seriously. Likewise it skipped over the fact
that, according to Genesis, the first human sin seems to be that of
Eve rather than that of Adam. But it did in general affirm that
there was a first human sin, call it the sin of Adam, from which
severe consequences flowed. St Paul, in a famous passage which

---

[11] 'Man sinned at the suggestion of The Devil,' declared the Fourth Lateran
Council (M. Denzinger, *Enchiridion Symbolorum*, 23rd edn. (Freiberg, 1963), no.
800).
[12] Gen. 3: 16–19.

takes up the Genesis story, wrote that 'through one man sin entered the world and death through sin; and so death passed unto all men, for that all sinned'.[13] St Paul does not here mention Adam's sin as the cause of later suffering, only of death and sin; but many later Christian theologians have seen it as the cause of later suffering.

However, the view that the sin of Adam had a role in causing the death of later humans is a view somewhat more central to the Christian tradition than the view that Adam's sin had a role in causing the suffering of later humans. I shall be arguing later that death is not, as such, a bad state; it is simply the absence of a good state—although it may be closely connected with bad states of suffering in the dying or those close to them.

If this claim that the sin of the first human caused the subsequent proneness to suffering and death of later humans is read as the claim that the first human was naturally immortal and not prone to suffering, and that his (i.e. Adam's) sins changed that nature, it seems a claim very unlikely to be true in view of the close similarity of the nature of humans to that of animals. It seemed very unlikely even to many ancient thinkers who knew nothing of our common ancestry with the animals. Mortality and suffering seemed to them to be involved in the embodiedness of an organism as such, quite apart from any bad choice that it or an ancestor might have made. Hence the claim that Adam's sin caused the subsequent proneness to sin and death has often been read as the claim that while Adam was born liable to suffering and death, if he had not sinned, God would have intervened in the natural order to preserve him and any descendants from suffering (from which in his privileged position in Eden he had so far been preserved) and from death. And given the Christian doctrine that, in consequence of Christ's resurrection, God will give everlasting life (of some kind) to all (or at any rate to the good), it seems natural to suppose that if humans had not sinned and so needed Christ's redeeming work to restore them to wholeness, everlasting life (in this world or another one) would have been theirs anyway. That the effect of Adam's sin was to stop God acting supernaturally to prevent

---

[13] Rom. 5: 12. Rom. 5: 12–21 was the source used by Augustine for his doctrine of Original Guilt (see later). I have argued (*Responsibility and Atonement*, additional note 8) that St Paul gives no warrant for that doctrine in this passage.

suffering and death was the view of Augustine,[14] Aquinas,[15] and Scotus.[16]

Augustine and almost all who followed him in Western Christendom until the last two centuries held that Adam's sin caused (directly, or in the indirect way elucidated alone) not merely our suffering and death, but our sinfulness, i.e. the bad desires or inclinations, the proneness to do wrong both of later generations and of Adam himself, who did not (before his sin) suffer from this proneness. This proneness—as a major part of what theology has called 'Original Sin'—subsequent Christian theology has normally claimed, was transmitted by nature, not nurture, that is by some genetic means rather than by bad example.[17] Even if this claim is read (analogously to the preceding claims) as the claim that Adam had a suppressed sinfulness, while being given supernaturally a temporary non-proneness to sin; and that but for Adam's sin, God would have intervened to bestow a similar supernatural gift on subsequent humans, the claim is open to an initial difficulty not raised by the other claims: how, if he had no active bad desires, could he have sinned? I shall be arguing later that we cannot knowingly do wrong in the absence of bad desires. And Genesis emphasizes, as did subsequent theologians, that Adam sinned knowingly. There must have been the smallest of inclinations to sin already in him before it was abundantly magnified by Adam's subsequent actual sin.[18]

[14] Augustine writes of the 'privileged condition' of Adam and Eve in Paradise as 'a condition mysteriously maintained by nourishment from the tree of life, which would have been able to preserve them from sickness and from the ageing process' (*De Genesi ad Litteram*, 11. 32). That is, they needed external help to be preserved from mortality.

[15] Aquinas understands Adam's immortality to amount to the fact that God gave him a special supernatural grace which would have kept him from death, but which was withdrawn when Adam sinned (*Summa Theologiae*, Ia. 97. 1 and 2).

[16] *Quaestiones in Lib. ii sent.*, dist. 29. 5. See N. P. Williams, *The Ideas of the Fall and of Original Sin* (Longmans, Green, 1927), 409–10.

[17] See the Council of Trent (Denzinger 1513 and 1523) for its firm affirmation of the mechanism of transmission of 'Original Sin'. Original sin so transmitted included both sinfulness and some sort of responsibility for doing something about the consequences. This 'responsibility' has been understood by some as guilt, and so a bad state. I give in the text very brief reasons for rejecting that understanding. In my view the responsibility is a responsibility to deal with the consequences of a sin for which we later humans are not guilty. For justification of this understanding, see my *Responsibility and Atonement*, 145–6.

[18] Augustine distinguished the state of the Blessed in Heaven involving their inability to sin (*non posse peccare*) from the state of Adam, who had the ability not to sin (*posse non peccare*), but the latter did involve, according to Augustine, a

But Augustine had a rather different view of Adam from that of most of the theologians who preceded him, as well as of theologians in the East later than Augustine. Irenaeus wrote that 'man was a child, not yet having his understanding perfected. Wherefore he was easily led astray by the deceiver.'[19] That is, Adam was created as a weak creature and so already significantly prone to sin. If (non-suppressed) sinfulness was part of Adam's created nature, it follows that (barring divine intervention) we would have inherited sinfulness whether or not Adam himself had sinned.

For theologians before the fourth century, the 'Fall' was a fall from a lower pedestal than it was for later Western theologians. But beginning with Athanasius[20] a quite different doctrine of Adam developed mainly in the West, as a perfect man without significant proneness to sin, a doctrine of Adam's 'original righteousness' which reached its extravagant fullness in Augustine. He held that Adam was 'exempted from all physical evils, and endowed with immortal youth and health which could not be touched by the taint of sickness or the creeping debility of old age'.[21] If we had inherited that nature,[22] we would have had little proneness to sin; and so

certain openness to temptation—which it seems impossible to construe except as a very mild form of sinfulness. (See *Opus Imperfectum c. Iulianum*, 5. 61 and *City of God*, 12. 8.) Yet Augustine clearly did not want to put the matter in that way; and to impose consistency on anything Augustine has to say about the moral condition of human beings is a hard task.

[19] *Demonstration*, 12. See also his *Adversus Haereses*, 4. 38. 1. In the Eastern Orthodox tradition, a thousand years later St Gregory Palamas writes of 'our ancestors' 'being still in an imperfect and intermediate state—that is to say, easily influenced, whether for good or evil'. It was because of their immaturity that it was not good for them to eat of the tree of the knowledge of good and evil, which, however you interpret it, claimed St Gregory, clearly provided a superior kind of knowledge. Our ancestors ought instead first 'to have acquired more practice and so to speak, schooling in simple, genuine goodness' (*Topics in Natural and Theological Science*, in G. E. H. Palmer, P. Sherrard, and K. Ware (ed. and trans.), *Philokalia*, iv (Faber & Faber, 1995), 369–70).

[20] *Contra Gentes*, 2. 4.

[21] See Williams, *The Ideas of the Fall and of Original Sin*, 361, for references to Augustine's views on this.

[22] This doctrine of Adam's original righteousness was taken up in the Orthodox Confession of Peter of Moghila (as approved by the Council of Jassy, 1642), one of the important doctrinal statements of the Orthodox Church (though not one with authority similar to that of the Seven Ecumenical Councils). It claimed that Adam's innocence was joined 'with every perfection and innate righteousness, both on the side of intellect and on the side of will'. Williams (*The Ideas of the Fall and of Original Sin*, 543), whose translation I quote, comments that 'the definitely Augustinian tone' of these sections 'contrasts strongly with the vagueness which had previously characterised Eastern thought on this subject'.

Adam's sin was seen as the cause of our sinfulness. That view
became normal in the West. By contrast an important doctrinal
statement of the Orthodox Church (the confession of Dositheus,
ratified by the Council of Jerusalem in 1672) seems to support the
view that the consequences of Adam's Fall were confined to suffering and death.[23]

Even if one accepts that Adam's sin caused our sinfulness, sinfulness is only a proneness to sin; and, given that libertarian free
will remains, we can resist this proneness. If libertarian free will
does not remain, then of course it is predetermined whether or not
we will yield to temptation. Put another way, all theologians in the
West subsequent to Augustine held, against Pelagius, that we need
(in consequence of our sinfulness) God's gracious help—his
'grace'—in order not to sin when temptation occurs. But those who
believed that we still have libertarian free will believed that we then
have the free choice of whether to use this grace or not. Those who
did not believe that we have this free will believed that if sufficient
grace was not provided we would, if tempted, inevitably sin; and
that if sufficient grace was provided we would inevitably not sin.

Augustine claimed that, as well as causing suffering and death for
humans and our inclination to sin, Adam's sin made us guilty for
that sin. That view was in general unknown to earlier theologians,
except to several important ones who explicitly denied it.[24]
Augustine, however, fastened that doctrine on the Western Church
for many years, until the later medievals greatly toned it down or
abandoned it. Classical Protestantism temporarily reverted to the

[23] 'We believe that the first man was created by God and fell in Paradise, when,
neglecting the divine command, he obeyed the deceitful counsel of the serpent; and
that thence has flowed in succession the ancestral sin so that no one is born according to the flesh who does not bear this burden and perceive the fruits thereof in this
present world. And by the "fruits" and the "burden" we mean, not sin, such as im-
piety, blasphemy, murder . . . etc.: for many of the Patriarchs and Prophets, and
myriads of others of those both who lived in the shadow of the Law and in the truth
of the Gospel, and the divine Forerunner, and especially the mother of God the
Word, the ever-virgin Mary, had no share in these or like sins; but we mean those
things which the divine justice sends upon man as a penalty on account of the trans-
gression, such as the sweat of toil, tribulations, bodily infirmities, the pains of childbirth, a toilsome life during this pilgrimage, and finally bodily death' (Decretum 6,
trans. Williams, *The Ideas of the Fall and Original Sin*, 542).
   Much turns on how 'had no share in' is read. But the Decretum does not mention
increased proneness to sin, let alone guilt, as among the consequences of the Fall.
   [24] For references and fuller discussion of the doctrine of Original Guilt, see
Responsibility and Atonement, 144–6.

Augustinian doctrine. The Eastern Orthodox tradition has had little sympathy with this doctrine. I shall not discuss it further. It is clearly to be rejected on moral grounds: I cannot be guilty in respect of the sins of another.

As I wrote earlier, the Fall of Adam has played a role of varying prominence in the theologies of different theologians. While any theologian had to take account of the Genesis story, one could see it merely as describing an incident in early history without enormous cosmic significance. Alternatively, a few of the early Fathers thought of it not as history but as a representation by a myth of the state of each one of us. Gregory of Nyssa writes of Moses, the supposed author of Genesis, as 'placing doctrines before us in the form of a story'.[25] And that has been the view of many theologians of the past two or three centuries. In that case there is no doctrine at all of a historical Fall causing later bad states. I shall wish to accept a historical Fall, and give it some role in my theodicy, but not the kind of prominence which Augustine gave to it. In any case, as most theologians have seen, it could not solve the 'problem of evil' fully; it merely takes it one stage further back. There would still remain the problem why God allowed the moral evil of Adam's sin; or, if Satan had a role in this, the moral evil of Satan's sin—though it may be that, in this form, the problem is more readily soluble. And it is important to note that, although the Fall of Adam (and to a lesser extent of the angels) has had some importance in Christian theology, neither of them gets any explicit mention in Christian creeds and that not even the Fall of Adam has been seen as a doctrine right at the centre of the Christian faith.

Other Strands of Theodicy

The Old Testament contains several meditations, subsequent to that of the Book of Genesis, on theodicy, the best-known of which is that of the Book of Job. But exactly what is the final conclusion of that enigmatic book is much disputed. In any case it is a pre-Christian conclusion. The New Testament contains no systematic treatment of the source of all the world's bad states, though St

---

[25] *Catechetical Oration*, 5.

Paul's Epistle to the Romans contains a lengthy treatment of one particular bad state—the rejection of Jesus Christ by the Jews. The only clear conclusion of this section of the Epistle is that this bad state is only temporary and allowed to occur only for the sake of a great future good which it makes possible. And that is the theme prominent elsewhere in the New Testament with respect to other bad states. The parable of the tares and the wheat[26] emphasizes that the tares will be allowed to grow only until the harvest time, then they will be bound in bundles and burnt. But if the tares are dug up before the harvest, there is the risk that the wheat will be dug up with them before it is ripe. Jesus's reply to the question of his disciples (in St John's Gospel) about the man born blind, 'Who did sin, this man or his parents, that he should be born blind?', was: 'Neither did this man sin nor his parents, but [it happened in order] that the works of God should be made manifest in him.'[27] The explanation of the world's bad states lies not in their past causes but in the future good which they make possible.

Very many Christian writers have stressed the value of suffering for the human beings who suffer, in enabling them to form their souls for good. By showing courage and sympathy in the face of their suffering and that of others, people can become naturally good people. That is a theme especially prominent in the Eastern Orthodox tradition, which I shall warmly endorse. Then there has been the claim that the bad of much human sin is outweighed by the great good of the Incarnation resulting in Christ suffering with us[28] and above all redeeming us on the cross. While acknowledging that much bad is indeed mitigated by these subsequent good states, I shall deny that the subsequent good can possibly outweigh the bad which led to it. Another theme often deployed in Christian thinking is that some suffering is punishment for the sins of those who suffer. That is possible, but no major Christian theologian has claimed that this explains all suffering: how could it possibly explain the suffering of babies before they are capable of sin? (And note the words of Jesus cited at the end of the last paragraph.)

---

[26] Matt. 13: 24–30.

[27] John 9: 1–3. 'Nor his parents' is clearly to be read in a sense which rules out also more remote ancestors.

[28] In recent theology Jürgen Moltmann (*The Crucified God*, trans. R. A. Wilson and J. Bowden (SCM Press, 1974)) has emphasized the great good for us, that God in Christ manifests the love which suffers in solidarity with those who suffer. He does not, however, regard this as providing a full solution to the problem of evil.

The Christian tradition, while deeply worried about moral evil, has been less worried about natural evil, and less worried still about the problem of animal suffering. During most of Christian history, natural evil was often seen as an inevitable consequence of finitude, in the form of being embodied and mortal (the latter in the case of humans being a consequence of the Fall). For embodiment involves being at the mercy of the natural world: fire can burn us and water can drown us. And embodiment involves 'corruption'; our bodies decay, are subject to disease, and become weak and worn out. But it seems to me logically possible to have disease, even incurable disease, without agonizing pain; and those who write in this way do not give any rigorous arguments to show that this is not possible. Augustine, among many others before and since, pointed out that the natural causes of suffering can be used for good purposes, if we choose to use them for these purposes: 'Poisons which are destructive when used injudiciously, become wholesome and medicinal when used in conformity with their qualities and design; just as, on the other hand, those things which give us pleasure such as food, drink and the light of the sun, are found to be hurtful when used immoderately or unreasonably.'[29] True, but it was surely not beyond the power of God to make medicines which could not poison, and food in which we felt no inclination to indulge immoderately.

This same unthinking assumption about the inevitability of suffering for creatures embodied in a natural world has continued in a lot of modern theology. Schleiermacher, who may be considered the founder of the tradition of modern continental theology, derived this from the interdependence of the nature in which we are embodied: "The very same activity or condition of a thing by which it enters on the one hand into human life as an evil, on the other hand is a cause of good, so that if we could remove the source of life's difficulties the conditions of life's progress too would disappear.'[30] F. R. Tennant has argued with somewhat greater persuasiveness that we need to live in an orderly world (i.e. one governed largely by laws of nature) if we are to learn and make choices; and that an orderly world is inevitably one in which natural evil occurs. So 'if water is to have the various properties in virtue of which it

[29] *City of God*, 11. 22.
[30] F. Schleiermacher, *The Christian Faith*, sect. 48 (Eng. trans. ed. H. R. Mackintosh and J. S. Stewart (T. & T. Clark, 1989), 187).

plays its beneficial part in the economy of the physical world and the life of mankind, it cannot at the same time lack its obnoxious capacity to drown us'.[31] That may be so if water and humans are made as they are. But it seems to me far from evident that there could not be a different system of chemistry (deriving from a different system of physical laws), such that there was a substance which played the beneficial role of water without embodied rational creatures being at risk of death by drowning in it.

I think, nevertheless, that despite these evident difficulties, there is something right in the claim that embodiment and finitude, in which creatures have an ability to learn, involve natural processes producing suffering as well as good. One of my tasks in this book will be to show in just which qualified form this claim is correct.

So I shall want to use many of the various strands in the Christian tradition of theodicy, emphasizing some and downplaying others, in the articulation of my own theodicy. But what I shall also use from the Christian tradition is its understanding of what is good and bad for the inanimate world and for human and animal life. In listing the good and bad states in Part II, I shall bring out there and in my final chapter that the insights on this of the Christian tradition (most of which could be attained without religious assumptions, by reflective secular thought) provide the materials for a satisfactory theodicy. I shall want to stress not only the value of human free will, but above all the value for us of our lives being of use to others. There have in the Christian tradition also been many writers who affirm that since we know that there is a God, we know that there is some true theodicy (a true account of possible, and indeed actual, reasons why God would allow moral and natural evil to occur), but deny that we have any idea what it is. In communities where the apparently knowledgeable people (whom we have reason to trust on theoretical matters) tell us that God exists; where the apparently knowledgeable people can produce arguments from the natural world or from scripture purporting to show that God exists; where some people purport to have direct awareness of God; and where there are no counter-arguments in circulation, a belief that there is a God will be strongly justified. It will be so well justified as to overwhelm any apparent objections from the bad states of the world, so that people

---

[31] *Philosophical Theology*, ii (Cambridge University Press, 1930), 201.

in those communities will all have a well-justified belief that God has good reason for allowing the bad states to occur—even if they have not the slightest idea what that reason could be. Many in the past were in that situation, but many of us today are not; and hence the need for theodicy or at least progress towards one. And so I move to set out my theodicy. Part II will describe the good purposes God may be expected to have (and the Christian revelation claims that he does have). Part III will show that if God seeks to realize these, he inevitably allows the bad states of this world to occur; but that (given the Christian revelation) he does all else he can to secure the good. Part IV will argue that God has the right to allow the bad, and that the good outweighs the bad.

II
The Good Goals of Creation

3

Beauty

In the beginning God created the heaven and the earth. And
the earth was waste and void; and darkness was upon the face
of the deep: and the spirit of God moved upon the face of the
waters. And God said, Let there be light: and there was light.
And God saw the light, that it was good: and God divided the
light from the darkness. And God called the light Day, and the
darkness he called Night. And there was evening and there
was morning, one day. And God said, Let there be a firmament in the midst of the waters, and let it divide the waters
from the waters. And God made the firmament, and divided
the waters which were under the firmament from the waters
which were above the firmament: and it was so. And God
called the firmament Heaven. And there was evening and
there was morning, a second day. And God said, Let the
waters under the heaven be gathered together unto one place,
and let the dry land appear: and it was so. And God called the
dry land Earth; and the gathering together of the waters called
he Seas: and God saw that it was good. And God said, Let the
earth put forth grass, herb yielding seed, and fruit tree bearing
fruit after its kind, wherein is the seed thereof, upon the earth:
and it was so. And the earth brought forth grass, herb yielding
seed after its kind, and tree bearing fruit, wherein is the seed
thereof, after its kind: and God saw that it was good. And there
was evening and there was morning, a third day. And God
said, Let there be lights in the firmament of the heaven to
divide the day from the night; and let them be for signs and for
seasons, and for days and years: and let them be for lights in
the firmament of the heaven to give light upon the earth: and
it was so. And God made the two great lights; the greater light
to rule the day, and the lesser light to rule the night: he made
the stars also. And God set them in the firmament of the
heaven to give light upon the earth and to rule over the day and
over the night, and to divide the light from the darkness: and

God saw that it was good. And there was evening and there
was morning, a fourth day.

(Genesis 1: 1–19)

A perfectly good God will seek to do many good actions and no bad
ones. Good actions often derive their goodness from bringing
about states of affairs which are intrinsically good, i.e. good because
of what they are and not because of how they were brought about
or what they cause. Although it is not always, as we have seen, a bad
action to bring about an intrinsically bad state of affairs, it requires
the special conditions described in Chapter 1 to make it not a bad
action. Other things being equal, a good God will seek to bring
about much good and no bad. I plan in Part II to list many of the
good states which a perfectly good God might seek to bring about,
and many of the bad states which (barring special conditions) he
will not bring about. I shall point out also that Christianity has
claimed, with respect to many of these good states, that God does
indeed have the purpose of bringing them about. The goodness of
good states and the badness of bad states arise from their being good
or bad for someone or something; and every state which is good (or
bad) for someone or something is (in that respect) good (or bad).
We shall need to be clear about who or what the person or thing is
which is being benefited or harmed. This is because, as I shall argue
in Chapter 12, if God is to have the right to allow some bad to come
about, that can only be if God gives to the individual to whom
the bad happens a life in which on balance the good outweighs the
bad.

I have no general formula for picking out good (and bad) states
of affairs; I believe them to be too diverse to fall under any such formula. That that is so was one of the main conclusions of chapter 6
of G. E. Moore's *Principia Ethica*. There is, he wrote, 'a vast variety' of 'great intrinsic goods' and 'great intrinsic evils'. Another
main conclusion of that chapter is that most of them are 'highly
complex wholes composed of parts which have little or no value in
themselves'.[1] While wishing to emphasize that the goodness or

---

[1] G. E. Moore, *Principia Ethica* (Cambridge University Press, 1903), 224.
Moore held, however, that while 'evils' could be necessary constituents of great
goods, in fact the 'evils' of this world always outweigh the goods which they make
possible. Hence (p. 220), 'we cannot admit the actual validity of any of the arguments commonly used in theodicies'.

badness of complex wholes is often very different from that resulting from any arithmetical sum of the goodness or badness of parts,
I demur from Moore's suggestion that many ordinary things have
no value in themselves. Surely every concrete thing—stick or
stone—has value in itself; it is intrinsically good that it exists. And
since this goodness does not arise solely from it being good for
someone or something else that it exists, we should say (odd though
it may sound initially) that it is good for it that it exists.

The existence of all concrete things—of stones and icebergs, of
wind and fire, and mountains and valleys—is good in itself. The
more of them, the better. And better that they be arranged in a
beautiful way. Could anyone who has come to admire sculpture
possibly deny that? But better still is a moving sculpture—a process
whereby trillions of trillions of concrete things emerge from simple
beginnings. Could anyone who has come to admire dance possibly
deny that? And good that they should come in kinds with marvellous patterns of colour, new kinds emerging from old—a living
painting. The goodness of the existence and beauty of the non-
conscious world—both the simpler inorganic world and the more
complex world of plants, of trees and grasses and flowers—is so
obvious; and yet it needs a poet to bring it alive. Some of the prose
poetry of the more popular science books does quite well in bringing alive the simplicity of the principles of behaviour (laws of
nature) which governed the behaviour of the immensely hot and
dense quanta of matter-energy at the time of the Big Bang; how
they cooled to form the chemical elements and then larger molecules; how the vast clouds of stuff coalesced into stars which
formed galaxies, and cooler bodies—planets; and how the larger
molecules came together to form simple and then more complex
plants. My poor pen is ill equipped to depict the greatness of the
dance of the Universe. But is it not obvious that a good God would
seek to bring about such beauty?

The Bible begins with the affirmation cited above (expressed in
the form of a hymn, representing the process of creation as taking
place in idealized day-stages) that God did bring about the inanimate world, because it was good in itself. And this has been a constant theme of subsequent Christian theology. All the medievals
thought that everything that exists (i.e. every concrete thing
that exists) is good in virtue of that very fact that it exists. They
disagreed among themselves about whether that goodness was

intrinsic to anything existent; or whether it belonged to created things in virtue of their being created by, and so in some sense 'participating in', a good God. I suggest that we take the former position, which was that of Augustine:[2] the goodness of stones is not dependent on who created them; God created stones because for other reasons (i.e. intrinsically) their existence is good.

It may be objected that there is nothing good in a work of art if no one observes it. This objection, which is of a type which we shall meet several times in this book, seems to me mistaken. When people admire a beautiful work of art, they are not admiring the effect of the work on their own consciousness; they do not say 'This is a wonderful painting because it produces these feelings in me and other people who look at it'. Rather, it is because they believe that it has some beautiful feature, which they have been fortunate to notice, that it does produce the appropriate feelings. The 'feeling' involves as an essential part the belief that the painting is beautiful in itself, that it has a beauty which it would still have even if no one had the right sensory equipment to notice it. Of course it is also good that people admire what is beautiful; but the beauty of the beautiful does not depend on being recognized. How could it? For recognition of beauty, as of anything else, depends on the existence of the feature before and independently of being recognized.

But anyway, even if I were mistaken about this and there is only a point in the existence of beautiful things if someone admires them, God has a very good reason for making a beautiful Universe, namely that he himself will admire it (not admire it because he made it, of course; but because what he made is admirable). And of course it is good that the beautiful Universe also be admired by very many other conscious beings; that is a good for them. That is a further point in creating it. And at the end of the twentieth century we humans on Earth are in the privileged position of being able to look through our telescopes and see it, not merely as it is now, but as it was in the early stages of its emergence from the Big Bang.

While the existence of any concrete thing is a good, its non-existence is not a bad state of affairs; it is just the absence of a good state. If the non-existence of things was intrinsically bad, then any

---

[2] 'Whatsoever things are, are good' (Augustine, *Confessions*, 7. 12). For analysis of medieval discussions of why existent things are good, see Scott MacDonald (ed.), *Being and Goodness* (Cornell University Press, 1991), introd.

world would be a very bad place indeed—because there would be so many things it did not contain. If one thinks of ugliness as a negative quality, as opposed to being the mere absence of beauty, one would be hard put to think of any part of the pre-human world which is ugly; ugliness in this sense seems to arrive with the arrival of humans, who, knowingly or unknowingly, make something which could be beautiful ugly instead.

The goodness of the inanimate world (in its very existence and its powerful beauty) and so (if there is a God) God's interest in creating it are too obvious to need further prose discussion. 'Consider the lilies of the field,' said Jesus, 'how they grow; they toil not, neither do they spin: yet I say to you that even Solomon in all his glory was not arrayed like one of these.'[3]

[3] Matt. 6: 28–9.

4

Thought and Feeling

And God said, Let the waters bring forth abundantly the
moving creature that hath life, and let fowl fly above the earth
in the open firmament of heaven. And God created the sea-
monsters, and every living creature that moveth, which the
waters brought forth abundantly, after their kinds, and every
winged fowl after its kind: and God saw that it was good. And
God blessed them, saying, Be fruitful, and multiply, and fill
the waters in the seas, and let fowl multiply in the earth. And
there was evening and there was morning, a fifth day. And
God said, Let the earth bring forth the living creature after its
kind, cattle, and creeping thing, and beast of the earth after its
kind: and it was so. And God made the beast of the earth after
its kind, and the cattle after their kind, and every thing that
creepeth upon the ground after its kind: and God saw that it
was good.

(Genesis 1: 20–5)

Good though the inanimate world is, clearly the animate world of
animals and humans is even better, and a major reason for this is
that animals and humans have mental lives[1] of belief and thought,
desire, sensation, and purpose. I shall consider in this chapter the
involuntary mental states, and in particular beliefs and desires—
which are states with which subjects find themselves, not through
their own choice and which they cannot change in the short term
(though they can take steps which will lead to change of these in the

---

[1] I understand by a 'mental' state one to which the subject has privileged access,
one about which—if she so chooses—she can know better than can anyone else.
Mental states include conscious states, such as sensations (e.g. an image of blue in
my visual field) of which we must to some extent be aware while we have them; and
states such as beliefs which continue while we are not aware of them. On the nature
and taxonomy of the mental life, see my *The Evolution of the Soul*, rev. edn.
(Clarendon Press, 1997), pt. I.

long term); and go on in the next chapter to consider purposes manifested in intentional action. I seek to list the many good such states which a perfectly good God might seek to bring about, and to contrast them with the bad states which (barring special conditions) he will not bring about.

Beliefs

Beliefs are views about how the world is. We find ourselves with certain beliefs—that I am in Oxford, that today is Monday, that there is no greatest prime number—which we cannot change in the short term. We can, however, investigate them further and then come to believe what our investigations reveal (which may or may not be different from what we believed to start with). (Or we can sometimes brainwash ourselves over time into having some belief which we desire to have; and then try to forget that we have done this.) But a 'belief' would not be a belief if we could change it readily at will (and so realize that we are doing it). For if some attitude is to be a belief we must think of it as corresponding to how things are in the world and so as liable to change as things change in the world and thus as caused by the world. If we could choose our 'beliefs', we would have no reason to suppose that they corresponded to how things are, and thus we would not regard them as beliefs.[2]

True belief is a very basic good. Many true beliefs are of course instrumentally good. A true belief about which road leads home will enable me to bring about the fulfilment of my desire to be at home. But my suggestion is that true beliefs are also intrinsically good (both for the believer and for the objects of belief)—all true beliefs, but especially ones which concern rational agents (e.g. humans) and other sentient beings (e.g. animals), and the history of the environment in which they have lived. One of the greatest misfortunes that can happen to a person, the ancients realized, is for his 'memory' (i.e. memory about him) to be 'blotted out'.[3] And even today we recognize it as a great misfortune for someone who is dead when he is falsely believed to have done something wrong: hence

---

[2] For fuller justification of the involuntary character of all beliefs, see ibid. 126–8.
[3] See e.g. Dante, *Inferno*, III. iv. 9.

public campaigns to 'clear' someone's 'name'. This is because what people did and what happened to them matters; and recollecting these things consciously (and so having them available in accessible memory or written record) gives them a certain life after death (in a metaphorical sense) and constitutes an acknowledgement of their importance and a tribute to them. It is good for those who do things and to whom things happen that they be 'preserved'—truly; a false memory does not acknowledge the actual deeds and happenings.

True beliefs about past individuals are especially worth having where what is believed is to the credit of those individuals, e.g. that they did great things, despite much suffering.[4] But so long as there is some good in their lives, they are worth remembering; and remembering the bad things as well fleshes out the memory of the good things, and makes the whole person 'come alive'. And mere living—the existence of an animate being which itself has beliefs— means that there is some good in that life.

As it is a good for the past individuals to be recalled, and as it is a good for anyone to have the privilege of benefiting others (a point I shall wish to emphasize a lot more in due course), so it is a good for present individuals to have the privilege of recalling past indi- viduals—of having true beliefs about individuals worth recalling, and of being the vehicles of telling others about them. The greater the connection of the past individuals with ourselves, the more appropriate it is that it is we who recall them. And even the inani- mate merits respect: it is a good for the Universe that we have a true belief about its constitution and history, and in so far as it has formed us, it becomes more appropriate that we pay that tribute to it.

These things are also a good for us, not only because we give a certain life after death to the past, but because we acquire thereby, also in a metaphorical sense, a certain control over them. To under- stand is already to begin to master. Control over things is a good for us (a point which also I shall need to emphasize a lot more)—like so many goods, capable of abuse, but a good all the same. The good-

---

[4] The Wisdom literature of the Old Testament is a very powerful advocate of the value for those who achieve worthwhile things, of being recalled. 'In the memory of virtue is immortality, because it is recognized both before God and before men' (Wisd. 4: 1). The famous passage from Ecclus. 44, so often read at 'Com- memorations of Benefactors', contrasts the blessedness of those who 'have left a name behind them' (v. 8) with the wretchedness of those who 'have no memorial' (v. 9).

ness of true beliefs on important matters constitutes, I think, the major reason why benefactors give large sums of money for research into the distribution of the galaxies, the 'initial state' of the Universe, the history of science and culture. Of course such research, like research into the life stories of our immediate relatives, may have some instrumental value. But it is implausible to suppose that many of those who finance and pursue it do so primarily because of that possibility. They clearly regard the acquisition of true beliefs on these matters as intrinsic goods, and I have tried to explain what makes them such.

Especially important is to have true beliefs about moral matters—to believe that it is good to give to the starving and bad to torture children. Obviously there are instrumental reasons why true beliefs here matter: they guide our actions. And the 'control' reason also applies. But there is clearly a further reason here: we are intrinsically better people for having the right outlook on moral matters. Our goodness is in part a matter of how we view the world; someone with false moral views is the worse for that, even if he is in no position to act on them.

It is good that our true beliefs should be strong ones: they guide our actions more firmly and enable us to see more clearly how the world is. Is strong true belief the better if it amounts to knowledge, if it has also that extra something—let us call it 'warrant'—which turns it into knowledge? That depends on what 'warrant' is. My view is that 'knowledge' is a fairly vague notion and that there are different ways of spelling it out, some of them largely internalist, some more or less externalist. An internalist theory of knowledge claims that the 'warrant' which turns a true belief into knowledge arises (in major part) from something internal to the subject (i.e. something to which she has ready access). A belief has warrant, for example (to put the point loosely, at this stage), if it is supported by the subject's other beliefs, or is based on immediate experience. An externalist theory claims that warrant arises solely from something external to the subject to which she may have no access. The most common version of externalism is reliabilism, which holds that a belief has warrant when it is produced by a process such as perception which normally produces true beliefs.[5]

---

[5] For an extended statement of reliabilism, the most common version of externalism, see A. Goldman, *Epistemology and Cognition* (Harvard University Press, 1986), pt. I. For a traditional statement of internalism, see Roderick Chisholm,

Now clearly it is a good thing that our beliefs satisfy the reliabilist requirement, for the fact that they do means that (given the evidence of their method of production) they will probably be true. But, if a given belief of mine is true, I cannot see that it is any more worth having for satisfying the reliabilist requirement. So long as the belief is true, the fact that the process which produced it usually produces true beliefs does not seem to make that belief any more worth having: just as so long as a desk is beautiful and useful, it is no better for having been produced in a factory that normally produces beautiful and useful products rather than in one which normally produces ugly and useless products. An alternative form of externalism spells out 'warrant' in terms of 'proper functioning': a belief has warrant if it arises in us as a result of the proper functioning of our cognitive apparatus. If there is no God, then proper functioning will amount to (roughly) functioning the way Evolution (in some sense) planned us to function; but I cannot see why a true belief would be the better for functioning in this way. If there is a God, then proper functioning amounts (roughly) to 'functioning the way God intended it to function'. This sort of proper functioning might well add to the worth of a true belief and that would be because thereby it constituted the fulfilment of a desire or purpose, in this case God's desire or purpose—on the goodness of the fulfilment of which I shall be commenting in due course.

What about 'warrant' in an internalist sense? The core component of 'warrant' for an internalist is 'justification'. To amount to knowledge, a (strong) true belief must be 'justified'. But there are different ways of understanding 'justification', according to whether the justification is a matter of satisfying the subject's own immediately accessible criteria or whether it is a matter of satisfying the true criteria, which a subject might not have initially in a clear form but which he can reach by reflection. The true criteria are the necessary a priori inductive criteria of what are the proper starting-points for belief, and of what makes what probable. The a priori is internally accessible; that is, what is true in this field does

Theory of Knowledge, 3rd edn. (Prentice-Hall, 1989). For an introduction to epistemology, contrasting internalist and externalist theories, see Keith Lehrer, *Theory of Knowledge* (Routledge, 1990). A full statement of the proper functioning version of externalism is to be found in Alvin Plantinga, *Warrant and Proper Function* (Oxford University Press, 1993).

not depend on how things are in the world outside ourselves but solely on the relations between concepts which we can discover by inner mental reflection. Yet the a priori is not necessarily what we believe it to be on first thinking about it. This can be illustrated by mathematical beliefs, which provide a paradigm example of beliefs which can amount to a priori knowledge. I might initially think that $5 + 7 = 13$ or that there is a greatest prime number; reflection will lead me to see that $5 + 7 = 12$, not 13, and that there is no greatest prime number. Similarly, with our inductive criteria I might think initially that the fact that a coin has landed ninety-nine 'heads' in a row after one 'tail' makes it probable that it will land tails next time (the 'Monte Carlo' fallacy), but later realize that that is not so: rather the fact that it has landed heads ninety-nine times out of 100 is evidence that the coin is biased and so will land heads next time.

I considered the subjective internalist sense of justification in Chapter 1, because our concern there was with subjects having beliefs which they were not epistemically at fault in having. In that sense a belief is justified if (by the subject's own criteria) it is rendered probable by the subject's other justified beliefs, or it is properly basic. Following an earlier terminology of mine,[6] let us call such beliefs 'justified$_1$' or 'rational$_1$'. But while a subject may not be at fault in operating in accordance with her own criteria, clearly it is better if she operates by true criteria: a belief is justified in an objective sense either if it is rendered probable by the subject's other justified beliefs or if it is properly basic. A belief thus justified I shall call 'justified$_2$' or 'rational$_2$'. The difference from the previous definition arises from the omission of the words 'by the subject's own criteria' which govern both of the following clauses. We all believe that there are true criteria for what makes what probable, for what is evidence for what. To hold that e makes h probable is to hold that it does so by true criteria; we believe that the criteria each of us applies in making such judgements are the true ones; otherwise we would regard it as equally permissible to hold the wildest beliefs on the grounds of present evidence—to think, for example, that ninety-nine heads in a row makes it probable that five blue parrots will fly into the room. In fact, not merely do we hold that there are true criteria for what makes what probable and that we have these, but that it is also the case that almost everyone has very

---

[6] See my *Faith and Reason* (Clarendon Press, 1981), 45.

similar criteria and so a very similar view about what are the true criteria. I need, for later purposes, to summarize briefly what (as almost all will agree) are some of these true criteria.[7] (Note that I use the word 'likely' with the same meaning as 'probable'; and sometimes write elsewhere of the probability of something happening as the chance of it happening.)

First, a hypothesis is more likely to be true, in so far as it renders probable what we observe (e.g. gives true predictions). Secondly, the probability given to a hypothesis by the fact that it makes it probable that we will observe what we do is diminished in so far as those observations are ones which are fairly probable anyway (that is, even if the hypothesis in question is false). Thirdly, a hypothesis is more likely to be true in so far as it is simple. It is an important consequence of the second criterion that a hypothesis of the form 'All *A*s are *B*' is more likely to be true if we observe many *A*s which are *B* (and none which are not *B*) than if we observe only a few. For the more we observe, the less probable it is that we will find what we observe (namely, more and more *A*s all being *B*) if it is not the case that all *A*s are *B*. For the same reason such a hypothesis is more likely to be true if the *A*s which we observe are observed under varied conditions; if all *A*s which we observe are observed in certain narrow conditions, *C*, it is almost as probable that there is no general regularity that all *A*s are *B*, but only the regularity that all *A*s under conditions *C* are *B*. And, finally, what *A*s and more varied *A*s, all found to be *B*, show is not a coincidental connection between being *A* and being *B*, but a physically necessary connection—most simply that being *A* causes something to be *B*, or, less simply, that being *A* and being *B* have a common cause.[8]

---

[7] If you do not believe that there are these true criteria of probability, then among the wild criteria which there is no reason not to adopt are criteria from which it follows that the fact that other people are screaming is no reason for supposing that they are in pain; and that (even if she cannot recall so asking) anyone's suffering is always suffering which she has asked God to give her. With criteria like this, we would conclude that there is very little suffering, apart from what we have asked God to give us; and the problem of evil would be solved very quickly. The problem is a serious problem only because we assume that our criteria of probability are correct ones.

[8] I am assuming that '*A*' and '*B*' are projectible predicates, e.g. predicates like 'emerald' or 'green', rather than predicates defined in complicated ways in terms of such predicates, such as 'grue' (where an object is said to be grue at a time if and only if the object is green and the time is before AD 2000 *or* blue and the time is after AD 2000). It will not be appropriate to discuss here the important issue of how projectible predicates are to be recognized as such. On the latter, see e.g. Nelson

Other important evidential criteria which I believe to be a priori include criteria for inferring to people's thoughts and feelings from the way they behave, and to their beliefs from what they say; and a criterion to the effect that (in the absence of counter-evidence) we should believe what people tell us about what they themselves believe. For people are aware of what they believe; if we do not trust what they tell us about their beliefs without further positive evidence of their reliability, we would have no grounds for most of our beliefs about the lives of those close to us or about history or geography etc. We have beliefs about these matters because others have told us what they believe, and that they have their beliefs because they are rendered probable by others of their beliefs. I believe what I do about history because others have told me (in writing) what they believe and that their beliefs are based on certain documents which they believe that they have seen. If I could not trust what others write about history without checking them out, I would have very little by way of justified historical beliefs. All of these criteria are criteria of what is evidence for what—that is, of which of our beliefs (about what we have seen or experienced, or others have told us) make other beliefs probable.

We also have our a priori criteria, and believe that they are in general true criteria, of proper basicality—that is, of which beliefs have some degree of probability simply on the basis of it seeming to the subject that they are true; criteria, that is, for what sort of content a belief has to have in order to be a correct starting-point for the process of forming other beliefs. Clearly any belief which is necessarily false (e.g. that $2 + 2 = 5$) is not a properly basic belief. And although perhaps even in this objective internalist sense it is right for us to start from whatever beliefs (about contingent matters) we find ourselves with, a belief about the apparent deliverance of perception forms a better justified starting-point for belief-building than some general world-view (e.g. the truth of quantum theory) or some claim about the future (e.g. that it will rain tomorrow) of which we are convinced. There is an important reason for this which we can reach by reflection. Our beliefs about what we are currently perceiving are caused by a short causal chain from a state of the public world to which those beliefs purport to correspond. For the beliefs to be true, only that short chain has to operate

Goodman, *Fact, Fiction and Forecast*, 2nd edn. (Bobbs-Merrill, 1965), ch. 4; and my *An Introduction to Confirmation Theory* (Methuen, 1973), ch. 7.

correctly. But if we have a belief about what will happen tomorrow or which scientific theory is true, there can be no direct causation (given the logical impossibility of the future causing the past). Any mechanism correlating belief and state believed will be indirect, in the sense that it will depend on two separate causal chains (some earlier unobserved state causing both the belief and the state believed). Such a mechanism will be more liable to incorrect operation and so to producing false beliefs than one where the belief concerns what we currently observe. A basic belief that the sun rose today will inevitably be a more properly basic belief (i.e. have a much greater probability, be a better justified starting-point for belief) than a basic belief that it will rise tomorrow. For the same reason a belief about what I am currently observing is as such a more properly basic belief than a memory belief about what I saw yesterday (where the causal chain is much longer).

All of these criteria—both of what is evidence for what and of proper basicality—are a priori. They are part of the armoury with which we come to experience and in virtue of which we can extrapolate from it to the past, the future, the unobserved, and very general theories. Unless we had a priori criteria we could take no step beyond experience. (We do of course use other rules as well for judging what makes what probable and what are proper starting-points for belief, which are empirically based, e.g. that this kind of witness often lies, or that fingerprints at a place make it probable that the one and only person with prints of that shape was present at that place. But we use these rules because it can be shown probable that they yield correct results by a priori properly basic beliefs in virtue of a priori criteria of probability.) Scientists would never agree—as they almost always do—about which theory their evidence supports unless they had these common criteria, and we would regard their results as arbitrary unless we thought that in general their common criteria were the correct ones.

Now again it is good that our beliefs should be justified$_2$ because it matters that we have true beliefs, and if they are justified$_2$ they are probably true. But the best any of us can do towards having justified$_2$ beliefs at a given time is to have justified$_1$ beliefs, beliefs which seem to us at that time to be probable on our criteria (i.e. the ones which seem to us correct). Over time we can try to improve our criteria. But because it is the best we can achieve at a time, it matters also that we should at each time have justified₁ beliefs. The internal coherence of our beliefs gives us in a different important respect the good of a rational outlook on the world. However, if knowledge is understood in an internalist sense as involving 'justified true (strong) belief', clearly 'justified₂' is the more plausible candidate for the justification involved. Someone who by a lucky accident had strong beliefs which are true and rendered probable by his own crazy standards could not be said to have knowledge. The person who claims to know that the coin will land tails because ninety-nine of the 100 past tosses have been heads does not really know that—even if the coin does land tails.

In order to have an account of knowledge in anything like the ordinary sense, the internalist needs to add two further conditions to the account so far of knowledge as justified true (strong) belief. First, he needs a condition to deal with the 'Gettier effect', that if the justification for a true belief 'proceeds via' some false belief, then we do not have knowledge.⁹ Clearly it is a good thing that this condition be fulfilled also, if only for the reason that it is good that all our beliefs should be true. An internalist will also need to add a condition to the effect that to amount to knowledge a belief must be 'based on' its evidence. That is, if what justifies the belief *B* is that it is rendered probable by other beliefs of the subject, these other beliefs must cause the subject to hold *B*.¹⁰ The objective relations of probability must be those which affect the subject in her belief formation. Even if the subject's belief *B* is made probable by her other beliefs, it must not be a mere coincidence that this is so; it

---

⁹ The simplest kind of example to illustrate the case where someone has a justified true belief the justification for which proceeds via a false proposition is as follows. I believe with justification that you own a Ford car (because I have seen you drive one). But if I am justified in believing that you own a Ford car, I am justified in believing any proposition which that entails, for example that 'Either you own a Ford car or you will win the lottery'. Suppose I do believe this latter proposition. You do not, however, own a Ford, but you do win the lottery. So I have a justified true belief that either you own a Ford car or you will win the lottery. But plausibly this does not amount to knowledge, because my justification for believing it proceeds via a false proposition—that you own a Ford. This kind of example was drawn to philosophical attention by Edmund L. Gettier, 'Is Justified True Belief Knowledge?', *Analysis*, 23 (1963), 121–3. For discussion of the kind of extra condition needed, see Keith Lehrer, *Knowledge* (Clarendon Press, 1974), ch. 1.

¹⁰ The 'basing' clause may need to be phrased more carefully than this, but the main point of such a clause should be clear. For more sophisticated accounts of this, see K. A. Korcz, 'Recent Work on the Basing Relation', *American Philosophical Quarterly*, 34 (1997), 171–91.

must not be the case that B is formed by wishful thinking and the subject has not seen the force of evidence in favour of *B* constituted by her other beliefs.

Now if knowledge is construed as justified$_2$ strong true belief based on its evidence (that is, on our properly basic beliefs) (where the justification does not proceed by a false proposition—the Gettier condition), is it a better thing to have than is mere strong true belief (with a Gettier condition satisfied)? If we respond to our evidence in accordance with correct criteria for assessing it, it is more probable that we shall get true beliefs than if we assess it in accordance with incorrect criteria. But why should it matter if an individual true belief has been formed in accordance with incorrect criteria? I claimed earlier that it would not matter if an individual true belief was not formed by a reliable process. But there is a difference here, arising from the fact that forming beliefs in accordance with criteria is normally a process of which the subject (at any rate the average human subject) is almost always at least half-conscious. We are at least half-conscious of the criteria we use in inferring from evidence to hypothesis (though it may need a philosopher or psychologist to make them fully explicit). But then, one who operates on false criteria will have false beliefs about what is evidence for what, about the right way to assess beliefs. And false beliefs here are false beliefs about something very central to human rationality. So if true belief matters, true belief which is justified is even more valuable. Furthermore, we value the great scientists of the past not just for getting the answer right, and not just for having true beliefs about justification, but for being influenced by those beliefs in forming their scientific theories; for seeing the force of complex evidence and being guided by it; for responding consciously to the world in their beliefs in the right way. A person who does this does not merely have rational beliefs in an important sense, but is a rational being. I conclude that knowledge in the internalist sense is a better thing to have than mere strong true belief; though knowledge in the most common externalist sense, the reliabilist sense, is not. A capacity for knowledge in the objective internalist sense is one of the hallmarks of human beings.

The Christian tradition has always seen its capacity for having knowledge of deep truths, with the allied capacity to reach such knowledge by reason (see next chapter), as one of the great-making features of humans. The Greek background of the tradition of course stressed this. Plato emphasized the difference between 'true opinion' and 'reason', holding that 'only the gods and a small group of humans partake of reason'.[11] Aristotle's *Metaphysics*, however, begins with the claims that 'all humans by their nature desire to know . . . Animals other than humans live by sense, impression and memory with but a small share in connected experience, whereas the human race lives by art and science.'[12] For both writers the knowledge that mattered was knowledge of the underlying principles of things. For all Christian theologians from the beginning of the Christian tradition, man was made in the image of God; and a primary element of that image was the power of reasoning. What makes man different from the animals which were created before him is his intellectual nature. John of Damascus said about this what all others also said: God 'creates with his own hands man of a visible nature and an invisible, after his own image and likeness: on the one hand man's body he formed of earth, and on the other his reasoning and thinking soul'.[13] In stressing its connection with the reasoning power of humans, theologians make it clear that the knowledge which they see as so good is knowledge in the internalist sense.

But it is not only human beings who have knowledge. The higher animals know things about their environment: where the food or predators are, where their young are, how to feed the young, and so on. These are not mere beliefs. They are true beliefs, either properly basic ones or ones formed on the basis of experience, namely on the basis of other beliefs which make them probable (though of course animals do not have an explicit concept of probability). And the other conditions for knowledge are also normally satisfied. It is good that higher animals act in the light of knowledge rather than respond instinctively as do the lower animals. It is good that birds get worms, because they know that their young want them and they seek to feed the young. It is good that the deer avoids the fire, because it knows that the fire is dangerous. If knowledge is the good we believe it to be in humans, a lesser degree and amount of knowledge in animals is a lesser good.

Reason is shown not merely in the possession of beliefs which amount to knowledge, but in responding to new evidence with changing beliefs. Learning from experience (as opposed to being

---

[11] *Timaeus* 51e.   [12] *Metaphysics* 980^{a-b}; my italics.
[13] *De Fide Orthodoxa*, 2. 12.

told by some expert) is, I suggest, a further good beyond the mere possession of knowledge. We value the great scientists not merely for having beliefs based on evidence in the right way, but for changing and developing their beliefs as new evidence turns up, for learning from experience. Consider some scientist Smith who originally held (with justification$_2$, given his evidence) some quite false theory of the Universe T_1; and then, being shown new evidence with which that theory was not compatible, and suddenly thinking of a new theory T_2 supported by all the evidence new and old, comes to hold the new theory. Contrast him with Jones, who was shown in his youth all the evidence which Smith eventually saw and, told about T_2, comes to hold it because of the evidence. Both are equally rational in their response to evidence, but Smith alone in a crucial sense learns from experience. He alone manifests a rationality prepared to give up old views in the light of new evidence. When we look at the history of science, we see that our heroes are not as such those who hold true theories on good grounds, but those prepared to abandon old theories in the light of new evidence, in order to adopt the true theories on good grounds. We value the process of knowledge acquisition in the light of new evidence additional to the product, knowledge.

I began this section by dwelling on the goodness of true belief. By contrast all the reasons that make true belief good make false belief bad. To believe that people have done and suffered things that they have not done and suffered is not merely not to acknowledge them as they are, but is clearly worse than that. I have already commented on the bad state of falsely believing someone to have done wrong. But it is also a bad thing (though a less bad thing) to believe someone A to have done good when they have not. It means that we regard them in the same way as someone B of whom we believe truly that they have done some similar good—and that is an injustice to B, for it involves failing to recognize what is special about B. It means too that our relation to A depends on a falsehood and so that any true beliefs about the good that is in A become distorted because we do not have a proper picture of A.

Desires

I understand by a 'desire' or 'want' an involuntary inclination with which an agent finds himself to do some action or to have something happen.[14] Desires may be for almost anything—for mental states, including sensory states, for bodily states, for states of the world far distant from the agent. I may desire to have a certain tingling sensation or for a piece of poetry to run through my mind, to waggle my ears, or to be President of the United States. Or my desires may be focused on others—that my children be happy or successful or inherit my wealth when I am dead. The satisfaction of desire is an evident good for the desirer (unless the desire is for something bad). It is good that a conscious being who wants something shall have that want satisfied. It is good for it that its longings for how the world should be should be respected by the world. The satisfaction of desire is also a very basic good in the sense, as we shall see, that its goodness contributes to the greater goodness of many other states of affairs.

Enjoyment or pleasure consists in the believed satisfaction of present desire; and that is also an obvious good (for its subject) unless the desire is for something bad. It normally comes on top of the actual satisfaction of desire and therefore is an additional good. Pleasure then includes doing what you are inclined to do, or letting happen what you are inclined to let happen, when you believe truly that you are doing the action or letting the state occur. I enjoy eating cake or playing golf if I am inclined to do so, do so while inclined, and believe that I am doing so. I get pleasure out of sitting in the sun if I let myself continue to sit in the sun when inclined to do so (do not struggle against sitting there) and believe that that is what I am doing. I get pleasure out of being President of the United States if I am inclined to be President, and am, and believe that I am President. I stress that pleasure consists in the believed satisfaction of present desire. This may be a desire which I have had for a long time but which has been until now (I believe) unsatisfied; or it may be a desire which came to me simultaneously with it being (I believe) satisfied.

---

[14] For a fuller account of desire, see my *The Evolution of the Soul*, ch. 6.

The most primitive kind of pleasure is sensory pleasure, pleasure in the having of certain sensations, such as the occurrence of a warm feeling in my throat. I do not see any reason to suppose that there are any sensations which are intrinsically pleasant or intrinsically unpleasant. For consider any sensations which most humans dislike, say, the sensation of burning. That sensation can occur in a very weak form in which we do not dislike it (we may even like it), and in some exceptional people in a somewhat stronger form in which they do not dislike it. Masochism is a genuine phenomenon. What seems rather to be the case is that humans (and animals) are (almost) all so made that they like (desire to have) the same sensations (to approximately the same degree) and dislike (desire not to have) the same sensations. To call a sensation a 'pain' would seem to imply not merely that it is of a certain kind, but also that it is disliked. Also, not all disliked sensations are naturally called 'pains'— a disliked feeling of nausea is not naturally called a pain. The occurrence of any disliked sensation, whether we call it 'pain' or not, is a bad state of affairs (for the one who has the sensation); and the occurrence of any liked sensation is a good state of affairs (for the one who has the sensation).

Conscious states such as sensations are states of affairs about the occurrence of which I can hardly be mistaken. However, the more remote from my immediate environment is the state of affairs on which my inclinations are focused, the more serious is the possibility that I may believe some inclination to be satisfied when it is not. I may believe that I am President of the United States when I am not. I still get pleasure out of this, for pleasure consists merely in the believed satisfaction of desire, but there is not here also the good of the actual satisfaction; and when I am disabused of my false belief, there is nothing left out of which I can get pleasure.

Pleasure is the believed satisfaction of present desire. Is there good in the present satisfaction of past desire? I suggest so, if the desire is unabandoned in the sense that while the agent still has desires, he still has that one. Suppose that, aged 5, I long to be an engine-driver but I cease to have this desire when I am 10, when I desire to be a naval captain instead; if I am then declared medically unfit for the Navy when conscription arrives and am drafted to become an engine-driver instead, there would seem little (if any) good in this. But this is because my earlier desire has been replaced by a different desire. Yet contrast this with the desire of a dying man for being buried here rather than there when he is dead. That desire is not abandoned; it is the man's last wish. And in that case surely it is good for him that his relatives should bury him here rather than there, even if but for the dead man's known past desire, there would be nothing particularly good about burial here rather than there. The reason why it is good does not arise solely from any consequences that it may have in leading other people to believe that they too will be buried where they desire and get pleasure out of that belief. For the goodness of the satisfaction of the dead man's desire would remain even if a law is just about to be passed making cremation obligatory in future; we would say then of the dead man 'Thank goodness he, at any rate, got what he wanted'. The reason is simply that it is good that longings be satisfied; they matter, and that could not be unless it matters that their goal is reached.

Both the satisfaction of desire and the believed satisfaction of desire are good things (for the desirer), unless the desire is for what is bad. Conversely, the non-satisfaction of desire is a bad thing (for the desirer), again, unless the desire is for what is bad. (A desire is not satisfied if it is not fulfilled at the time to which the desire relates. A desire to go to London tomorrow is today neither satisfied nor non-satisfied.) I suggest that non-satisfaction is bad even if the desirer does not believe that the desire is unsatisfied. The non-satisfaction of my desire to be buried here rather than there is a bad thing for me. Suffering—to use a more general word than pain for this bad state—is the believed non-satisfaction of desire. That is a bad state, even more evidently. For therein consists unhappiness. The believed non-satisfaction of desire is a bad thing even if in fact the relevant desire is satisfied. It is bad if I believe that my desire to be in California is not satisfied when in fact it is. In such a case there are good and bad states to be weighed against each other. But of course things are worse if the desire which the subject believes not to be satisfied is in fact not satisfied. Such non-satisfaction I call 'frustration' of desire. Sensory pains are one species of such frustrations. They involve two components: a sensation and a strong desire that it cease (which I shall call an aversion to it), known not to be satisfied. But an unfulfilled longing to be President of the United States (known to be unfulfilled) is a bad thing for just the same sort of reason.[15]

---

[15] See Additional Note 2.

The goodness of a desire is, however, affected by what it is a desire for. The satisfaction (or believed satisfaction) of desires for things intrinsically bad is itself a bad thing. The satisfaction of a desire that others, or even one's later self, suffer pain, or lose their reputation, fortune, or family is of course a bad thing (for them); and any pleasure derived from these things is not merely not a good, but very much a bad state—for the one who is pleased.[16] Only the pervert rejoices at the sufferings of others. Also, I suggest, pleasure is not on balance a good where the belief needed to sustain it is false. The pleasure which a man gets from believing his son to be a successful businessman when in fact he is unemployed is not a good thing for the father. We can see this when we consider that if we had the opportunity to plug into an 'experience machine' which would inculcate in us the false beliefs that our desires were currently being satisfied, we would—almost all of us—refrain, under normal circumstances (i.e. unless life without the machine was so intolerable that plugging in was the lesser of two evils). While, I am claiming, the satisfaction of any desire for anything (so long as it is not a bad state) is good, the satisfaction of a desire is the better if it is a desire for a state of affairs good for other reasons. Desires to read great novels rather than low-quality thrillers, to understand quantum physics or to develop a correct theodicy rather than know Wisden's Cricketers' Almanack by heart are like this, because of the width and depth of the knowledge we desire to attain in the former cases.[17] Since the satisfaction of desire is as such a good thing, it

[16] The situation is different when the desire is not for a state of affairs bad in itself but for one associated with a bad state of affairs. If my desire to win the lottery being satisfied involves the frustration of your desire to win the lottery, but is not in itself a desire for the latter, then the satisfaction of my desire is still a good. But whether the total state of the satisfaction of my desire and the frustration of yours is overall a good depends on how great are the good and bad components respectively.

[17] J. S. Mill implausibly suggested that the fact that those who are 'capable of the higher pleasures' often choose them showed that the higher pleasures were more pleasurable (see his *Utilitarianism* (1861), ed. M. Warnock (Collins, 1962), ch. 2). But that of course does not follow at all, unless you already assume that the only things which move to action are desires to have pleasure and avoid pain; a theory even more dubious than Mill's ethical theory. The point is surely that some things are more worth enjoying than others; and even if by some measure there is a greater quantity of pleasure to be had out of the latter, it is (up to a point no doubt) better to have the former. Mill's famous sentence 'it is better to be a human being dissatisfied than a pig satisfied; better to be Socrates dissatisfied than a fool satisfied' (p. 260) is true. And, as Mill says, Socrates or the human being who know 'both sides' can see that. But they can also see, as Mill omits to note, that the pig or the fool may well (if it could be measured) get more pleasure—but those who see both sides

must be that the satisfaction of a strong desire is as such a greater good than the satisfaction of a weak desire.

The satisfaction of joint desires—e.g. the desires of two creatures for the common end of their nest being built—is very good (for both creatures) because of the goodness of sharing and cooperation. And it is yet better that the desire of one for the satisfaction of the desire of another—e.g. my desire for the satisfaction of your desire to eat cream cake, or more generally the desire of a mother for the satisfaction of her offspring's desire—be satisfied, than that the desire of each of us for the satisfaction of his or her own desire be satisfied. This is because of the goodness of mutual concern and involvement. Much better that my desire that your desire to eat cream cake be satisfied than that the desire of each of us for the satisfaction of his or her own desire be satisfied. (All this, given that the desires are not for what is bad.) It follows, because of the goodness of mutual concern, that even better is the satisfaction of joint desires for the satisfaction of the desire of a third creature, e.g. the satisfaction of the desire of both parents for the desired success in examinations of their child. Even better still is the satisfaction of desires to perform *actions* of certain sorts benefiting oneself and others, to the goodness of which actions (desired or not) I shall come in due course.

In cases such as those just described, where one person, *A*, desires the well-being of a second person, *B* (e.g. the satisfaction of some desire of *B*), and the desire is satisfied, there is a triple good. There is the primitive good for *B* of *B* being benefited, e.g. by the satisfaction of *B*'s desire. There is the greater good for *A* of the satisfaction of *A*'s desire, greater because *A*'s desire is focused on something intrinsically good, e.g. the fulfilment of another's desire. And there is the further good for *B* that *A*'s desire for *B*'s well-being, e.g. his (*B*'s) desire to be satisfied, was satisfied. We are fortunate if our well-being gives happiness to others, even if we do not know that it does. We can see this by the fact that we regard ourselves as fortunate when we discover that another was made happy by our being happy. Although the discovery causes us to regard ourselves as fortunate, what we regard ourselves as fortunate in respect of is what we discover (not the fact of our discovering it)— and that is something which could occur without our having

do not think that that in itself makes a difference to the relative goodness of the two states.

discovered it. (Note the similarity of this argument to the argument about beauty in Chapter 3, and other arguments in later chapters.)

There is special good in the eventual satisfaction of a strong desire which persists through varied experiences and other desires, even though temporarily frustrated (so long, of course, as it is not for something bad). Hence the special good of the satisfaction of an animal's desire for the return of its offspring lost for hours or days. The greater good of the satisfaction of persisting desire is yet greater when what is desired is the success of some action of some kind. It is good that someone persist in attempting to search for food, and eventually find some; stick at trying to learn to type or drive or swim and finally succeed.

And note of course that in these as in other cases, the good of the satisfaction of desire does not lie solely in its known satisfaction. It follows that there is significant good in a persisting desire being satisfied after the desirer's death. The greater good of the satisfaction of persisting desires is yet greater, the better their object; and so there is especial good in the satisfaction of shared persisting desires for the satisfaction of the persisting desire of a third individual.

It is not just the satisfaction of desire which is in general a good, and especially when it is of a desire for a state of affairs good for other reasons. The mere having of desire for anything at all, so long as it is not for a bad state, is good. It is good for me that I want things, long for things, am inclined to try to bring about things. It is better that I be someone to whom things matter rather than a 'cold fish' who acts under the guidance of reason alone. Desires in themselves are good, except when they are desires for what is bad; but they are better, the better for other reasons are the states desired. It is good that I should desire everything that is good; then my system of desire will be rightly attuned to the values of things. And if my desires are focused on your well-being, that is a good not merely for me but also for you: how fortunate we are if people care about us, mind what happens to us.

All the features which make good desires better make bad desires worse. It is bad for me and for you that I should desire your harm— it is bad for me to be a hater; and, as it is good to be loved, so it is bad to be hated—even if you do not know about it. Joint desires and cooperative desires for states of affairs bad in themselves are the worse for their joint and cooperative elements. A's desire that B's hatred for C be fulfilled is bad not merely because both A and B

desire *C*'s harm, but because *A* desires what is bad for *B*, the satisfaction of a bad desire. And a persistent desire for the bad is worse than a casual intermittent one.

The absence of a desire for something good cannot as such be considered a bad state. There is nothing the matter with me if I do not desire that some child in China of whom I have never heard pass her examination. But the absence of a desire for a goal which I ought to pursue is, I suggest, a bad state. I ought to educate my children. If I do not mind whether they are educated or not, if I have no desire for their well-being in this respect, then there is, I suggest, something bad about me—even if I do my best to see that they are well educated. Obligations are limited and, in principle, knowable. There is something bad about us if we do not know our obligations; and, if we do know them, and find it difficult to act on them, then that will be due to bad desires deterring us (see p. 86) and our having these is a bad thing.

While other-centred desires are clearly a good thing for us—we are the better for wanting other people to be happy—it is important to note that self-centred desires are also a good thing for the desirer. For, as we have seen, it is good that you desire my well-being rather than some ethically irrelevant state of me, because the former is a good thing; and in that case it is good that I too desire it, for it is good that I desire whatever is good. Now it is good that any good desire be fulfilled. But if my well-being consisted solely in promoting your well-being, and your well-being consisted solely in promoting my well-being, and so on in a circle, there would be nothing ultimately in which the well-being of either of us would consist. There would be nothing which I could do to promote your well-being—if doing the latter consisted in causing you to cause me to cause you to cause me . . . and so *ad infinitum*. A few really self-centred desires are needed if there is to be any altruism. If I want to eat chocolate, there is something you can do for me: give me some. And if you also want some, there is something I can do for you, as well as or perhaps instead of indulging my own desire: give you some. Only with a bit of self-centredness (perhaps taking a higher form than a desire for chocolate) is there scope for generosity, for altruism generally, for individuals with differing natures, and for moral choice. But of course self-centred desires need to be properly balanced, in a morally perfect individual, by strong other-centred desires.

I draw attention to one important class of desires and two important particular desires on which I shall need to comment later. The class is that of instrumentally useful desires: desires to get something which goes with some good, or to get rid of something which goes with some harm. Let us call the former incentive desires, and the latter deterrent desires. Biologically useful desires are the obvious examples of instrumentally useful desires. Among biologically useful incentive desires are desires to eat, drink, sleep, and have sexual intercourse. Such desires are in themselves good to have and satisfy (except in those cases where the state desired is overall bad, e.g. when the sexual intercourse involves adultery). But their satisfaction also has further consequences, not necessarily envisaged by the desirer, of biological utility for individuals and the race; e.g. sleep making the sleeper fresh for the next day, and sexual intercourse leading to the survival of the race. Among the biologically useful deterrent desires are the desires to avoid pains of various kinds. When we put a hand into the fire, we get a strong burning pain; this involves a desire that it cease, which can only be satisfied by removing the hand from the fire. Such desires are again good to have and satisfy (except of course where the state desired is overall bad, which in this example would only be the case under very peculiar circumstances); but it is of course bad that this desire should be initially unsatisfied. The satisfaction of the desire has biologically useful consequences, e.g. that the hand is not destroyed. (But it is not always the case that the sufferer who seeks to stop some pain realizes the biological consequences of doing so.) Pain arises in the first instance because of its biological utility; it can also occur when not biologically useful, but it is important to have in mind that that involves its occurrence outside the context where it has its main use.

The (incentive and deterrent) useful desires may be immediate, or delayed in the sense of being desires for the satisfaction of some future desire, or not to have some future frustrated desire. When we acquire some knowledge of how the world works we know that under certain circumstances we shall have desires which we can then satisfy or ones that we cannot then satisfy. Our present desires to have the former then act as incentives; and our present desires to avoid the latter act as deterrents. Among the useful delayed incentive desires are the desires that when we desire to eat or sleep, we shall be able to do so, which lead to our buying food and securing accommodation. Among the useful delayed deterrents are the desires that we do not have pains which we cannot there and then remove: the desire to avoid the hangover we shall get if we drink more than eight pints of beer, influencing us not to drink those pints now.

There are instrumentally useful desires other than these simple biological ones. In so many (but not all) economic systems, for example, the desire of one person for fortune is instrumentally useful in developing technology and bringing prosperity to others. In our world all desires for longer-term goals are instrumentally useful in leading us to seek and acquire theoretical knowledge. Desire to communicate with distant relatives, to fly in the air, and to cure disease and prolong life require us to seek knowledge of how the world works which we can then use to achieve our goals. I have argued that true belief about how the world works, and more so, knowledge in at least one sense of the latter, is a good thing to have. But while most of us do desire that knowledge for its own sake, that desire is not initially in many of us a very strong one. Desires for most other good things therefore have an instrumental utility.

The first particular desire to which I draw attention is the very good desire to be thought well of. We like to be liked, and it is very good that we do. For what we desire—that we shall be valued by others, that they shall seek our company and respect our opinions and achievements—is a great good for us. And it is a great good for them that we believe their good opinion worth having, and desire their company. A world in which people could not care less what others thought of them would be a terrible world. Of course there are occasions on which the achievement of a greater good (e.g. standing up for justice when that will make us unpopular) may require that we resist the desire to be thought well of. But to have the desire is good and it is normally good that it be satisfied.

The second particular desire to which I draw attention is involved in many of the good desires to which I have been drawing attention. It is simply the desire to continue to exist in what is a good state, including happiness. Existing in what is objectively a good state is a good thing, and even better is enjoying it. So it is very good that we should desire (in this sense) our own future well-being.

Emotions

Many mental states to which we give names are mixed states in involving certain combinations of belief, desire, and sensation; and those which involve the right combinations are very valuable. The right combinations are ones in which the desires are to perform actions and have things happen which, given true beliefs, are good to happen, and in which sensations 'chime in' naturally.

An emotion such as anger, for example, includes a belief that someone has done wrong (to oneself or someone else), a desire to hurt them for that reason, and often also a sensory element of tightening round the eyes and in the stomach, which we do not welcome, but which 'fits' the desire in that satisfying the desire to hurt would involve an 'uncoiling' which would get rid of the tightening. There is a 'righteous anger' in which we have a true belief that someone has done a wrong and a good desire to bring this home to them by word or deed (urged on by appropriate sensation), good for us and (on balance) good for them.

Respect is a good emotion to have towards those who deserve it. It involves a belief that someone is great in some way—greatly knowledgeable, powerful, wise, good, or has achieved various things (in spite of hardships), for example—and a desire to acknowledge this. All people deserve to be acknowledged for what they are, and so for the great-making qualities they possess. I have argued that knowledge (in one or more senses) is a good for the knower, and I shall be arguing in Chapter 5 that causing, and so power—the ability to cause—is a good for any agent, and especially for a free intentional agent. Those who have these qualities deserve respect; and for us to fail to show it to someone would be bad for them and bad for us, for we would not then be rightly attuned to things as they are. Respect is good if and only if the belief involved in it is true—if its object deserves respect. But if it does, respect is acknowledgement of worth. Of course if power is misused, the powerful may not overall deserve respect. Yet someone whose natural inclinations are to be disrespectful of the powerful, cynical about the saints, supercilious about the learned as such, has got something the matter with them.

Aesthetic contemplation of beauty seems to involve a belief element (the belief that the work of art is beautiful) and a desire element (the desire that the work should exist). True beliefs and right desires correctly focused on what is in fact beautiful is clearly a considerable good.

'Love' is a word used in many senses. But in many of these senses it involves a whole complex of beliefs, desires, and sensations, as well as an active component of performing various intentional actions. I confine myself in this chapter to reflecting on the goodness of the various involuntary components. Loving another involves believing that some aspects of them are good. It may be that we believe them beautiful, or successful or charismatic, or sympathetic, or honest, or whatever; but of course it does not involve believing that all aspects of them are good. Centrally it involves desire: desire that things go well in all ways with the beloved; and desire that we may interact closely with them in shared activities, and that we may share desires and beliefs with them; desire that we know all about what they desire and believe, and that we desire and believe the same things. And it involves the desire that the beloved should desire all of these things with respect to us (that they should desire to share our desires and beliefs etc.). And it involves (though less centrally) sensations peculiar to the having and satisfaction of the desires: the tinge of excitement at the beloved's presence, a sensation which we desire to continue; and the sensation involved in frustration at lack of closeness, a sensation which we desire not to continue. Given that my beliefs about them are true, and that the desires are for good states, it is good (for them and for me) that I love all animate beings, but especially those with whom I have contact and in particular those greatly dependent on me or on whom I am greatly dependent. It is good that I love these latter more than others—otherwise I do not pay proper tribute to their connection with myself; I trivialize our personal relations. And again, the love that persists despite inadequate satisfaction has its own special greatness. And if the beloved suffers, it is good that the lover feels frustrated in his own desires. And if the beloved dies, it is good that the lover mourn the beloved. We could be so made that immediately we lost a loved one, we ceased to miss him or her. But how horrible that would be! If love is good, it matters that we grieve, that we pine for the loss of a loved one. It constitutes the proper tribute of a lover to the lost loved one. Someone is indeed unfortunate if no one is sorry when they die. A love is only worth having if it is still there when unsatisfied; that is what constitutes its serious nature. What goes for grief goes also for so many other unsatisfied longings: if what is longed for is good, then there is good in our caring that we do not have it. We creatures of desire pay with our desires the tribute of our nature.

It is good that I feel joy at the other's success, at being close to them; and that I feel compassion for the sufferer, sadness at failure, and grief at the loss of the departed (both in this package which constitutes love, and more generally). Again, these attitudes are both good for him who has these right attitudes and good for him on whom they are focused—very good if the latter knows about them and that gives him some pleasure, but good even if he does not—for the reason given earlier. What gives him pleasure is the knowledge of the existence of a good state (e.g. someone else's compassion for him), and that state can exist without his knowing about it.

The love of embodied persons, such as humans, for each other will naturally involve a bodily element—for bodily proximity (so that we may desire sensations from the other's body, being that material object over which the beloved has most immediate control; and may convey sensations in the same way to the beloved). But sexual desire—to derive sensations out of a very special kind of interaction with the other—is of course not necessarily involved in love as such; and, notoriously, may exist without the other aspects of love. But of course it can and often does go together with other aspects of love in a wonderful package.

Human and other finite beings can only interact with a limited number of other beings, and while it is good that they shall love many others, only a love for a few others can possibly be satisfied. But, quite apart from that limitation of finitude, there is special value in special kinds of love which are not shared. It is a very great good for someone *A* to be loved by another *B* in a way and for qualities for which *B* loves no one else. If we are valued only for qualities which can be shared with others, our particularity—what makes me me—is not recognized. The qualities which cannot be shared are those which consist in interactions at particular times with particular individuals. If I am valued for being someone's first-born child, or spouse, or sole doctoral supervisor, then I am valued for something special to me.

Only emotions which are rightly focused are good. An anger driven by a false belief that wrong has been done, or in which the desire to hurt is quite out of proportion to the wrong done, is clearly bad. So too is respect for those who do not deserve it. Love too can sometimes be misplaced. A love which (is not merely caused by, but) has as an essential constitutive part a false belief is not good: if I love you because I believe that you are my faithful spouse but in fact you are cheating on me badly, then my love is not good, possibly even bad. And if I love you for something which is bad in you— if I love you for your cruelty—that is a bad love. And a love which if realized would spoil another love—such as a love which seeks a sexual relationship with the wife of someone else to whom she is happily married—is also clearly bad. But of course in general love is good—very good indeed, the best of all the emotions.

True beliefs, good desires, and thereby rightly focused emotions are good for the individual who has them, independently of their consequences; and good for the individuals on whom they are focused. It is good that they should be interdependent in the various ways described, and very good that they should be fulfilled. This has been the argument of this chapter. Hence one would expect a good God to create individuals who have such beliefs and desires; and (if there is a God) clearly he has done so in abundance.

The higher animals have all of the simpler kinds of belief and desire which I have described, and humans have the more sophisticated kinds of belief and desire. One might come to think that, in that case, because the beliefs and desires which humans can have are better than those which animals can have, God would create only humans. But that thought would be mistaken for more than one reason. It will suffice to mention here just one reason; I will come to others in the next chapter. This one reason is that among the great goods available to humans are those of responding in the right way to those with lesser abilities and so to love and to care for animals. Although animals can respond with great love to human love, they cannot love in the same way; and hence human love of animals will have a uniquely valuable character (because reciprocable only in a limited kind of way). To be able to love those who cannot love you in the same way is to have a unique opportunity for generous love. 'If you love them that love you, what reward have you? Do not even the publicans the same?'[18]

---

[18] Matt. 5: 46. The context of verses 43–8 suggests that the 'reward' is not an after-death reward, but the present 'reward' of being perfect. On the general point of how to interpret the 'rewards' promised by the Sermon on the Mount, see Ch. 13.

There are, however, many false beliefs and bad and frustrated desires of the types which I have described, both among animals and—more strikingly—among humans. The pain of incurable disease and accident, grief and disappointment at failure, the feelings of hatred which individuals and nations have for each other, are all too evident to need much further comment; and we shall need to inquire in due course why God should allow these to occur.

In general the Christian tradition has recognized and praised God for all the true beliefs and good desires of the types described. But at times there have been thinkers and groups of Christians who have judged that desires focused on mere human goods (as opposed to desires for closeness to God) are not good.[19] Of course all the tradition has recognized what I have stressed earlier, that the desires for mere human goods need to be kept under control—we must not yield to desires for food or sexual intercourse under many circumstances (e.g. when others need the food more, or when the one sexually desired is married to another)—and that desires for what it is bad that we should have are themselves bad. And because it has recognized that it is often difficult for humans to get their desires rightly attuned to the good, it is often necessary for them deliberately to frustrate desires which tend to exert in general more influence than they should, even when it would otherwise be good to indulge them. Thus the tradition has commended fasting in Lent, abstaining from food which it would otherwise be good that we should have, in order to be able to keep our desire for food under control during the rest of the year, so that it does not influence our conduct more than it should. But the tradition has on the whole maintained that desire for mere human goods and their indulgence is as such a good thing. The Christian thinker who above all said this very clearly was St Thomas Aquinas. Question 2 of part 2(1) of the *Summa Theologiae* discusses what human blessedness (*beatitudo*, often misleadingly translated 'happiness') ultimately consists in. Aquinas's final answer is that it consists in the Vision of God. But, before reaching that answer, he considers whether it consists in riches, honours, fame, power, bodily well-being, sensory pleasure, or in 'some good quality of the soul' (e.g. intellectual achieve-

---

[19] This tendency in Christian thought reached its culmination in the writings of some later medieval mystics and in the Quietist movement of the 17th century, which denied the goodness of any desire, even desire for God. On this tendency, see K. E. Kirk, *The Vision of God* (Longmans, Green, 1931), 451–66.

ment). With respect to each of them, he holds that they are goods, but they are lesser goods: blessedness cannot consist 'principally' in being honoured, the 'perfection' of human good cannot consist in being acknowledged by other people, and so on. But all these things, even 'external goods', are 'required' for the 'imperfect blessedness open to us in this life'.[20] And since all these things are good for us, it is good that we should desire these things.

[20] *Summa Theologiae*, IaIIae. 4. 7.

5

Action

And God said, Let us make man in our image, after our likeness: and let them have dominion over the fish of the sea, and
over the fowl of the air, and over the cattle, and over all the
earth, and over every creeping thing that creepeth upon the
earth. And God created man in his own image, in the image of
God created he him; male and female created he them. And
God blessed them: and God said unto them, Be fruitful, and
multiply, and replenish the earth, and subdue it; and have
dominion over the fish of the sea, and over the fowl of the air,
and over every living thing that moveth upon the earth. And
God said, Behold, I have given you every herb yielding seed,
which is upon the face of all the earth, and every tree, in the
which is the fruit of a tree yielding seed; to you it shall be for
meat: and to every beast of the earth, and to every fowl of the
air, and to every thing that creepeth upon the earth, wherein
there is life, I have given every green herb for meat: and it was
so. And God saw every thing that he had made, and, behold,
it was very good. And there was evening and there was morning, the sixth day.

(Genesis 1: 26–31)

Causing Spontaneously and Causing Freely

In the last two chapters I was concerned with the goodness of involuntary states—both non-conscious and conscious. Now I move on
to consider the goodness of action, that is causing or bringing
about. All causing is, as such, good (for the agent); even if it is unin-
tentional (of plants say, which produce seeds to produce new
plants), but especially if it is intentional. An intentional action is
one which an agent does because he or she means to do it. Causing

is as such a good thing because in causing the agent contributes. It is only causing what for other reasons is bad, which is itself bad. Causing what is good, e.g. the states of affairs described in the last two chapters, is very good; and not just for the reason that those states of affairs are good, as examples will bring out in due course.

An intentional action may be objectively or subjectively good, or both. It is—to repeat from Chapter 1—objectively good if it is good in its nature or (likely) consequences, apart from what the agent believes about it; and typically this will be a matter of its consequences. Other things being equal, an action is good in virtue of having good effects. It is subjectively good if the agent believes that in the respect in which it is intentional (i.e. in respect of what he or she is seeking to achieve) it is a good action; and is doing it for that reason.[1] An intentional action is the better for being both objectively and subjectively good.

An objectively good intentional act is good, even if it is not done intentionally in the respect in which is good. Performing some intentional action (e.g. I buy your house), I may unintentionally do something else good (e.g. I save you from bankruptcy). Such a good action will derive its goodness not from its intention but from its effect. What is achieved is a good, and it is also a good for the agent who effected it, even if unintentionally; he is lucky to be a vehicle of benefit. His agency is not a wasted agency; it contributes.

Conversely, an unsuccessful action which aimed at something believed good is also a good for the agent. It is good that people try to help the starving even if they do not succeed. We can perhaps see the good of unintended success better than in my earlier example by bringing in this latter point, and considering an action which is aimed at a good but fails and is better for having an unintended good result than it would be otherwise. I toil to save a life and fail; but the record of my efforts makes possible the development of a technique for saving other lives in future. Is that better than if I failed and by chance someone else hit on the new technique? Yes, because my efforts are crowned, and therefore it is a good for me, not merely for those whose lives were ultimately saved. But clearly things are better if the good which I achieve is intended. While it is good that I try to feed the starving even if I do not succeed, it is better if I do succeed—but not just because it is good that the

---

[1] For fuller analysis of the distinctions of this paragraph, see my *Responsibility and Atonement* (Clarendon Press, 1989), ch. 1.

starving have enough to eat; it is a good for me that I am privileged to help them, that I am of use. It is even good that I aim at something believed good, even if falsely—for I am better for a direction of will towards the good, even if somewhat misinformed about wherein it consists.[2] But it is better if my moral beliefs are true; and, while keeping in mind the possibility of false moral beliefs, I shall for the present, for simplicity of exposition, assume that agents have true moral beliefs; that is, true beliefs about the moral worth (good or bad) about the consequences (intended or foreseen) of their actions.

An intended good action, when fully caused, is the better if the agent is fully behind it; if the inclinations (i.e. desires) which lead him to act are not in conflict with each other. We value the spontaneous pursuit of the good, the pursuit of the good which the agent fully desires to pursue. We value the willingly generous action, the naturally honest, spontaneously loving action. But we value even more that the pursuit of the good should result from a free choice of the agent between equally good actions, that is, one resulting from the exercise of (libertarian) free will. It is a good for any agent to have such a free choice; for that makes him an ultimate source of the way things happen in the Universe. He is no longer totally at the mercy of forces from without, but is himself an autonomous mini-creator. And in both of these cases—the spontaneous good action and the freely chosen good action—the action is better if efficacious, if it does make the intended difference to how things are in the world outside the agent.

But the good of freely forwarding the good is better if the agent has a free choice between a greater and a lesser good; better still if he has a free choice between the good and the bad, and even more so if the possibility of doing bad includes the possibility of doing wrong (see Chapter 1 for this distinction), not just between alternative equal goods. (In this discussion I am counting 'doing nothing' as one alternative open to an agent.) I shall call free will involving a choice between good and bad 'serious free will', and if wrong is also a possibility, 'very serious free will', to be contrasted with 'unserious free will', where the choice is only between alter-

---

[2] For reasons which I give in *Responsibility and Atonement*, ch. 1, I do not think that anyone can be totally mistaken in their beliefs about which actions are good. To have a concept of the good, you need quite a few true beliefs about which actions are good.

native goods (and if the goods are equal goods, 'very unserious free will'). An agent who has serious and efficacious free will is in a much fuller way an ultimate source of the direction of things in the world; he is not pre-programmed to make a choice within a range of choices all of the same moral kind—good. And he is an ultimate source in an even fuller way if the choices open to him cover the whole moral range, from the very good to the very wrong. Having the opportunity thus to influence the way things go is a great good for the agent, whether or not he exercises it in favour of the good. But an agent who exercises his very serious free will in favour of the good is blessed indeed. He rejects contrary desire and directs the flow of events in favour of the good rather than the bad. The agent has used his choice to make a significant difference to the world for good.

Now agents, such as ourselves, capable of recognizing reasons for doing an action and so something good about doing the action, will always do the action which they see the most reason to do, i.e. regard as the best to do, unless some influence diverts them from that. To have the belief that there is a reason for doing an action is to acknowledge that, thus far, it would be sensible, appropriate, reasonable, rational, to do the action, that it is the thing to do. Really to believe that some action would be sensible, appropriate, etc. to do is to acknowledge, to put the point dramatically, the summons of the action to me to do it; and thereby to have an inclination to do the action, other things being equal. I could not recognize R as a reason for doing A unless I accepted pressure from how I see things to be in the direction of doing A. To admit that R was a 'reason' for doing A but to deny that I had any inclination at all in consequence to do A would be to say something apparently contradictory, and to suggest that, when I said that R was a 'reason', I was using the word in an 'inverted comma sense' and meant something like 'what most people would consider a "reason"'. To recognize a reason for doing A is only to have an inclination to do A, other things being equal. But other things may not be equal. There may be other and better reasons for not doing the action. To believe that there is reason overall for doing the action is to believe that, on the balance of reason, it would be sensible, appropriate, reasonable, rational to do the action. I may still not do the action because I may yield to non-rational forces which influence the purposes I form. But to believe that the balance of reason supports doing it entails being inclined to do it, and doing it in so far as one is unimpeded by non-rational forces.[3]

It follows that if an agent is to have the option of doing what he regards as less good or bad actions—and so, on the assumption that he has true moral beliefs, doing less good or bad actions—he must be subject to a stronger desire to do an alternative action. (The alternative may of course simply be the action of 'doing nothing'.) With such desires, i.e. temptations, alone can he have a free choice of pursuing the best or not pursuing the best. We regard as blessed and honour those who freely do the good when they overcome the temptation to do instead the bad or less good.

Just as if reasons alone influence action, an agent inevitably does what he believes to be the best, so if desires alone influence action, an agent will inevitably follow his strongest desire. Free choice of action therefore arises only in two situations. One is where there is a choice between two actions which the agent regards as equal best and which the agent desires to do equally; which—on the assumption that his moral beliefs are true—is the situation of very unserious free will. The other is where there is a choice between two actions, one of which the agent desires to do more and the other of which he believes it better to do.[4] This latter is the situation of temptation. Temptation may come in three forms: where the desire to do an action other than that believed best and which is stronger than the latter is a desire to do a less good action, or a bad but not wrong action, or a wrong action.

For any situation of temptation there are possible different degrees of free will. Our desire to do the bad (or whatever) may be only marginally stronger than the desire to do the good and in that case it does not require great effort of will to conform to the good. On the other hand the temptation, e.g. the desire to do bad, may be almost irresistible; immense effort will then be required if we are to conform to the good.

---

[3] See Additional Note 3.

[4] There is a further circumstance under which free choice is possible. That is where an agent has a choice between an infinite number of good actions, each of which is, he believes, less good than some other such action; there is, he believes, no best or equal-best action. However, since only a being whose power is unlimited in some respect will be in such a situation (as, I elucidated in Ch. 1, is God), humans or animals on Earth are never in such a situation; and so for the sake of simplicity of exposition, I ignore this possibility in the text at this point.

How is the value of the different forms of free will (serious, un-serious, etc.), and different degrees of each with respect to a given action, to be weighed against each other? Fairly clearly to do good out of very serious free will despite strong contrary temptation is the best exercise of choice. It is a marvellous thing for an agent to be the ultimate source of things going well rather than very badly. And the agent is more ultimately the source of that happening the more the passive forces at work in the world were sweeping it along in the wrong direction and by his effort alone the current was turned in a different direction. To generalize: the more serious the free will and the stronger the contrary temptation, the better it is when the good action is done. So much seems fairly evident. But the agent's having good desires is a good in itself, and so when they are added to the good of the good action which follows naturally from them, it becomes unclear just how much better it is overall to do a good action out of serious free will rather than generously and naturally. Fairly evidently too if the less good, bad, or wrong is cho-sen freely, the free exercise of choice is worse, the worse the action chosen (e.g. if it is wrong rather than merely bad), and the less strong the temptation to do it. (Then the agent has less excuse.) And the desires for the less good, the bad, or wrong which make possible the choice of the latter are bad. But also, as I have already suggested, the very fact of the agent having a free choice is a great good for the agent; and a greater good the more serious the kind of free will, even if it is incorrectly used. It is good for the agent that the world goes the way he chooses rather than the way someone else imposes on him.

All the above, I suggest, most people can accept. But where views will differ in a way not easy to resolve is in how these dif-ferent goods and bads are to be weighed against each other. To give someone free will makes it up to him what will happen. That is a great good, and (from the viewpoint of his creator, who does not make his choice for him) there is a certain chance of a further good that he will use it to choose the best. Both of these—the actual good of the free will and the chance that it will be used for the best—have to be weighed against the chance that the agent will do the less good, bad, or wrong act, and the badness of the bad desires which make the latter choices possible. The chance that the agent will do (what he believes to be) the best will be greater, the less is the temptation to do the alternative. But the less the

latter temptation, the less is the goodness of the act done in resisting it. I have no easy algorithm for working out which kind of free
will is the best to have.

The good of the good free act, and the bad of the bad free act, will
be greater if the act is efficacious than if it is not (i.e. if we succeed
in doing the act rather than merely attempt it but fail), both because
of the goodness or badness of the effect, and because the agent is the
instrument of it. The extent of the possible consequences for good
or ill will clearly affect the equation, make a difference to whether
it is a good or bad thing for a creator to give creatures free will of a
certain kind. But in itself (i.e. apart from the bad desires which are
needed to make it possible, and the chance of bad consequences) I
suggest that having a free will which can make a big difference to
the world is a greater good than having one which can only make a
small difference. In a later chapter I will have to face the issue of
how great a chance of how much bad is too much for God to give us
a certain sort of efficacious free will. But meanwhile I wish to reflect
on the goodness of various good actions which it is good that agents
should do spontaneously, and better that they should have the
opportunity to do freely rather than various alternative actions.
The range and importance of the effects which they can bring about
constitutes the significance of their actions. If those actions result
from free choice, then the choices have corresponding significance.
I shall talk of agents having responsibility for things in so far as the
way those things go results from their free choice. Agents have
great responsibility in so far as they can make free choices of great
significance. 'Responsibility' *simpliciter*, as I shall use the term,
belongs only to free agents, though I may need to talk of unfree
agents having an unfree responsibility for others when their actions
have significance for those others (as do the actions of animals for
their offspring). All I am claiming at present is that it is good in
itself (i.e. good for those agents) that free agents have such responsibility, even if the chance of their misusing it is so great and the
resulting bad so great that on balance it is not a good thing that God
give agents such free will.

So in summary the goodness of having free will is a function of
its freedom, namely its kind (serious, unserious, etc.) and degree
(strength of temptation); and its significance (the greater the
importance and range of difference its exercise makes to the world;
the difference made by it being efficacious). The significance of a

choice is a matter of the amount of responsibility for ourselves and others involved in it. Given that we have true factual beliefs about the consequences of our choice and true moral beliefs about their moral status, any serious choice will be to some extent a significant choice. For it will mean that our choices are not merely good or bad in themselves, but make a further difference in the world for good or bad. But choices between good and bad may be choices which have big (good or bad) effects or small ones. The importance and range of difference we can make to the world constitutes the significance of our choice. The goodness or badness of the exercise of free will, as opposed to merely having it, will of course depend also on the goodness or badness of the choices actually made and the difference which they make to the world.

I assume throughout most of this chapter that agents have true moral beliefs. The goodness of an agent's choice is clearly largely a matter of its subjective goodness, its choice between the alternatives as he views them; what is good is that the agent shall make the choice which he believes to be the best. But, as the discussion on pp. 83–4 showed, the goodness of the efficacious free act depends, as well as on the goodness of the choice, on the objective goodness (not believed goodness) of the act—and typically this will be a matter of the goodness of its actual consequences (not just, to repeat, the goodness or badness of those consequences for those to whom they happen, but their goodness or badness for the agent as the agent of those consequences). In cases where the agent has false moral beliefs, we must make the corresponding adjustment to the equation, taking into account also the fact (considered in Chapter 4) that false moral beliefs are in themselves (and so for the agent) a bad thing.

The Scope of Responsibility

It is good that agents have the opportunity to make the world beautiful or ugly; we reflected briefly in Chapter 3 on the goodness of the beautiful states. It is good that agents have the opportunity to benefit or harm themselves, in the short and long terms, by imposing on themselves any of the good or bad states described in Chapter 4. These opportunities will include the primitive giving of pleasure in the short term (e.g. by eating chocolate) or the primitive allowing of pain (by not bothering to remove a stone from one's shoe); and of taking steps to provide for long-term happiness or through negligence allowing long-term unhappiness (e.g. by not taking steps to cure an incipient disease). But, as we saw, there is more to the good than what is enjoyed; and there is more to the bad than what is disliked. And it is also good that animals, albeit unfreely, should benefit themselves, each other, and humans in as many of these ways as their nature allows.

It is good that the choices open to agents should include the choice of whether or not to seek to acquire knowledge (in the objective internalist sense) through observation, experiment, and reflection; rather than that they should be born with all the knowledge they can ever have or acquire it by accidental observation or being told by some expert. Knowledge of empirical and moral matters, I argued in the last chapter, is valuable for practical purposes. I may initially have no idea what will be the effects of some of my actions, short- or long-term; and among the choices which it is good for God to give me is whether to bother to find out or not to take the trouble. I have the choice of investigating, by seeing the effects on other people and asking experts, the effects of different kinds of diet and lifestyle; or of not bothering. It is good too that I should have the opportunity of working out for myself whether some of the effects my actions have are good or bad, rather than have true moral views foisted upon me. In a liberal society we have come to see that it is a good that people should make up their own minds about moral issues. That need not imply that there is no truth about what is morally good or bad—only that it is good that we have the opportunity to choose freely to seek to discover those moral truths for ourselves, or, alternatively, not to bother; and to admit them honestly to ourselves when we find them, or to try to hide them from ourselves.[5] Moral inquiry takes the form of talking to other people of different kinds, hearing about their experiences, becoming involved in their lives; seeing television programmes, reading novels, and even reading books of moral philosophy.

[5] While it is unavoidable which beliefs we have at a given time, we may refuse to admit some of them even to ourselves (see *The Evolution of the Soul*, rev. edn. (Clarendon Press, 1997), 292–6). And it is always up to us whether we choose to investigate further the truth of some proposition, and so open ourselves to new evidence which will lead us (by involuntary processes) to change our beliefs; but if we investigate, we cannot predetermine the results of our investigation.

Animals cannot recognize moral truth, but the higher animals can discover empirical truths, and it is good that they should do so; and it is good that they should learn not merely by accidental observation or being taught, but that they should actively seek to find out for themselves where the food is, what food is nourishing, and so on, rather than just being born with that knowledge. I claimed in the last chapter that it is intrinsically good for us—not merely instrumentally good—to have both moral knowledge and general theoretical knowledge, and that is a further reason why it is good that we should have the choice of seeking such knowledge or not bothering to do so. Theoretical inquiry into fundamental matters of no immediate practical importance—such as the origins of society and the Universe, and the forces at work in it—and the deepest philosophical thinking about it involves cooperative study and discussion over centuries.

It is good too for agents to have the choice of whether to increase their power or not to bother. In order to have this choice we need to know how to increase our power; and getting into that situation may involve inquiry. The acquisition of knowledge may by itself give us power: knowing how a radio works may give us the power to build one. But it may be necessary to do other things as well: build our muscles to increase our bodily power; practise the language or the musical instrument in order to be able to speak or play it well.

A person's character is her system of desires and beliefs (principally moral beliefs); and just as it is good that agents have the choice of seeking to improve their beliefs or of not bothering to do so, so it is good that they should have the power to modify their desires over time. It is good that they be able to develop good desires and strengthen the best desires (including, for example, the desire for knowledge); or allow themselves to be captured by bad desires. But, given my earlier analysis that a free choice between the (believed) best action and lesser goods and bad and wrong alternatives involves desires for the latter stronger than desires for the former, such character modification will involve a restriction of the kind and degree of free choice. In so far as we eliminate bad desires, our freedom of choice will be restricted to good alternatives.

One way in which this could happen is the way it does happen in humans. Humans are so made that, by forcing themselves to do good actions when it is difficult, it becomes easier and easier to do them, until finally we desire to do them—our inclinations naturally lead us to do them. As Aristotle famously remarked, 'we become just by doing just acts, temperate by doing temperate acts, brave by doing brave acts'.[6] We can so dedicate ourselves to doing good by constant commitment over time that bad desires cease to have any influence over us.

And it does seem to be also the case that we can yield so frequently to whatever desire happens to be the strongest that we lose the habit of choosing between desires on the grounds of the goodness of acting on them. So often our strongest desires are bad desires; and there is good in us beginning life like that, for only so, as we have seen, do we have a choice between good and bad. But if we allow ourselves continually to yield to those desires, we close the possibility of choosing the good because it is good. We cease to have a free choice between alternatives on the basis of their overall goodness (that is, on moral grounds). We become a theatre of competing desires, in which the strongest (and so often the worst) wins. It does seem to be the case that the evil men of history have got themselves in this situation. I shall need to say a little more about the condition of such persons in Chapter 8, to consider whether it involves the elimination of conscience. Meanwhile, I note the immense significance of the choice of character formation open to us. The choice of our own characters involves many very serious choices over time and is in itself clearly of the deepest significance, quite apart from the consequences for others which may follow from our good or bad characters.

One of the greatest goods which agents can have is responsibility for others. We recognize this when we recognize it as a good gift to our own children to give them the responsibility for things, animals, and even other humans, and do not pressurize them too much as to how they are to act. The paradigm situation of responsibility for others is the situation of the parent. We humans have the awesome responsibility of choosing to bring into the world another human individual—initially helpless, without knowledge and without free choice—and of helping that individual to understand the world, to know what is good and bad, perhaps also to develop a capacity for very serious free choice; but also to help that individual to resist bad desires and to encourage good ones; so that in turn he or she can help yet others to do the same.

6 *Nicomachean Ethics* 1103[b].

So just as (for limited periods) a human parent may entrust a younger child to the care of an elder child (despite the risk that the elder child may abuse that trust and hurt the younger child) because of the goodness of the elder child having responsibility, so God may entrust creatures to the care of each other. It is good that God be generous in giving creatures such as us a share in moulding the world and each other, and the deep responsibility that that involves, but if we are to have such a share, good and bad must both be available to us. Otherwise God would not have given us a choice of great significance; he would have reserved for himself the all-important choice of the kind of world it was to be, while simply allowing us the minor choice of filling in the details. He would be like a father asking his elder son to look after the younger son, and adding that he would be watching the elder son's every move and would intervene the moment the elder son did a thing wrong. The elder son might justly retort that, while he would be happy to share his father's work, he could only really do so if he was left to make his own judgements about what to do within a significant range of the options available to the father. A good God, like a good father, will delegate responsibility.

The responsibility of humans for their children is indeed an awesome one. But it is good that the responsibility of free creatures for each other should not be limited to responsibility for children. It is good that there be a web of interactions of different kinds and degrees between creatures, in which they have responsibilities of various kinds and degree for each other. And of course it is like that with the human race. Children eventually become responsible for their aged parents. We have limited responsibilities for other relatives, and some of us can often make big differences to the societies in which we live, through teaching, community work, or political campaigning. Our influence is in no way limited to the present. The way we educate our children makes a very great difference indeed to the way in which they educate their children. And so on.

When A benefits B, it is of course a primitive good for B. If A educates B, the acquisition of knowledge is a good for B. But, I have also been claiming, it is a good for A that he is privileged to make all the difference to B. I need now to add that it is a further good for B not merely that B acquires knowledge, but that some-one else is the intentional vehicle of that knowledge—has taken an interest in him. We are fortunate if people mind about us, and the natural expression of minding is seeking well-being. Sometimes those who 'don't like to be beholden to others' do not see this. 'I wish that I were not so dependent on my parents for money', says the undergraduate. But 'so' is the crucial word: dependence can come in irksome forms or be too complete. What the undergraduate understandably resents is his own impotence to benefit himself, not that the good comes to him from a parent rather than from some chance lottery. And he may also rightly resent it if the parents give unwillingly or stingily. But how awful it would be for us if nobody ever cared for us enough to give us anything. Fortunately, if there is a God, no human or animal is ever in that situation.

Just as it is good that there be a criss-crossing of desires and their satisfaction, so it is good that our actions support each other's actions, and cooperate with each other's actions in forwarding further goods. It is good that my wife and I pursue a common good—the happiness of our daughter. It is good that we pursue it, not independently, but each contributing to a total direction: she does this for her and I do that; or, better still, I do this which is no use on its own, and she does that which is no use on its own, but together the two bits make our daughter happy. It is good for me, for my wife, and for our daughter.

Some of the good actions which I have been describing are obligatory, others are supererogatory. Obligations, we noted in Chapter 1, arise from voluntary undertakings (explicit promises, or implicit undertakings—as when in begetting children, I become obliged to feed and educate them) or from benefits received (as is the obligation to care for parents who have cared for us).

One great good which an agent can do is (given that the promise is not to do something bad) to make an explicit promise. He has the power thereby to make some future action obligatory which would not otherwise have been obligatory; and some future action wrong which would not otherwise have been wrong. If I promise to pay you £100 next week, I make it obligatory that I pay you and so wrong if I do not. Having this power over the moral status of future actions is a good for creatures; and exercising it constitutes a gift which one gives to another. If my promise is to you (as opposed to a mutual friend) that I will pay you £100, you now have it in your power to hold me to the promise or let me off it (i.e. keep it obligatory, or make it no longer obligatory that I pay the money).

Promises are promises to others, from the obligation to keep which they can dispense us. But there is another form of commitment which I call 'vows'; the vow-taker gives a commitment in a form which gives no one the right to dispense him from it. By making the vow to do action *A*, either absolutely or under certain circumstances (e.g. if another person does action *X*), the vow-taker makes it a bad act not to do *A* (at all, or under the relevant circumstances). If not doing *A* would be a bad thing anyway, the vow makes it bad for a further reason.[7] There are two reasons why anyone should make a vow. The first, which only applies if not doing the action would be bad for other reasons, is to make it harder for the vow-taker to avoid doing the action when or if the relevant time comes. Suspecting that I shall not take exercise otherwise, I make a 'New Year resolution' to go for a run once a week. The second reason is that by making the vow known to others, that serves to influence their behaviour. If the state solemnly vows (by passing a law which cannot be repealed and whose application does not depend on the discretion of judges) that all who commit a certain crime will be punished in a certain way, that will deter people from committing that crime. But it will only do so if people believe that judges will execute that penalty, even if those judges believe that that penalty is not the best one (for the particular criminal or for the future of society). Deterrence only works if people believe that the penalty will be executed whether or not other later reasons suggest that it is a good thing that it should be. One way in which people will come to believe this is by seeing that that is what has happened in the past. But with a new authority or new circumstances or a new kind of penalty, we cannot infer from what has happened in the past that a particular penalty will be imposed. We can, however, infer it in so far as the authority has vowed to impose it, and we have reason to believe that the authority is good and regards vow-keeping as good.

A promise to do something bad is not, however, a good thing; though if we have the right to give it, giving it surely does make it obligatory to fulfil it. It may not be good to give you £100 if you will only waste it; but if I promise to give it, I ought to give it. But a

---

[7] Failing to fulfil a vow can only be a bad thing, and not a wrong thing, if I am right in my contention that obligation is always obligation to someone else. For fuller discussion of this point, and the role of vows, see *Responsibility and Atonement*, *passim*, and esp. pp. 104–6.

promise to do what we have no right to do cannot bind. A promise to murder your mother-in-law is not merely bad to make but can create no obligation—such is the surely correct traditional view. Likewise a vow to do something bad would be bad to make; but, once made, it is good to fulfil it unless we have no right to do the bad action. If that were not so, vows by morally good authorities to punish for crimes which could not be repeated would have no deterrent force.

For consider the case of the utilitarian parent who wishes to deter his child from doing a certain wrong act of a non-repeatable kind. The child has stolen from the parent in the past and the parent has left only one valuable item—a picture, say, worth £1,000—and no prospect of acquiring any more valuables nor any income apart from that needed for immediate expenses. The parent wishes to deter the child from stealing the picture, selling it, and spending the money on drink and drugs. So the parent threatens, 'If you steal the picture I will punish you'. But the child knows that the parent is a utilitarian and that if the child does steal the picture the parent will then consider whether he should punish or not according to whether there will be subsequent beneficial effects of punishing, e.g. whether punishment will deter from future crime. But if the child has stolen the parent's only valuable item, sold it, and wasted the proceeds, there will be no possibility of future crime from which to deter. It is only if the parent believes that the threat constitutes a vow which it would be good to keep despite the badness otherwise (i.e. on pure utilitarian considerations) of imposing the punishment, and the child believes that the parent believes this, that deterrence will work. And a good parent could only make such a vow if it is good that vows should be kept when it would be for other reasons bad to keep them. But of course a vow to do something which the vow-taker has no right to do does not make it obligatory, or even good to do it.

Vows, like promises, are then yet more ways in which agents can influence the future. Vows and promises are not always made by uttering such formal words as 'I vow' or 'I promise'; but may be made in any way which shows that the agent has committed himself in the ways described here. I shall need to return later to the particular way in which a vow can influence the future.

There are certain sorts of good action which can only be done in the face of bad states of affairs. Showing sympathy to the suffering (which I distinguish from being in the passive state of feeling compassion), helping the suffering, and showing courage of a certain sort are like this. I cannot show sympathy to the suffering, nor help the suffering unless there is suffering, nor bravely bear my pain unless I have pain to bear.

Other good actions which can only be responses to bad states of affairs include those which are responses to the malevolent or negligent actions of others or ourselves. I can only successfully apologize or make reparation to you if I have harmed you; or forgive you if you have harmed me and apologized. Other good actions are the appropriate responses to good states of affairs. There is an obligation to show gratitude to those from whom we have accepted benefit, and also to acknowledge the achievements of those whom we have benefited and who have put those benefits to good use.[8] I claimed earlier that it is a good for me if my efforts to achieve some good are successful. I am indeed fortunate if my pupils all pass their exams. They have done me a good turn, and I ought to acknowledge that. So more generally communities should recognize and honour those of its citizens who have put to abundant good use the nurture and education which it provided for them.

There are also actions similar to these just described which are not obligatory but supererogatorily good. It is good to show gratitude beyond the minimum obligatory; good for a wrongdoer to give reparation and penance beyond the minimum; and good to show respect in recognition of the worth and achievement of others, even when the achievement has no connection with ourselves. So many of these actions are actions which acknowledge the past, in which an agent acknowledges his identity with a certain past agent and the identity of others with certain other past agents. They consecrate past actions by giving them a present significance; and so they sanctify history. History does not get lost, it matters. Wrongdoing is not left as a blot, but wiped out in so far as it can be. Gratitude too consecrates the past; and the making of promises also makes for bonds of significance crossing the passage of time, which are strengthened as the promises are fulfilled.

If responsibility is a good thing, then (barring the chances of bad consequences, to which we shall come later) the more of it the better. It is good that I be able to influence not only my family now,

---

[8] For analysis of such notions as reparation, forgiveness, gratitude, and reward, see *Responsibility and Atonement*, chs. 4 and 5.

but, through cooperative action, distant communities and future generations. Among the choices we have, both as individuals and (in cooperation) as a community, is, as I have already noted, whether to seek to grow in knowledge. On the large scale, this means that we have the choice of whether to invest money in universities and research institutes, to find out about our past history, the laws of nature, and the truths of philosophy; or whether not to bother.[9] We have also the choice of seeking (partly through growing in knowledge) to grow in power. We were able to choose whether to take steps to learn how to ride horses, build boats, make combustion engines and computers—and so to go places, build things, and destroy things. And by our choices now—to pursue certain kinds of scientific research and invest our wealth in certain sorts of technology—we may be able in centuries to come to affect for how long the human race lives and on which planet. To have the choice of whether or not to seek to grow in knowledge and power, we must start from a position of relative ignorance and impotence; and there has to be a way which we can recognize as available to us by which we may try (with some reasonable chance of success) to extend our knowledge and power.

One evident way for God to create creatures with this sort of choice is for him to create embodied creatures. An agent has a body if there is a chunk of matter through which alone he or she can make a difference to the world, and through which alone he or she can learn about the world. We humans are embodied because only through such a chunk (our body) can we make a difference to other things: I can only move the furniture with my hands, or give you some information by using my mouth to tell it to you or my hands to write it to you. I can only learn about the world by light rays landing on my eyes or sound waves landing on my ears. And (barring a possibility to be discussed in Chapter 11) I can only acquire knowledge or exercise power if my body is situated in a world governed by simple natural laws which I can come to comprehend.

---

[9] Good though the search for knowledge is, it can only be good in so far as knowledge is a good thing to have, and our search has some prospect of success. There is clearly no point in searching for something you will not reach and is not worth having. Hence the famous remark of Lessing is a gross exaggeration: 'If God were to hold out enclosed in his right hand all truth, and in his left hand just the active search for truth, though with the condition that I should always err therein, and he should say to me: Choose! I should humbly take his left hand and say: Father! Give me this one; absolute Truth belongs to Thee alone' (G. E. Lessing, *Eine Duplik*, pt. 1).

Only if, when I move my hands in certain ways, the furniture above them moves and stays put when I let go of it, can I successfully move the furniture. And only if light travels in straight lines day after day will the visual images in my mind and the beliefs about the world correlated with them caused by the light impinging on my eyes be reliable guides to how things are in the world.

Now an embodied agent is one who starts with limited power and knowledge: he can move his limbs, and know about his mental states. But if his body is situated in a world governed by simple natural laws, then he will note that moving his limbs in certain ways leads to different mental states: putting my hand in a fire leads to pain and putting chocolate in my mouth leads to pleasure. We come naturally to explain these correlations in terms of our bodies being situated in a world of material objects which we can influence and which influence us. This interpretation of our situation comes naturally. Further experience will add a little to our knowledge unsought (if we are rational in our response to it). But for significant expansion of knowledge, we need to choose to seek it actively. We can investigate the effects of making various machines and pulling various levers, and test hypotheses about the causes of things. We can do this because different states of the outside world have different effects on our bodies and so on our minds; and our different actions through our bodies have different effects on the world, which we can study through the effects of the latter on us. Embodiment in a world governed by simple laws of nature secures the goal of an initial limited repertoire of power and knowledge, and a means (by discovering those laws) for extending it. God has this reason for making a universe with simple laws of nature: to provide for embodied beings to have a limited repertoire of power and knowledge and a means of extending it. But a universe governed by simple laws of nature will also have the beauty which our Universe has, and which I set out in Chapter 3. In creating such a universe, God will fulfil two major purposes.

So God has a strong reason for creating creatures of limited power and knowledge: that they can choose whether or not to grow therein. And he also has strong reason for creating creatures already having much power and knowledge—in the goodness of power and knowledge. There is no particular best amount of power and knowledge in a creature; and so God has reason for creating creatures of varying amounts of power and knowledge, and varying capacities for acquiring them—freely or spontaneously. All of which provides another reason for God to create animals (with very limited power and knowledge, but some capacities to grow therein, both by learning passively, and by actively seeking knowledge, yet spontaneously rather than freely) as well as the reason mentioned at the end of Chapter 4: the goodness of having available for love those who cannot respond in quite the same way. There is too the great goodness of the special kind of love that animals can have for humans, and the special kinds of cooperation which can exist between animals and humans. And there is the great good of mere variety of kinds of power, knowledge, and embodiment. Similar argument suggests that God has reason for creating non-embodied creatures who have so much knowledge and power that they do not have much capacity to grow therein. Much Christian tradition affirms that God has created creatures just like this—the angels. A principle powerfully influential in the history of thought from Plato until at least the eighteenth century was the principle of plenitude:[10] nature or God would create all the possible kinds of being.

In considering love in the last chapter, I considered only its involuntary aspects: desires to share things, including beliefs; and desires that the beloved desire to share things including beliefs; and so on. But love also involves of course the crucial component of action. It involves doing and seeking to do things with and for the beloved. And love is much the better for being not merely mutual, but seeking (through a shared desire to do so) the well-being of others. Hence the very great good of procreative love—bringing into being new agents who will be loved and live good lives. And despite the value of animal love, obviously there is especial value in love which is freely given, in which the actions are freely chosen. Is love the better if the loving actions are chosen, despite contrary temptation? Clearly it is good that the lover sometimes persevere in dedicating himself to the beloved, despite contrary temptation. But

---

[10] See A. O. Lovejoy, *The Great Chain of Being* (Harvard University Press, 1936) for the history of this principle. Aquinas, strongly influenced by this principle, claims that diversity requires that there exist both immortal and mortal things; and also things that cannot cease to be good and things that can cease to be good; he holds that what can happen, at some time will happen, and so there is bound to be an absence of good which, for Aquinas, constitutes the bad (see *Summa Theologiae*, Ia. 48. 2). But of course that is carrying the principle too far: the goodness of diversity as such provides inadequate reason for God to create what is bad.

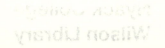

generous service in which there was little desire at all for the beloved could not be called love and, though a good thing, would be significantly deficient. All desires for what is good are good, and the lack of desire for the well-being of someone towards whom it is good that we perform loving actions is clearly a deficiency.

The Greatness of Being of Use

It is, this chapter has tried to bring out, a good thing to have power—to be able to make a difference to things for good or ill. This I have called responsibility for things. But it is also a good thing to be of use, to help, to serve, either through freely exercising power in the right way, or through doing it naturally and spontaneously, or even by being used as the vehicle of a good purpose.

That helping is an immense good for the helper has always been difficult for humans to see, but it is especially hard for twentieth-century secularized Western man to see. It is, however, something quite often near the surface of New Testament writings, as I shall illustrate much more fully in Chapter 13. For the moment let me just quote St Paul's farewell sermon to the church at Ephesus when he urged them 'to remember the words of the Lord Jesus, how he himself said, It is more blessed to give than to receive'.[11]

We do not, most of us, think that most of the time. We think that our well-being consists only in the things that we possess or the experiences we enjoy. Sometimes, true, all people find themselves in circumstances in which they ought to give; alas, the starving appear on our doorstep and we ought to give them some of our wealth, perhaps something large which will deprive us of future enjoyments. But that, the common thinking goes, is our misfortune, good for the starving but bad for us. Life would have been better for us if they had not turned up on the doorstep. But what the words of Christ say, taken literally, is 'not so'. *We* are lucky that they turned up on the doorstep. It would have been *our* misfortune if there had been no starving to whom to give; life would have been worse for *us*.

And even twentieth-century people can begin to see that sometimes: when they seek to help prisoners, not by giving them more

---

[11] Acts 20: 35.

comfortable quarters, but by letting them help the handicapped; or when they pity rather than envy the 'poor little rich girl' who has everything and does nothing for anyone else. And one phenomenon prevalent in end-of-century Britain draws this especially to our attention—the evil of unemployment. Because of our system of Social Security the unemployed on the whole have enough money to live without too much discomfort; certainly they are a lot better off than are many employed in Africa, Asia, or Victorian Britain. What is evil about unemployment is not so much any resulting poverty but the uselessness of the unemployed. They often report feeling unvalued by society, of no use, 'on the scrap heap'. They rightly think it would be a good for them to contribute; but they cannot.

It is not only intentional actions freely chosen, but also ones performed involuntarily, which have good consequences for others, which constitute a good for those who do them. If the unemployed were compelled to work for some useful purpose, they would still—most of them—regard that as a good for them in comparison with being useless. Or, if they would not so regard it, I suggest that most of us who are employed, and not directly involved in their plight, can see it as a good for them. Or consider the conscript killed in a just and ultimately successful war in defence of his country against a tyrannous aggressor. Almost all peoples, apart from those of the Western world in our generation, have recognized that dying for one's country is a great good for him who dies, even if he was conscripted.[12]

And it is not only intentional actions but experiences undergone involuntarily (or involuntary curtailment of good experiences, as

---

[12] This good, others have recognized, exists as a this-worldly good, quite apart from any reward for patriotic behaviour which might accrue in the afterlife. The hope of such reward was not a major motive among Romans and Greeks who died for their country. 'The doctrine of future life was far too vague among the pagans to exercise any powerful general influence' (W. E. H. Lecky, *History of European Morals from Augustus to Charlemagne* (Longmans, Green, 1899), ii. 3). 'The Spartan and the Roman died for his country because he loved it. The martyr's ecstasy of hope had no place in his dying hour. He gave up all he had, he closed his eyes, as he believed for ever, and he asked for no reward in this world or in the next' (ibid. i. 178). The well-known lines of Horace *dulce et decorum est pro patria mori* ('it is sweet and proper to die for one's country'; *Odes* 3. 2. 13) were written by a man whose belief in personal immortality was negligible (see the famous ode 3. 30, in which he sees his 'immortality' as consisting in his subsequent reputation); and so those lines would seem to convey the view that dying for one's country was as such good for him who died. It was of course a Socratic view that doing *just* acts was a good for him who does them (see Plato, *Gorgias* 479).

by death) which have good consequences—so long as those experiences are closely connected with their consequences—which constitute a good for him who has them (even if a lesser good than that
of a free intentional action causing those consequences, and a good
often outweighed by the bad of the experience in question).
Consider someone hurt or killed in an accident, where the accident
leads to some reform which prevents the occurrence of similar accidents in future (e.g. someone killed in a rail crash which leads to the
installation of a new system of railway signalling which prevents
similar accidents in future). His relatives often comment in such a
situation that at any rate the victim did not suffer or die in vain.
They would have regarded it as a greater misfortune for the victim
if his suffering or death served no useful purpose. It is a good for
us if our experiences are not wasted but are used for the good of
others, if they are the means of a benefit which would not have
come to others without them, which will at least in part compensate
for those experiences. It follows from this insight that it is a blessing for a person if the possibility of his suffering makes possible the
good for others of having the free choice of hurting or harming him;
and if his actual suffering makes possible the good for others of
feeling compassion for him, and of choosing to show or not show
sympathy or provide knowledge for others. Thus it is a good for
the fawn caught in the thicket in the forest fire that his suffering
provides knowledge for the deer and other animals who see it to
avoid the fire and deter their other offspring from being caught in
it.[13] I emphasize that I make this comment and similar comments
in this and other paragraphs without for the present raising the
question who, if anyone, has the right to impose a bad state on an
unwilling agent 'for the sake of' some good. We will come to that
issue in Chapter 12. But I should make it clear here that I am *not*
saying that humans have any right to cause train crashes or forest
fires of the kind just described. Nor am I yet passing any judgements about whether the good is as great a good as the bad is bad.
Nevertheless, I am claiming, the supreme good of being of use is
worth paying a lot to get. It is much better if the being-of-use is

---

[13] Those familiar with recent philosophical writing on the problem of evil will
realize that I choose the example of a fawn caught in a forest fire because of its prevalence in that literature. It was put forward by William Rowe ('The Problem of Evil
and Some Varieties of Atheism', *American Philosophical Quarterly*, 16 (1979),
335–41) as an example of apparently pointless evil. I shall be pointing out from time
to time the good purposes which the fawn's suffering subserves.

chosen voluntarily, but it is good even if it is not. Blessed is the man or woman whose life is of use.

Someone may object that the good is not (for example) dying for one's country, but knowingly dying for one's country when one believes it good to do so—having the experience of 'feeling good' that one is sacrificing oneself. But that, for reasons similar to those given in connection with similar claims earlier, cannot be right. It could only be good to have the experience in question if one's beliefs were correct—we saw in Chapter 4 how a false belief can ruin the worth of a mental state. There would be nothing good about believing one was dying for a good cause, when in fact it was a lousy cause. And so the experience will only be good if what one believes is true, and one's beliefs include the belief that it is good to die for one's country (which could occur even if one did not know it). What one rejoices in is that one's life is of use, not that one knows that one's life is of use.[14] The good for the subject of being able to be of use to others (as well as use his life in other good ways) does, however, make available to him the possibility of self-respect; he is in a position (justifiably, not through self-deceit) to think well of himself as a person. Unjustified pride is of course a bad thing, but proper pride is a good thing, and people who have it have a good worth more than many thrills of pleasure.

Actions which consist in bringing about what is bad or believed to be bad are as such themselves bad whether done spontaneously or freely through yielding to temptation. Any failure to bring about what is good, when there is an obligation to do good, is wrong. And actions may be wrong, because they involve a breach of obligation, even though they do not consist in bringing about a bad state of affairs. When I talk with you, I implicitly accept an obligation not to deceive you. So a lie is wrong, even if its consequences are good and even if the agent believed that its consequences would be good. And being the victim of wrong is bad for the victim, not just because of the harm done but in so far as it was done knowingly, or, worse, deliberately by an agent who sought the victim's harm. It is bad for someone to have someone else seek their harm. No one likes

---

[14] In the Old Testament, it is the Wisdom literature which saw most clearly this great good. The curse (in Wisd. 3: 11) for the ungodly is that their 'works' are 'useless'; that, for example (3: 16), 'the children of adulterers shall not come to maturity'. The ungodly are compared to a 'ship passing through the billowy water, whereof, when it is gone by, there is no trace to be found' (Wisd. 5: 10).

to be hated—there would be something very wrong with us if we did—and seeking the harm of another is the natural manifestation of hate.

A good God will seek to create agents not merely with good desires and beliefs but ones who have the opportunities to do good actions and take those opportunities. If the good actions are not free, or do not involve a choice between the perceived good and the temptation to do bad, God can ensure that not merely do the agents have the opportunity to do good, but actually do it. And so he may well create many who do inevitably good actions.

God's Provision of Human Freedom

Clearly (if there is a God) he has created animals who (on the reasonable assumption that they do not have free will) do inevitably many greatly good actions, such as feeding and caring for their young. Sometimes of course they do bad actions, such as neglecting their young, and we shall need in due course to consider why God allows that. Clearly too (if there is a God) he has created humans who make many serious responsible choices with all the characteristics described in this chapter, and are (like animals) of use in many ways. But what is open to question is whether human choices are free in the sense of not being fully predetermined by prior causes. This issue has of course been the subject of (so far) unending philosophico-scientific controversy, to enter into which there simply is no space here. But suffice it to make here two brief points.

The first is that it does often seem that it is up to us how we are to choose, and it is, as we have seen in Chapter 1, a mark of rationality to believe that things are as they seem to be, in the absence of counter-evidence. The second is that the mental life (of sensation, thought, desire, and purpose) is, evidently, so very different from normal physical events in the inanimate world that the brain (in sustaining a mental life) must be very different from other physical systems (which do not sustain mental life); and so there is not too much reason for supposing that any virtual determinism which operates outside the brain operates within it. Hence there is not too much reason from science for supposing that things are not as they

seem to be in respect of our freedom of choice. But that does not of
course settle the question finally; and the reader will need to take
into account the fuller philosophico-scientific arguments available
in the literature.[15]

That humans have free will (free will, that is, in the libertarian
sense) is a doctrine which, I argued in Chapter 2, has been strongly
affirmed by a significant majority of the Christian tradition. Those
who have affirmed it have seen it as a central feature of the fact that
humans are made 'in the image of God'. Free will, they are telling
us, is one of the best, perhaps the best of all the characteristics with
which God endowed humans. But the greatest glory of humans
consists in using it in the right way. Thereby humans will be
conformed to God's 'likeness'. In the fourth century, for example,
St Gregory of Nyssa wrote that 'pre-eminent' among all the facets
of this image 'is the fact that we are free from necessity, and not in
bondage to any natural power, but have decision in our own power
as we please'.[16] In the eighth century St John of Damascus wrote
that 'every man is said to be made in the image of God as regards
the dignity of his intellect and soul—as regards, that is to say, the
quality in man that cannot be scrutinized or observed, is immortal
and endowed with free will, and in virtue of which he rules, begets
and constructs'.[17] And at the end of the Eastern patristic period, in
the fourteenth century, St Gregory Palamas wrote that 'it is not by
virtue of natural qualities, but by virtue of what one achieves
through free choice that one is close to or distant from God'.[18] And
St Gregory stressed, as others did also, echoing the passage from
Genesis with which this chapter begins, that part of the greatness
of the human soul is that it has 'a capacity for sovereignty':[19] the
human soul 'overlooks the universe and has all things in its care'.[20]
That is, in my terminology, the glory of humans is not just their
very serious free will, but the responsibility for so much which that
free will involves.

[15] For my own philosophico-scientific arguments in favour of human free will,
see my *The Evolution of the Soul*, ch. 13.
[16] *On the Making of Man*, 16. 11.
[17] St John of Damascus, 'On the Virtues and Vices', in G. E. H. Palmer,
P. Sherrard, and K. Ware (ed. and trans.), *Philokalia*, ii (Faber & Faber, 1981), 341.
[18] St Gregory Palamas, 'Topics of Natural and Theological Science', in G. E. H.
Palmer, P. Sherrard, and K. Ware (ed. and trans.), *Philokalia*, iv (Faber & Faber,
1995), 382.
[19] Ibid. 374.		[20] Ibid. 356.

Because of the weight of Christian tradition in its favour, and the absence of good philosophico-scientific arguments to the contrary, I am therefore taking the doctrine that humans have free will for granted. I have argued that it is a good thing that we should have it with the resulting responsibility for ourselves and others. It thus forms a central part of the package of Christian doctrine in terms of which I seek to explain why God should allow the world's bad states to occur. Given the omnipotence of God, humans have free will only in so far as God continually sustains it in them and allows their actions to have their intended consequences. But just as it is good that human parents should allow their children to make choices which are not good, and it is the mark of a good parent that she should allow her children, as they become older, to rebel; so surely a good God will do the same. An objector may, however, question whether, if there is a God, he allows humans too much free will and responsibility; I shall come to such quantitive issues in Chapter 13.

The great good of so much free will and often cooperative human action has gone with the bad of so much negligence of ways to prevent harm, and so much deliberate infliction of harm (often cooperatively). Our bad actions, like our good actions (especially if done in cooperation), have effects in distant places and distant centuries. The Holocaust was made possible by the continued denigration of Jews over many centuries, by professed Christians of Central Europe. I need to argue in due course for the greater good which allowing (and when we are dealing with free human actions, it is only allowing, not causing) such horrible things to occur makes possible. But it is right to start by dwelling at some length on the very great and (as far as much of this chapter is concerned) manifest goods of the created order.

The Influence of Angels and Ancestors

There are two further Christian views about the range of responsibility of free creatures for the state of the world, suggesting that it is much greater than may at first appear in the light of mere secular considerations, to which I drew attention in Chapter 2.

The first view is that there are angels, non-embodied creatures who have some influence for good or ill over the world. Given that there is a God, this ancient view has some a priori probability (reinforced by any probability it might gain, if seen as part of the Christian revelation). There are many, many kinds of good state. Embodied humans are not the only kinds of rational agent with free will there could be. God might well create non-embodied free agents; and some of them might indeed choose the bad. We may perhaps regard the initial choice of character by the angels as one extended in time, and, given that, if it is good that God should give us the ultimate choice over the period of our lives on Earth of being allowed to fix our characters beyond further change, it would seem to be similarly good that God should give to angels also the ultimate choice of being allowed to fix their characters. And he might well also, in giving them that initial choice, have promised them temporary and limited power over the world when they had fixed their characters. That would have given a deeper significance to their choice than it would otherwise have, for they would know that in choosing the bad, they would be choosing to exert a bad influence on the world. If freedom and responsibility are good things, it is good that there be angels who have it, as well as humans. The power of the angels might have been exercised by their influence on the structure of the world which God created (e.g. ensuring that natural processes sometimes produced incurable pain) rather than by intervening in an already created order. However, the Christian tradition has on the whole seen the influence of bad angels (and so of the chief bad angel, the Devil) as operative mainly in tempting humans to wrongdoing, rather than in causing suffering. And in view of the limited place of such demons in the Christian tradition, it would seem *ad hoc* to attempt to explain too much of the bad in the world as due to their operation; there is not enough independent evidence to suppose that any bad angels have very much power. Analogously there is not enough independent evidence to suppose that any good angels have very much power. In any case, since angels could only choose the bad if they were tempted so to do, being already subject to bad desires, the bad must have pre-existed any bad choice by angels.

Then, secondly, there is the view that human free choice has more distant effects than we realize. There is in particular the doctrine that it was through the knowingly wrong choice of the first human being, i.e. the earliest of our ancestors with free will and moral awareness, traditionally called Adam, that natural evil and

death and at any rate much of the proneness to moral evil came to
the human race. We saw in Chapter 2 that this is most plausibly
expressed as the view that, but for the sin of Adam, God would
have conferred on humans an immunity to suffering, to bad desires
and other natural evil, and to death.

Now clearly (whether he lived many thousands or millions of
years ago) there must have been a first human being in the sense of
an earliest of our ancestors who had moral awareness and (given
that we have free will) also free will. For the primitive organic
material out of which humans and animals developed did not have
those characteristics, and, I am assuming, we do. And plausibly
enough—at any rate given the view of Adam as a weak character
which Irenaeus and other early theologians advocated and which is
far more plausible given our knowledge of evolutionary history
than the rival view—the first human yielded at some time to his bad
desires and so was also the first sinner. (I write this without any
implication that the sin consisted in eating an apple in any literal
sense.)

It may be that Adam's bad action had more distant effects and
bigger effects than at first appears, because God allowed human
mortality and the extent of human suffering and proneness to sin to
be affected by that choice. But as with the angels, so with Adam:
Adam could not have sinned without already having some bad
desires to which he yielded—and bad desires are themselves a natural evil. Adam must have inherited from his animal ancestors such
desires as the desire to eat more than his share of the available food
and the desire to order others about. What was different about
Adam is that because he had moral awareness and free will (that
was what his having a human soul amounted to), such actions
became sinful, and because of his moral awareness he came to see
such actions as wrong and (given that he had also some awareness
of God) as sinful. By inheriting, genetically, his desires and his free
will; and by inheriting, no doubt in part culturally, his moral
awareness, we later humans inherited that sinfulness. But we would
have inherited the sinfulness anyway, whether or not Adam had
sinned, but for divine intervention.

As we have seen, the traditional account of the Fall claims that
God would have saved us from death and suffering (and on some
versions from sinfulness also), but for the sin of Adam. Perhaps so.
As I am arguing throughout this book, although the bad in the

world serves good purposes, God would have been no less than perfectly good if he had produced a world with a lot less bad and so a
lot less of that good for which the bad is needed. And maybe God
allowed which of the worlds he would produce (a world without
human death and much human suffering; or a world with these and
also the other good states which they make possible) to depend on
the choice for good or ill of the first human being. But there must
be much other good, than the good of Adam having the responsibility for the future of so many millions of subsequent humans,
served by our subjection to suffering. For good though human
responsibility is, it would surely have been bad if God gave to one
human being the choice of whether all subsequent humans suffered
or not, unless much other good was served by that suffering.[21] This
would be especially bad since, given the implausibility of the 'original righteousness' account of Adam,[22] he would not have understood much of what would have followed from that choice. If
Adam's choice made all the difference, God would only have been
good in allowing him to have that choice if overall the alternative
consequences of his actions did not differ enormously in their
goodness. There must be a lot of other good served by our suffering than the good of Adam's responsibility for future generations.
For this reason the Fall must not be given too central a place in
theodicy. My own theodicy will be concerned to bring out how
suffering and sinfulness make possible good states for those who
suffer and sin and their immediate victims, rather than give too
much importance to the role of Adam or the Devil; I believe that I
am following the best traditions of earlier Christian thought in this
respect.

[21] And plausibly it would have been almost equally bad if God had given to a
human the choice of whether all subsequent humans were mortal or immortal—
though the issues here are different, if death is not itself a bad state but merely the
end of a good state, as I shall be arguing.
[22] See pp. 39 and 101.

6

Worship

And there came one of the seven angels . . . And he carried me
away in the Spirit to a mountain great and high, and shewed
me the holy city Jerusalem, coming down out of heaven from
God, having the glory of God . . . And I saw no temple therein:
for the Lord God the Almighty, and the Lamb, are the temple
thereof. And the city hath no need of the sun, neither of the
moon, to shine upon it: for the glory of God did lighten it, and
the lamp thereof is the Lamb. And the nations shall walk
amidst the light thereof: and the kings of the earth do bring
their glory into it . . . And he shewed me a river of water of life,
bright as crystal, proceeding out of the throne of God and of
the Lamb, in the midst of the street thereof. And on this side
of the river and on that was the tree of life, bearing twelve
manner of fruits, yielding its fruit every month: and the leaves
of the tree were for the healing of the nations. And there shall
be no curse any more: and the throne of God and of the Lamb
shall be therein: and his servants shall do him service; and they
shall see his face; and his name shall be on their foreheads.
And there shall be night no more; and they need no light of
lamp, neither light of sun; for the Lord God shall give them
light: and they shall reign for ever and ever.

(Revelation 21: 9–22: 5)

The good states of which I have written so far are good whether or
not there is a God. But there are some states which are good if and
only if there is a God. And most of them fall under the central head-
ing of a right relation to God himself. A good God, for his sake and
for theirs, will seek to have creatures rightly related to himself. He
will seek for those creatures who have the capacity to do so to know
him, interact with him, and love him.

We saw in Chapter 4 what a good thing knowledge (in the objective internalist sense) is, propositional knowledge, knowledge of

facts, that is. All knowledge is good, but especially knowledge of deep truths about the Universe and our place in it, who or what is the source of our being, and moral truths about our duties and the good actions beyond duty which we can do. Humans and maybe rational beings elsewhere in the Universe (if any such there are) are capable of understanding true answers on these issues—at any rate to some degree. So if God is the creator and sustainer of the Universe, he will want us to have such knowledge, and so to know (for our sake, of course; not for his sake) that among our moral duties are the duty to express our gratitude to God and seek to do his will. For, as we have noted, there is a duty to please benefactors. God is our supreme benefactor: we owe our existence from moment to moment, and our powers and pleasures, our knowledge and desires, to his sustaining power. And everything that everyone else does for us they can do only because God sustains in them their power. We owe him so much by way of expression of gratitude and service; and, as was noted in the last chapter, it is supererogatorily good to do more for benefactors than duty requires. And since God, seeking our well-being and theirs, will want us to be good, to fulfil our duties to others, and to do things for them and ourselves beyond the call of duty, it will become doubly our duty and doubly good to do so.[1]

All human wrongdoing to other creatures is also wronging God. For, first, anyone who misuses a gift from a benefactor wrongs the benefactor. God gives us life and all our powers and knowledge. If we use them to hurt someone else, we wrong God also. And secondly, just as anyone who wrongs a child wrongs the parent who brought him into existence, nourishes, educates, and loves him, so wronging another creature is wronging God whose creature they are. Wronging God is sin; and so all wrongdoing is sin.

But God is not just our benefactor deserving our grateful service. I reflected in Chapter 4 on the goodness of having and expressing respect for the powerful, wise, and good. It follows from God's omnipotence and perfect goodness that he is holy, so other and different from anything else that a truly awesome reverence is the only proper reaction to him. And God will want us for our sake to respond in the proper way to his own ultimacy.

---

[1] For fuller justification of the claims of this paragraph, see my *Responsibility and Atonement* (Clarendon Press, 1989), ch. 8.

God will, for these and other reasons to which I will come
shortly, want us to know that he exists. He could do that by showing us that some argument for his existence from evident features
of the world is deductively valid or gives high inductive probability to its conclusion. Or he could give us a very powerful experience
of his presence. Although the human concepts in terms of which we
attempt to describe and recognize God are inevitably hopelessly
inadequate for the purpose, on the traditional Western view with
which we are operating, they give us some idea of God. God is powerful, rather than weak; wise, rather than foolish; good, rather than
bad. But also on that view they are just adequate enough for us who
use them to realize how inadequate they are. To quote those haunt-
ing words of Kant: 'Unconditioned necessity, which we so indis-
pensably require as the last bearer of all things, is for human reason
the veritable abyss. Eternity itself, in all its terrible sublimity, as
depicted by a Haller, is far from making the same overwhelming
impression on the mind; for it only measures the duration of things,
it does not support them.'[2] It is natural to suppose that the inadequacy of our ordinary categories for talk about God arises from
the fact that they have their primary application for talking about
ordinary mundane beings. We learn the contrast between 'wise'
and 'foolish' by having examples of wise and foolish humans
pointed out to us; and then we are told that God is more like the
former than the latter (in the respect in which the former are like
each other and unlike the latter). But if God gave us a more direct
awareness of himself, we could devise words and thus designate
categories for describing the God of whom we are aware in experience, which would capture more nearly what God is like. God will
surely want to give us this knowledge.

As our creator, God will seek to interact with us. He will want us
to feel his presence, to tell him things and ask him to do things; and
he will want to tell us things (to be the source, and known to be the
source, of all the deep truths to which I have referred), and to do
things with us, to cooperate with us in producing further good. No
parent would be a good parent who did not seek all this for their
children; and God, as so much more the source of our being than
our earthly parents, must seek all this for us. So he will manifest his
presence to us, not merely give us the knowledge that he is present.

[2] I. Kant, *Critique of Pure Reason*, B641.

He will persuade us to tell him things (even if he knows them already; many a parent knows already what his child tells him, but wants the child to tell him all the same). He will want us to ask him for good things for ourselves and for others, which he will bring about if and only if we ask; for in that way, the good which he brings about is better for our involvement in its production. And God would wish to involve us in his projects, and his concern with each of us would be shown by giving us different jobs to do, by tailoring jobs to fit us rather than just saying 'Do something useful'.

When we do wrong, God will want us to hear his angry rebuke; when we apologize, God will want us to hear his message of pardon. And as a loving parent, he will want us to love him; and he will cultivate in us the beliefs about him and desire to interact with him which make this possible.

While all loving interaction, alias friendship, is good, such interaction with those with whom we are deeply involved for other reasons is especially good. Friendship with our benefactors and beneficiaries and so with parents and children is especially good because it consecrates with liking (i.e. saves from formality) relations of deep significance. And friendship with good people is especially good. This is because it involves sharing good thoughts and good activities, and liking those who are especially worthy of being liked because they do good actions and have good characters, and so will involve having the right attitude towards actions and characters. (I do not of course wish to imply that we should seek friendship only with the already good, but only that since friendship is better for being based on fully correct values, we should aim at turning any friendship into such a friendship.) All friendships, and especially those of the kinds just discussed, are intrinsically valuable. Friendships with the good, and especially with good parents deserving respect and gratitude, are also obviously enormously valuable instrumentally. The good influence of good parents is very great. The good influence of a good God would be enormous.

Now the Christian tradition teaches two doctrines relevant to such divine interaction with us. The first is that God does now have limited interaction with many Christians and others. And the second is that God will have full interaction with many of us after death. As regards his present limited interaction with us, God does, it is claimed, help some of us to see the force of arguments to his existence, give some of us experience of his presence, make known to some of us our 'vocations'. And certainly to some of us it seems that this is the case. If there is a God, it seems reasonable to suppose that our apparent experiences of him are genuine, and that often what he seems to be telling us he is telling us; and in so far as our arguments have force, it is God who is helping us to see that. The claim continues that humans have a duty to interact with God in prayer, and to make petitionary prayer for the removal of many bad states and the coming about of many good states; and that God answers many of the prayers of those who ask (in the way most expedient). God does not answer all prayers, and his goodness would not lead us to suppose that he would.[3] Good benefactors do not answer prayers for what is bad; and they only answer prayers for what is not bad only in a certain respect, in that respect. But God does answer some prayers, the claim is, in the sense that he brings about some state of affairs prayed for which would not otherwise have occurred. Some people cured from some disease would not have been cured but for prayer, and some people not cured would have been cured if others had bothered to pray for their cure with sufficient devotion. If human responsibility is good, then this extension to it—of exerting influence on (though not of course compelling) God to change things—would surely be also good.

It has been central to the Christian tradition since its beginning that God is an interactive God, guiding us and responding to our good and bad deeds individually. It has been so much taken for granted by the tradition that it has never been sufficiently a matter of controversy (before the last two or three centuries) to require formulation as a doctrine. If the investigator finds that science or philosophy has counter-evidence to this claim, she will have to take it into account; but in so far as the evidence is from revelation, it is very strongly in its favour.

---

[3] There were unanswered prayers both of St Paul (2 Cor. 12: 7–9) and of Jesus himself (Mark 14: 36). On the other hand the Gospels have sayings seeming to say that all prayers, at any rate of Christians, will be answered (e.g. Matt. 21: 22). The usual Christian compromise is to suppose that the Gospel overall is saying only that prayers for things which are not contrary to the will of God will be answered. They may be either for states neither good nor bad, or for good states (or the removal of bad states) but ones which God will only bring about if asked—because he wants us to be involved in bringing them about.

The Mechanism of Providence

The good states—knowledge, good desires, efficacious desires, etc.—with which previous chapters were concerned are ones given to all or to large groups of creatures. Given that there is a God, they thus manifest what is known as his 'general providence'. (Apart from the possible influence of angels and of Adam) they are goods arising from the general structure of the world, the natural order of things; which, if there is a God, clearly he brings about.

God's dealings with particular individuals, however, in response to their particular needs and requests, not in accordance with any general formula, manifest God's 'special providence'. This involves his intervening in the natural order of things. The 'natural order' of things is simply their regular behaviour in accordance with the laws of nature. If this regular behaviour, the 'laws of nature', are deterministic, any intervention by God will involve his temporarily suspending the laws of nature, violating them. But if this regular behaviour is not fully determined (if the laws of nature merely make some future events physically probable and others physically improbable, but do not determine what will happen), then God's intervention will simply be a matter of inclining things to behave on a certain occasion in this way rather than that, which will be compatible with the probabilistic patterns of behaviour which humans may discover and formulate as 'laws'. Yet even if compatible with the 'laws', some divine interventions could cause states of affairs very improbable given those 'laws'.

Quantum theory indicates that the most fundamental laws of nature, the laws governing the behaviour of very small-scale particles, are probabilistic, i.e. indeterministic; but that, in general, small-scale indeterminacies cancel out on the large scale, leading to virtually deterministic behaviour of the medium-sized objects with which we interact—tables and chairs, trees and persons. The human brain may well be an exception—here small-scale indeterminism may well lead to large-scale indeterminism. Hence the possibility that our free actions,[4] and any effects of divine intervention in our mental life, are not merely compatible with the laws of nature, but not improbable given those laws. But other divine

---

[4] On how quantum theory makes room for free will, see my *The Evolution of the Soul*, rev. edn. (Clarendon Press, 1997), ch. 13.

interventions in the world, God moving material bodies over several metres, for example, would require the occurrence of events immensely improbable given natural laws, which we may call 'quasi-violations' of natural laws. If we are to know that some event is or is not a quasi-violation, we need to know not merely what are the laws of nature but what was the previous state of the world. Suppose that the desk seems suddenly to move several metres from here to there before our very eyes. We need to know that there are no ropes pulling it, that no magnets are at work, that it really is a desk and not a hologram, that we are not subject to a sudden hallucination, etc. Occasionally we are in a position to know this. But with respect to events crucial for human well-being (health, crops flourishing, accidents, defence against enemies, success in business), we would be very seldom indeed in any position to know that some event which constituted in a wide sense what was prayed for did or did not occur in accordance with natural laws. This is because all events, and particularly events of this kind, are such that which subsequent events will follow earlier events in accordance with laws of nature depends on a whole multitude of interacting earlier events (many of them very small-scale ones).

We are normally only aware of some of these earlier events, and when some subsequent event occurs we suppose it caused by the previous events of which we were aware, combined with whatever other events would be sufficient in accordance with laws of nature to produce the subsequent event. That is, we 'read back' into nature causes sufficient to produce whatever we observe. We are almost always able to do this, and very seldom would we be in a position to say that some event *could not* be explained by ordinary causes operating in accordance with known natural laws. Someone recovers from cancer. We would hardly normally be in a position to know enough about the previous state of their body to know that natural laws would not lead from the latter as cause to the recovery as effect. Pharaoh's army is drowned by the Red Sea suddenly rushing in and covering a previously shallow crossing. Natural causes could well have combined with the state of wind and rain at that place on the previous day to cause Pharaoh's army to drown. Alternatively, God may be bending nature to answer prayers and thus interact with individuals and groups all the time; we would not normally know. Just occasionally we are in a position to know that a violation or quasi-violation has or has not occurred.[5] And maybe one day we will be in a position to know this with respect to a lot more events, and if so maybe there would be evidence to show that God very seldom intervenes in nature, and if so that would show something very much in error in the Christian tradition. But I cannot see that present evidence shows that future discoveries are more likely to show that than to show the opposite. And so I suggest that the doctrine that God intervenes in the natural order from time to time to answer prayers in the ways most expedient for us is not at odds with our knowledge of the natural world, and so to be adopted on grounds of revelation.

Yet if God answered all prayers for the removal of bad states of affairs promptly and predictably, that would become evident. Clearly that does not happen. Maybe God allows some bad states to continue in order to allow people the choice of whether to persist in prayer and allow more people to be involved in the prayer. Yet some bad states seem to be so evidently unaffected by much continuing prayer that natural evil cannot in general be accounted for by the absence of petitionary prayer. We need other reasons why God should often not answer such prayers, in terms of some good states (other than people having the free choice of whether or not to pray for the removal of bad states) promoted by allowing the bad states to continue.

Life after Death

The second doctrine is that God will take many of us after death, and—if the world ends before some of us die—many of us before dying, into his more evident presence, and we will be able to render proper worship and other service to him then. The last book of the Bible, from which the quotation at the beginning of this chapter is taken, describes the saints as worshipping God, and 'reigning', that is, exercising power with God for making the world or maybe new worlds ever better. The Catholic tradition has represented the state

<hr>

[5] For arguments about what would be evidence for and against such violations, see the papers in R. Swinburne (ed.), *Miracles* (Macmillan, 1989). For examples of a few modern cases where there is quite a balance of evidence in favour of the occurrence of a violation or quasi-violation, see D. Hickey and G. Smith, *Miracle* (Hodder & Stoughton, 1978) or Rex Gardiner, *Healing Miracles* (Darton, Longman & Todd, 1986).

of the inhabitant of Heaven as enjoying the 'Beatific Vision', a state of contemplation of God, an expression which seems to do less than justice to the activity which is so good a feature of the life of humans and other rational beings. The Orthodox tradition has described it as θεοποίησις; which, translated literally, means 'deification'. For most of the Fathers this meant simply 'enjoying the divine *relation* of Son to Father, sharing the divine life'.[6] The blessed, although not themselves divine, interact with the Father as closely as does the Son, and so are involved in the work of God as well as the adoration of God. Since the wider Christian tradition has in general held—although not describing it as 'deification'—that this latter is also involved in the life of Heaven, I shall in future understand the 'Beatific Vision' as including it.

Who will enjoy the life of Heaven is something about which the Christian tradition has been far from clear. Christian believers who have lived on Earth a good life which ended with a good death are clearly included. But 'believers' has been traditionally thought to include also those who have been baptized and died in infancy. It has been thought to include also the Jews who lived good lives before Christ; and more generally the good ancestors of the Jewish people, including Adam. Some early theologians, like almost all modern ones, have thought that all who have not heard the Christian Gospel presented with sufficient plausibility, but who have lived good lives and made themselves so sensitive to truth and goodness as naturally to worship God in Christ when after death they hear the Gospel, will also enjoy the life of Heaven. A 'good life' has not usually been thought of as 'many good works', but a life which ended with a readiness to do good works, even if little time remained in which to do them. But while some Christian theologians of the present century have been 'universalists', that is have held that necessarily all humans will eventually be 'saved', i.e. go to Heaven, that position was virtually unknown in earlier times. That humans who fall outside the limits stated above in their widest sense will not be saved has been the traditional Christian view (although it was always allowed that just maybe in fact every human falls within the limits in their widest sense).[7]

[6] Rowan Williams, *The Wound of Knowledge*, 2nd edn. (Darton, Longman & Todd, 1990), 51.

[7] For a more detailed account of what the Christian tradition has supposed about the life of Heaven and who would enjoy it, and the different fates of different groups in the afterlife, see *Responsibility and Atonement*, ch. 12.

Both of these doctrines, that God does and will interact with us in these ways, to be expected in virtue of his goodness and also further evidenced to the extent to which there is independent evidence for the Christian revelation, do raise obvious problems: why is God's present interaction with us so limited, and why is his future interaction not provided for all? But we need to reflect on whether and why the limited interactions are bad states of affairs rather than mere absences of a good. For, as we have seen, there is no end to good states, and not even an all-good and all-powerful being could produce all the good states that there are. The limitedness of God's interaction in the present would, however, seem to be a bad state. It is, first, a bad state for those humans who desire to interact with God and desire to interact with him more fully. For then they have a frustrated desire, and that is a bad thing, I have argued. If humans long to have a deep experience of God, to interact with him in prayer, or at any rate to know that he is there, and do not—here is something bad. To the extent to which humans want God and do not have him there is something bad. But mere ignorance of God's existence is a bad thing for quite a different reason. Humans have, as I have noted, a duty to worship and serve God; and if they are ignorant of his existence, they cannot fulfil those duties, and an inability to fulfil a duty is clearly a bad state. In these ways and to these extents lack of knowledge of and interaction with God in the present is a bad state for humans; and we shall need in due course to see what greater good that ignorance and darkness serves.

Would it be a bad state if God's future interaction is not provided for all humans, if not all humans will enjoy the Beatific Vision? Now that again will only be a bad state (as opposed to the absence of a good) if those deprived of that vision desire it all the same. If some do not desire it, it would not be a bad thing if they do not have it. As we have seen, the life of Heaven consists in adoration of the good and in pursuit of the good. It therefore involves wanting and seeking all that God wants and seeks—wanting the wrongdoer to be penitent, and wanting the good to be generous with their lives, and wanting to worship God for his goodness. It would indeed be a bad state if anyone who desired these things (including, if they have done wrong, their own penitence) were deprived of the life of Heaven.

Why should anyone be in such a condition of not desiring the good? Either because God has allowed them to get into this condition, even though once they desired the good, or because they never had a desire for the good in the first place. I pointed out in Chapter 5 that humans are so made that their good choices on one occasion make good choices easier next time. We are so made that we gradually form our characters—either so that we become naturally good (prone to do the good, as soon as we are rightly informed wherein it consists), or so that we naturally yield to bad desires such that they acquire permanent mastery over us. It is good that God should allow people the choice of forming their characters in such a way as not to be open to future change. For if God refused to allow someone to develop an irreformably bad character, that would be depriving her of an ultimate choice of the sort of person she is to be. If God always left the bad open to good influences, that would be refusing to recognize an ultimate choice by an independent moral agent. It would be like a jilted lover pestering the beloved on and on, not recognizing her right to say a final no. But if someone does form their character in such a way as to be unalterably bad and if that involved their having no residual desire for the good which they cannot choose, they do not then desire the Vision of God; and so it is not a bad thing that they do not get it. (Whether the continued choice of the bad does involve elimination of any residual desire for the good is an issue to which I shall come in Chapters 8 and 11.)

There may also be those who never had a desire for the good (i.e. the morally good) in the first place; and there would be nothing bad in them not obtaining the Vision of God. Many medievals believed that the unbaptized who die as babies are in this category. They have not committed actual sin, and so they are not punished, but they do not enjoy the Vision of God. They go to an intermediate Limbo (more technically, the *Limbus puerorum*) where their enjoyments are on a lower level. To all appearances animals also lack moral concepts, and so cannot desire the Beatific Vision; and so their not getting it is not a bad thing. Indeed it rather looks as if animals in old age have no desire to continue to live at all, and so if they have no life after death, that too requires no theodicy.

Christian tradition has, however, taught not merely that the incorrigibly bad are deprived permanently of the Vision of God, but that this is a punishment for their sins (*poena damni*, the penalty of the loss of God) and also that they suffer further felt punishment (*poena sensus*), i.e. punishment involved in frustration of desires.

That is a bad state, not merely the absence of a good one, and so requires a theodicy. I shall come to such a theodicy in Chapter 11.

While noting the need for theodicy in respect of the temporary lack of the Beatific Vision for those who desire it, and for the felt punishment of those who permanently do not, let us return, at the end of Part II, to reflect not merely on the goodness of an Earth so evidently good in the ways described in earlier chapters, but on the glorious state which, the Christian revelation affirms, God will give to those who desire it. Blessedness with the saints in the life of God himself, in adoration of the good and ever promoting that good further, is, according to the Christian revelation, what God, our loving parent, had in mind in creating us.

III
The Necessary Evils

7

The Fact of Moral Evil; and Free Will

[The Lord] himself made man from the beginning and left
him in the hand of his own counsel. If thou wilt, thou shalt
keep the commandments; and to perform faithfulness is of
thine own good pleasure. He hath set fire and water before
thee: thou shalt stretch forth thine hand unto whichsoever
thou wilt. Before man is life and death; and whichsoever he
liketh, it shall be given him.

(Ecclesiasticus 15: 14–17)

The Logical Straitjacket

God will seek to provide all the good things and none of the bad
things described in Part II. But he cannot—for reasons of logic.
For, as simple non-religious examples will make evident, some
good states are logically incompatible with each other. It is good for
John to be married monogamously to Mary for all his married life
and good for John to be married monogamously to her sister Ann
for all his married life, but it is not logically possible that he be in
both these good states. It is good for Bill to be the President of the
United States in AD 2000, to have the great responsibility of gov-
ernment; and good for Bob to be President of the United States in
AD 2000. But they cannot both be President of the United States at
the same time. And some good states are not compatible with the
absence of certain bad states. It is good to have games of football,
in which teams develop their ball skill and team skill in such a way
as to defeat other teams. And it is good that all the teams want to
win, and so are enthusiastic, and happy when they win. But if
a winning team is happy because its desire to win is being fulfilled,
a losing team will be unhappy because its desire to win is being

frustrated. Arsenal's team and Liverpool's team cannot both win, and Arsenal cannot be happy at winning unless Liverpool are unhappy at losing. And not even God who can do anything logically possible can bring about both of two incompatible good states; or a good state without the bad state, when the good state entails the bad state.

Actions may be logically impossible for reasons other than that they consist in bringing about logically impossible states. There is no logical impossibility in there being an uncaused state, but it is logically impossible for anyone to bring about an uncaused state; and there is no logical impossibility in there being a state of affairs uncaused by me, but it is not logically possible for me (though it is logically possible for you) to bring it about. God cannot do what is logically impossible for him to do—whatever the reason for that logical impossibility.

People sometimes think that a really powerful God ought to be able to do the logically impossible—bring it about that John is monogamously married both to Ann and to her sister Mary for all John's married life. But to say that some 'action' is logically impossible is just to say that what appears to be a description of an action does not make ultimate sense, i.e. there is nothing which would constitute doing such an action. It is obvious that there is no action of making my desk both exist and not exist at the same time: there is nothing which would amount to doing such an action. Whatever I or anyone else did, whether in consequence my desk existed or not, there is nothing which would constitute making it exist and not exist at the same time. There are other purported descriptions of actions which look as if they describe actions which someone (at any rate someone sufficiently powerful) might do, but do not really. The description in that case does not, I shall say, make ultimate sense. If we investigate more fully what it would be like for such a description to hold—e.g. make John monogamously married both to Ann and to her sister Mary for all his married life—we realize that there is nothing which would constitute doing such an action. The logically impossible action is not an action which is very difficult to do, but a purported description of an action which does not describe an action at all. But, having made that point, we can make the original point (without now, I hope, misleading) by saying, God cannot do the logically impossible.

It follows from that, I shall show in the next four chapters, that God cannot bring about (or at any rate cannot guarantee to bring about) many of the good things described in Part II at the same time as many other good things, nor many of the good things without many bad things as well. I shall consider in turn the various bad things of this world, and show how their actual occurrence or the unprevented possibility of their occurrence is required for the realization of the various good states listed in Part II. The most obvious example of this logical straitjacket to which even God is subject is that he cannot give us very serious free will, i.e. the free will to choose between good and wrong, without the natural possibility (unprevented by God) that we will do wrong.

The Free-Will Defence

So I begin with one of the obvious ills of this world—the core moral evil of agents making wrong choices. I argued in Chapter 5 that it is good for agents to have very serious libertarian free will—libertarian, in that it involves freedom to act in a way not fully determined by causes; and very serious, in that it involves freedom to choose between the good and the bad, including the wrong. It would seem logically impossible for God to give agents this freedom (to make it up to them how they will choose) without the probability of them making some wrong choices. The more agents who have this freedom, the more such choices they have, and the greater the temptation to wrongdoing, the more wrong choices there will probably be. (Just how probable will depend on the strengths of their wrong desires—on which see later.) If humans have libertarian free will (as I am assuming; see Chapter 5), then the unprevented possibility of human wrong choices makes possible the great good of human free choice between right and wrong.

Plantinga's Complication

Alvin Plantinga is a firm advocate of this position, the 'free-will defence' to the objection to theism from the existence of moral evil.[1] But he has raised a complication for his own position. He

[1] For Plantinga's initial discussion of the problem of evil, see his *The Nature of Necessity* (Clarendon Press, 1974), ch. 9, where his exposition involves logical

holds that, although God could not make people choose freely as they do, he foreknows how they will choose freely; not just 'foreknows' in the sense of 'is aware of their present desires and beliefs, and so knows how likely it is that they will do the good as they see it or alternatively capitulate to desire and do wrong', but knows necessarily (namely, without the possibility of mistake) exactly what they will do. Plantinga holds this because he holds to a strong traditional view of God's essential omniscience, as God knowing all true propositions; and combines this with the view that God is not timeless but everlasting, and so knows now how people will choose tomorrow, that is has foreknowledge of their free choices. Such omniscience on this view is essential to God: he cannot but know all this, or he would not be God. Plantinga also holds that God's omniscience includes (essentially) 'middle knowledge', that is, knowledge not merely of how actual beings will choose (freely); but also knowledge in advance, of how all possible beings would choose (freely) in all possible circumstances if he were to create them. God in the beginning, at stage one, knew all the worlds which he could create, in the sense of which free beings he could create and in which circumstances governed by which (deterministic or probabilistic) natural laws he could place them; and also which free choices each of them would make in the different circumstances. He then used this middle knowledge to decide to create one such world—that is, to create some of the possible beings and put them in some of the possible circumstances. Then in virtue of his decision, at stage two he acquired ordinary foreknowledge of what these beings will choose freely; and his middle knowledge became knowledge of what would have happened if he had acted otherwise.[2] God knows what I would have done if I had fought in the Second World War, been taken prisoner by the Japanese, and been offered a bribe

apparatus developed earlier in that book; and, for a simpler version, his *God, Freedom and Evil* (George Allen & Unwin, 1974), pt. 1.

[2] The doctrine of 'middle knowledge' was first put forward (under that name—but see my Additional Note 5) by Luis de Molina in pt. IV of his *Concordia* (1588). For an excellent introduction to and translation of the relevant parts of this, see L. de Molina, *Of Divine Foreknowledge*, trans. A. J. Freddoso (Cornell University Press, 1988).

If one thinks of God as outside time, then these 'stages' in God's knowledge acquisition are not temporal stages, but 'logical' stages in God's timeless knowledge possession; having 'ordinary foreknowledge' of how beings will choose is to be interpreted as having ordinary knowledge of how they will choose at times future relative to some time-bound human observer.

to become a spy. And God knows what some being A which he did not create would have done if he had been created instead of me, with my genes and brought up in my family circumstances. God's present knowledge of how beings which he did not or will not create would have chosen if he had created them, and of how beings which he did or will create would have chosen in circumstances which he will not bring about, is called knowledge of counterfactuals of freedom. These are conditional assertions of the form 'If p then q', where 'p' describes circumstances which, it implies, did not and will not occur, and 'q' describes an action which some agent would do freely, either some actual agent or a possible agent.

But, if God knows in advance how all possible beings would choose in all possible circumstances, then, since it might seem as if there were infinitely many such beings and infinitely many such circumstances, surely God, who does not want people to choose what is wrong (and only gives them choice in order to give them the opportunity of choosing rightly), would only create beings and put them in circumstances in which (he foresaw) they would freely choose the good. To save the free-will defence against this objection, Plantinga draws our attention to a further possibility: 'universal transworld depravity'. Maybe, he suggests, each of the (presumably infinite number of) possible beings whom God could create would in some of the circumstances in any world in which he created them freely choose what is wrong.[3] It is logically possible, Plantinga urges, that there is universal transworld depravity. He does not claim that it is probable that there is such depravity, but merely that, because this is possible, it does not follow from God having middle knowledge that he can create a world in which there are free beings who always choose the good. And that seems correct.

But, as R. M. Adams among others has suggested, the hypothesis of a universal transworld depravity *looks* highly implausible.[4] Surely there are possible beings who could live in some circumstances so that throughout their lives they freely chose only the good. Although no one, not even God, could cause that to happen, he could, if he had middle knowledge, create only those whom he knew would so choose. If you were allowed to create an infinite

---

[3] *The Nature of Necessity*, 184–9.
[4] See R. M. Adams, 'Middle Knowledge and the Problem of Evil', *American Philosophical Quarterly*, 14 (1977), 109–17: 116–17.

number of free agents and put them in any of an infinite number of different circumstances, and then see how they would act, surely you would find a few agents who in some circumstances would do nothing but good. But if God could see in advance, before creating agents, how they would act in different circumstances, he could create just those few and put them in just those circumstances where they would freely choose the good. The infinity of the number of beings and possible choices available to each in lives in different worlds shows that if this logical possibility of transworld depravity is to constitute a serious counter-objection to the difficulty raised for the free-will defence by the suggestion that God has middle knowledge, then the onus is on Plantinga to prove, or show it to some extent probable, that all creatures would do some wrong in some circumstances. Even if all creatures will do wrong some of the time, could not God give them freedom only at such times at which, he foresees, they will freely choose what is right? Plantinga would have to respond by saying that possible creaturely decisions are so interwoven—necessarily, so that 'the more God withholds freedom so as to prevent evil, the more evil would be done on the remaining occasions when creatures are left free'. But as David Lewis, who offers Plantinga this way out, comments, that is, though perhaps possible, 'not plausible, except as a last resort for heroic faith'.[5] It would seem to follow that if God did have middle knowledge, he could give humans on many occasions libertarian free will without their doing wrong; and he could do this knowing that no wrong would result. So the possibility of moral evil would not be required if God is to give to creatures libertarian free will.[6]

Adams has suggested that there are no counterfactuals of freedom, or at any rate ones with truth-value (i.e. ones which are true or false). In that case not even an omniscient being could know which counterfactuals of freedom were true or false and thus act to put creatures only in those circumstances in which they will freely choose rightly. Plantinga has urged,[7] however, that there must be counterfactuals of freedom with truth-value, for often we can have

[5] David Lewis, 'Evil for Freedom's Sake', *Philosophical Papers*, 22 (1993), 149–72: 162.
[6] Creatures might still need the natural evil of bad desires, which they resist, if they are freely to choose the good instead of the bad.
[7] See J. Tomberlin and P. van Inwagen (eds.), *Alvin Plantinga* (D. Reidel, 1985), 372–82.

a justified belief about what is the truth-value of some counterfactual of freedom. Knowing the strength of the desires to which some agent would be subject in certain circumstances, we may often justifiably predict that in those circumstances he would yield to them, even though he was free not to yield and could, if he had tried hard, have resisted the desires. Against Plantinga and in support of Adams, William Hasker[8] raised the question, if a counterfactual of freedom has a truth-value, what makes it true?

Consider the counterfactual 'If Elizabeth were offered the grant, she would accept it'. Suppose the counterfactual to be true. Being a counterfactual, this presupposes that Elizabeth is not offered the grant. So what makes it the case that the counterfactual is true? If the world were deterministic, its laws of nature would make it the case that there would be a certain outcome if Elizabeth were offered the grant; and it would be the fact that they operated which would provide the truth-conditions of the counterfactual. But if it is a counterfactual 'of freedom', there are no such laws. Yet whatever, if anything, does make the counterfactual true, it will not be Elizabeth, for (*ex hypothesi*) she has not been in a position to make the choice. But, Hasker urges, if it is not a counterfactual made true by Elizabeth's free choice, it cannot be a counterfactual 'of freedom' at all, for she is the agent with whose freedom it was supposedly concerned. If we suppose the counterfactual false, we reach the same conclusion that it cannot be Elizabeth's free choice that makes it false. However, the defender of counterfactuals of freedom may urge that nothing else makes the counterfactual true; it is just 'barely true'. Take a different sort of example. Suppose that it is not predetermined whether tossed coins land heads or tails. I did not toss a coin yesterday; but perhaps there is a truth about how some coin would have landed if I had tossed it.

So let us grant this point, and suppose that there are counterfactuals of freedom with truth-value. Even so, Plantinga has gone wrong in supposing that anyone could have incorrigible knowledge of the truth-value of a counterfactual of freedom. And this for the reason that no one can foreknow incorrigibly the future free actions of an agent in circumstances which *will* be realized. My argument for that is not original,[9] but it is, to my mind, of irrefutable

---

[8]   See his *God, Time and Knowledge* (Cornell University Press, 1989), 39–52.

[9]   This argument was set out very carefully and cogently by Nelson Pike, 'Divine Omniscience and Voluntary Action', *Philosophical Review*, 74 (1965), 27–46.

cogency. Consider such a free agent J faced with a choice tomorrow of doing x or not doing x; and any pre-cognizer G. If G were to know today what J will do tomorrow, he will have a belief about this—for knowledge entails belief. Given that, of logical necessity, the past is unaffectable by present actions (causes cannot follow their effects),[10] then G's belief today will be what it is before and independently of what J does tomorrow. Yet what J does tomorrow depends on J's choice tomorrow. If J is indeed free, he is free to make G's belief, whatever it is, false. He may not do so, but he has it in his power to do so, and so G's belief cannot be necessarily true, and so cannot amount to incorrigible knowledge. If no one can have incorrigible knowledge of the future free actions of actual agents, *a fortiori* they cannot know what they will do in unrealized circumstances, let alone what possible unactualized agents will do. If no one can do all this, even God cannot.

Plantinga has subsequently claimed[11] that God's belief today about what J will do tomorrow is not what it is before and independently of what J does tomorrow. More generally, God's beliefs at a time t are not 'hard facts' about t. A 'hard fact' about a certain time is a fact, all of whose truth-conditions, the states of affairs which make it a fact, are states of affairs at that time. A 'soft fact' about a certain time, by contrast, is a fact whose truth-conditions are (at least in part) states of affairs at some other time.[12] Thus 'John played the piano in 1984' (if true) expresses a hard fact about the world in 1984; whereas 'The next century's greatest pianist played the piano in 1984' (if true) expresses a soft fact about the world in 1984, for its truth depends partly on how things go in the next century. *The Times* having a prediction today about who will win tomorrow's Derby is a hard fact about today. But *The Times* having the *correct* prediction today about who will win tomorrow's Derby is not a hard fact about today, because whether it has a correct prediction today depends partly on (i.e. is partly constituted

---

[10] For argument on this, see my *The Christian God* (Clarendon Press, 1994), 81–90.

[11] A. Plantinga, 'On Ockham's Way Out', *Faith and Philosophy*, 3 (1986), 235–69.

[12] My definitions of 'hard' and 'soft' facts, taken from *The Christian God*, 132, are somewhat different from those of most writers, who construe a 'hard fact' about a certain time as one all of whose truth-conditions are states of affairs at *or earlier than* that time, and a soft fact as one all of whose truth-conditions are states of affairs *later than* that time. This difference does not affect the present argument.

by) what happens tomorrow. So, Plantinga suggests, while my having a certain belief today about what will happen tomorrow is a hard fact about today, *God's* having a certain belief today about what will happen tomorrow is not: it is a soft fact, because God's beliefs today about tomorrow are the beliefs they are in virtue of what happens tomorrow. The claim of the last paragraph that causes cannot follow their effects is to be read as the claim that whether some hard fact holds cannot be affected by what happens later; soft facts can be so affected. Hence, Plantinga claims, the argument of the last paragraph is unsound, and God can have an incorrigibly true belief today about what I will do freely tomorrow.[13] So, Plantinga puts himself in a position again to defend the logical possibility of God's having middle knowledge, and so to need the hypothesis of transworld depravity in order to explain the occurrence of moral evil.

However, the suggestion that God having a certain belief today about which action J will do tomorrow is a soft fact about today seems to empty of all content the notion that God has a 'belief' today. Of course whether the belief is true depends on what happens tomorrow, but what the belief is does not. That being so, it cannot be that God has necessarily true beliefs today about what J will do freely tomorrow; and more generally God cannot have incorrigible knowledge of the future actions of free creatures, let alone the actions which they would perform in circumstances which will not occur, or the actions which creatures never to be created would have performed if they had been created. So if God gives us freedom to choose between right and wrong, he cannot foreknow incorrigibly how we will choose; and so he inevitably allows the possibility of our doing wrong. (And if the freedom he gives us is limited to a choice between good and the bad which is not wrong, he inevitably allows the possibility of our choosing the latter.) And if he gives freedom for much time to many creatures, he makes very probable the occurrence of much moral evil. Plantinga's affirmation of the latter stands secure against the difficulties which he raised for his own position. Since Christian tradition has on the whole affirmed that humans have free will (see Chapter 2) God's omniscience must, I suggest, be understood (as I suggested in Chapter 1) as knowledge at every time of all that is

[13] See Additional Note 4.

logically possible for God to know at that time. This knowledge does not include knowledge of the true propositions about the future actions of free agents.[14]

Temptation

We saw in Chapter 5 that for agents[15] to have free will of any kind other than very unserious free will, they need desires to do actions of strengths out of proportion to the goodness of the actions desired. To have a free choice between a greater and a lesser good, they need a desire for the lesser good stronger than that for the greater good. To have desires out of proportion to the worth of the action desired is in itself a bad thing—mildly so. But to have a free choice between good and bad, agents need a desire for the bad stronger than for the good. Desires for the bad are bad. And to have a free choice between good and wrong—what I call very serious free will—agents need a desire for what is wrong stronger than for the good. The wider the range of free choice—in itself so good a thing—the worse the desires required to make it possible. It is bad to want to deceive, rape, hurt, maim; there is something badly amiss with an agent whose attitude for his fellows is to seek their harm in these ways, an attitude to which he will inevitably yield unless he makes the free effort to hold such urges in check. And the stronger the bad desires, the worse is the agent's condition.

In my view an action would not be intentional at all unless done because it was regarded as in some way a good thing. Intentional action is action seeking to bring about an effect which the agent aims at because he regards its fulfilment as good to achieve. If I believe that going to London would give me no pleasure, would give no one else any pleasure, would not enable me to do something else which was in some way good, would not enable me to avoid doing something in some way bad, would not involve fulfilment of duty, etc., then the movement of my limbs in the direction of London cannot be regarded as an intentional action. It would follow that we cannot aim at the bad as such, but what we can do

---

[14] See Additional Note 5.
[15] Other than an agent such as God in the special condition described in Ch. 5 n. 4.

is to aim at some good which can only be achieved by means of something bad, and so aim at what is bad, despite its badness. He who aims to deceive seeks some good (normally for himself) which the deception will achieve; he who aims to rape seeks thereby the good of sensory sexual pleasure; and even he who aims to hurt aims thereby at the good of punishment for wrongdoing or the exercise of his own power (a good in itself). The trouble is that these actions have effects or concomitants which mean that in pursuing a good agents aim at what they truly believe to be overall bad.

Although I do believe this—that all intentional action is action to realize a believed good—my present argument does not depend on it. It depends solely on the view advocated in Chapter 5, that if we do believe some action is overall the best, we will do it, unless non-rational forces, i.e. desires, provide a counter-influence. For humans to have libertarian free choice between good and bad, not merely is the possibility of moral evil required, but the actual occurrence of a certain kind of natural evil—bad desires—is required.

Bad desires, and above all wrong desires (as well as good desires), are an evident human phenomenon. They are often (though not always) desires for kinds of things which are good to possess in some circumstances but not in all, but the desires operate both when it is good that we indulge them and when it is bad that we indulge them. Often it is good that we should have and so desire to have food and drink (when we need them), sexual intercourse (with our spouse), fame (when we deserve it), and fortune (when we can rightly use it). The trouble is that we have the desires when it would be bad, and often wrong, to indulge them. And yet this natural evil is a necessary condition of the good of free choice between good and bad. I cannot exercise a serious free choice to give money to the starving unless I have some desire to possess money when it would be good to give it away (i.e. a certain miserliness). Since it is so often good to act, and less often good to do nothing, that inclination which will so often ensure that we have a free choice between good and bad is sloth, in the modern sense of idleness or the desire to do nothing. (I shall have more to say about the importance of sloth in the next chapter.)

The temptation to yield to a bad desire will be greater if the desire is the desire to do some action immediately. Since desires by their very nature act upon us, whereas we have to take positive action to resist them, it will be easier to resist bad desires if we have time to pull ourselves together. We are more likely to yield to desires which lead more instinctively to action.

I have been assuming (see Chapter 5) that we know the consequences of our actions and their moral worth. But of course we may not; and in that case the serious free choice is between the believed good and bad. Our situation is, however, very often an intermediate one. We do not *know* the consequences of our action, nor are we entirely ignorant of them. We believe it slightly probable or fairly probable that they will have such-and-such consequences; and there is quite a chance that these are bad consequences, and indeed that it is wrong for us to bring them about. The good desires are weaker and the bad ones stronger in so far as we doubt that the bad action will have bad effects. In a situation of doubt about consequences, the temptation also arises for self-deception, for refusing to admit to ourselves that the probability of the bad consequences is not really as high as in our initial honest moment we believed that it was. If the evidence only suggests that probably smoking causes cancer, we can tell ourselves that nothing definite is known about the matter. Uncertainty clouds, and allows us to cloud even more, the stark choice between exposing ourselves to a high risk of cancer and not smoking.

The choice between what is probably good and what is probably wrong is a very serious choice, but a blurred one; and does not provide the opportunity for going so deliberately against the good as does a choice where we know clearly what we are doing. Both the choice being a considered one and the wrongness of a wrong action being obvious are two marks of the choice of wrong being a mortal as opposed to a venial sin in the traditional distinction. The other mark is that the mortal sin involves worse wrong than the venial sin. The more the choice between right and wrong is considered and evident, in a way the better. Our libertarian free will is freer, more obviously in control of the way the world is to go. But the worse it is if we make the wrong choice; for we have set ourselves more deliberately against the good. It is good to be spared such stark choices in the early years of childhood; but good too to have the choice of improving our self-control (so as not to be swept away by desires) and our moral and factual knowledge, so as to make stark choices which express our stand.

I argued in Chapter 5 that the goodness of doing the best action is better, the stronger the contrary temptation and the more significant the good act, without espousing any view about how strong a temptation and how important the alternatives it would be best for a creator to give creatures, in view of the risk of bad resulting—both the bad intentional acts and the bad consequences following therefrom. There follows not merely the formal logical impossibility of God giving us free will to choose between good and bad without bringing about the natural possibility that (unprevented by God) we will do bad, but a whole range of more detailed logical impossibilities. God cannot give us certain kinds of free will (certain strengths of temptations to choose between certain kinds of important actions) and at the same time ensure that there is only such-and-such a probability that we will do such-and-such bad or wrong actions. The stronger the temptation to do bad, and the more significant are the good or bad actions, the greater the possibilities for good that God gives us and the less the chance that those possibilities will be realized.

This chapter has been concerned with intentional action as such, and in particular with free intentional action; and with the bad (and especially the wrong) inevitably involved in various kinds of good free choice, differing in seriousness and strength. The goodness of free intentional action will vary also, as we have seen, with its significance, with the kinds of difference which it makes to the world, the responsibility for which belongs to the agent in his choice. The next chapter will consider the various kinds of bad involved in various kinds of responsibility.

8

The Range of Moral Evil; and Responsibility

See, I have set before thee this day life and good, and death and evil; in that I command thee this day to love the Lord thy God, to walk in his ways, and to keep his commandments and his statutes and his judgements, that thou mayest live and multiply, and that the Lord thy God may bless thee in the land whither thou goest in to possess it. But if thine heart turn away, and thou wilt not hear, but shalt be drawn away, and worship other gods, and serve them; I denounce unto you this day, that ye shall surely perish; ye shall not prolong your days upon the land, whither thou passest over Jordan to go in to possess it. I call heaven and earth to witness against you this day, that I have set before thee life and death, the blessing and the curse: therefore choose life, that thou mayest live, thou and thy seed: to love the Lord thy God, to obey his voice, and to cleave unto him: for he is thy life, and the length of thy days: that thou mayest dwell in the land which the Lord sware unto thy fathers, to Abraham, to Isaac, and to Jacob, to give them.

(Deuteronomy 30: 15–20)

The Principle of Honesty

So the good of many agents having many free choices between good and bad involves the very high probability of much moral evil—the bad choices unprevented by God. But God could of course arrange things so that our bad choices never had any effects. When we chose kind words, they came out of our mouth; when we chose to insult, the air did not convey the message. When we chose to strike, we became paralysed; when we chose to stroke, our hands obeyed our commands. But for God to create agents permanently so placed would be a great deceit. He would have made it seem to us as though we had power—for we could not have a choice between uttering kind words and uttering insulting words, unless we thought our attempts to talk would be successful. God would not be the parent (of p. 93) who warned the elder son that he would intervene the moment the son did a thing wrong, but the parent who always gave the impression that he would not intervene, but always did the moment the son made a bad choice.

It is, I suggest, a moral truth which I shall call the Principle of Honesty:

> God has an obligation not to make a world in which agents are systematically deceived on important matters without their having the possibility of discovering their deception.

The principle is not concerned with what it is right for God to *tell* people, e.g. in words, by a propositional revelation (my view on that is that it would never be right for him to tell us anything false); but with what it is right for him to allow people to infer from the world which he makes. It does not rule out him allowing one person to get a false idea of how the world works; or allowing one person to tell another falsities about how the world works. But it does rule out God making a world which leads people to have false views on important matters, which they cannot discover to be false.

The principle is a natural extrapolation to God from the similar obligations to honesty of a human teacher. It would always be wrong for me to give a student a false piece of information, which I state to be true. But it is not always wrong for a teacher to include misleading elements in what he shows to his students, in order to force them to sort things out for themselves. I may give a student an apparently valid but really invalid argument, without saying either that it is valid or that it is invalid, in the hope that he will come to discover for himself that it is invalid. But it would be wrong for me to allow a student to get a false impression from my teaching if there was no possibility of the student finding out the truth. It would be wrong for a teacher to present a student with an apparently plausible account of history or geography, in which the various strands fitted with each other in such a way that the student could never find out that it was basically false. If the teacher is teaching a class, rather than individuals on their own, the

possibility of discovery will be a class one: to discover the falsity
may require cooperation between members of the class.

Now while individual humans teach other humans (or groups
thereof) over a short time-scale, God deals with the human race as
a whole over a long time-scale. Although he may sometimes intervene in the world, in general he has created a world where things
behave in regular ways; and it is individual humans who try to find
out how things behave and teach others, and who try to discover
moral truths and teach others. And of course the others may come
to correct what they have been taught. We have already commented
on the goodness of such an arrangement in Chapter 5. Therefore
what the Principle of Honesty says is that God must not create a
world in which in general people cannot discover the truth of how
it works and what is good and bad, at any rate over time, in cooperation. It allows the possibility of error (factual and moral) which
some can help others to discover—though not, I would suggest, too
much even of that.

For God to make a world in which we think that some of our
actions cause suffering when really they do not, or do not cause suffering when really they do, when the human race could never discover differently, would be to treat creatures with contumely.
Likewise if God is to give us a choice between actions which seem
to matter, say by causing pain or pleasure, they must in general
matter—namely, cause pain or pleasure; or we must be able to find
out that they do not. Just how soon we must be able to find out is a
difficult matter (as are all matters of drawing exact borderlines for
moral principles); though I would suggest that most, though not
all, errors ought to be discoverable by individuals or communities
within a few years. But God must not put us in a world of virtual
reality which we could never discover to be such. The Principle of
Honesty is a moral truth very important for the concern of this
book, and we shall meet it several times in the next few chapters. It
limits the ways in which God can give us good without bad.[1] Its
immediate consequences at this stage of the argument are that God
cannot give us apparently serious moral choices of doing good or
bad and yet ensure that our choices never make any real difference.

---

[1] That it would be wrong of God to deceive us is a point central to Descartes's
philosophy (see R. Descartes, *Meditations* 4, 5, and 6); but he does not add the qual-
ifying adverb 'systematically'.

The Bad Involved in Responsibility for Oneself and the Consequences of Ignorance

But, we saw in Chapter 5, the more significant the choices an agent has, the better it is for him. And indeed, even if it were permissible for God to create a deceptive world, it would be better for us if our choices do really make significant differences rather than our merely thinking that they do. So it is good for me if I can influence my present condition and my future condition—really influence it, and that means for good or ill. For God would have given me no real responsibility for myself if he ensured that I could do myself no harm. God will allow me to sustain my strength by eating or to neglect to do so. And God will allow me to do actions which risk harming myself, as well as ones which will certainly do so: to go rock-climbing or consume dangerous drugs. And God will allow me to do actions which will have (or probably have) long-term effects on myself for good or ill. He will allow me to ruin my health by smoking or alcohol, or to care for it with proper diet and exercise.

But if our choices are to be choices which make a difference to things for good or ill—not just choices made in a simulator—we need, as has been pointed out earlier, knowledge, factual and moral, of the consequences of our choices. And, as we saw in Chapter 7, our freedom is greater if we really realize what we are up to: we do not yield to the desire to do wrong through a cloudy perception of its wrongness. So an important choice which we each of us have with respect to our own future is the choice of whether or not to try to acquire knowledge, factual and moral. If we are to have these choices, we must begin in a position of (at any rate) relative ignorance. I cannot choose whether or not to bother to find out the effects of smoking if I know already. And I need ignorance of what is morally good and bad if I am to choose whether to seek the knowledge. Though in general ignorance is simply the lack of a good state, not the presence of a bad state, it is an absence of a good state necessary for choice. But certain sorts of ignorance will make it immensely more likely that I will act or neglect to act, with effects that I do not desire. If I do not know the effects of smoking, then I am much more likely to get lung cancer, something I do not desire. And ignorance of that kind would seem a bad state, not merely the absence of a good. And moral ignorance with respect to actions which I am likely to perform would also seem a bad state. It is bad if I do not think that it matters whether or not I hurt others or indeed myself. Yet if the great choice of whether to try to acquire knowledge, factual and moral, is to be open to me, I may not bother; and the bad consequences will flow.

I shall have much to say about factual knowledge and the way open to us to improve it in Chapter 10. The possibilities through experience and discussion for acquiring moral knowledge surround us, and thus we have the opportunity to follow them up or to hide from ourselves moral truths which they seem to be indicating. We can, through honest thought, cooperative discussion, and hard experience, come to have a deeper and deeper understanding of values; or, through idleness and self-interest, allow ourselves to have a trivial and false understanding of values, and even come to believe that there is no right and wrong. This good, of it being up to us whether we acquire a morality and of what kind, involves the necessary evil to begin with of us having inadequate moral views, and those views leading to bad actions, for example to cruelty in war against enemies regarded as entitled to no human rights because they are foreigners.

Growth in morality involves first understanding justice, that there is right and wrong; that we have duties to repay our debts and not kill or maim our fellows. And it involves understanding that if we do kill or maim, that gives others the right to take back from us an equivalent of what we have taken away—'an eye for an eye, and a tooth for a tooth'. Justice involves the right to punish.[2] But further growth in morality involves understanding that it is sometimes good to let people off their debts and not exercise our right to punish them—good, that is, to show mercy—and generally to be generous to others beyond the call of obligation. We could not understand the latter without understanding the former: that is a logical point. We could be born with both items of knowledge; or we could help each other (through discussion and encouragement) to move from the former narrower understanding to the wider one (or refuse to do so). Only the latter method makes moral outlook a matter for choice. So there is a point in a society starting with the

---

[2] For fuller discussion of this claim about the sources of the right to punish, its extent, and the frequent goodness of not exercising it, see my *Responsibility and Atonement* (Clarendon Press, 1989), chs. 5 and 6.

morality of the Books of Exodus and Leviticus and then gradually being encouraged to adopt the teaching of the major prophets and then to develop the morality of the Sermon on the Mount.

It is good that we should have power over ourselves, gradually to mould our desires for good or ill. But if we have this power, then there is the danger that we will let ourselves acquire bad desires, with all the ill that that constitutes and which will follow from it. The greater our power to affect our desires, and the greater the range of desires—good and bad—open to us, the better, in virtue of the choice that it makes available to us. But of course the more such power we have, the greater the probability that some of us will allow ourselves to have bad desires and indulge them: racists and misogynists are likely to emerge. It is good, as we saw in Chapter 5, that we should have the power (as apparently we do) gradually, over time, to mould our characters so as to fix them permanently. Our characters consist of our beliefs, principally our moral beliefs, and our desires. We saw there how, by always choosing the good, we can so weaken the force of bad desires that they cease to have influence over us. Now God could have given us merely the choice of whether to form a good character or to postpone doing so, so that the choice always remained open in future to initiate that process. But a God who only gave us that choice would have kept back from us the further possible choice—of so immunizing ourselves to any moral influence that we no longer had the possibility of forming a good character. A God who did not give us the latter alternative would have rigged the choices open to us in his own favour, i.e. in favour of the good. We saw in Chapter 5 that it does rather look as if humans have open to them this final alternative, of always so indulging our strongest desires (including a considerable number of bad desires) that we lose the power to choose between alternatives in virtue of their perceived goodness. Instead, we become a theatre of competing desires, often bad desires, in which the strongest always wins. It does rather look as if the evil men and women of history have got themselves into this condition.[3]

What will happen to our moral beliefs in this situation? Will we still believe that there are good actions to be done, but regretfully acknowledge that we have lost the power to choose them? Or will we cease to believe that there are good actions to be done? Would

---

[3] See Additional Note 6.

the failure to obey conscience leave it nagging at us for ever ineffectually, or will it lead to its elimination? Either alternative seems logically possible. Empirical psychology suggests that what in fact happens on a small scale in all of us when we continually refuse to do what we believe to be obligatory or even good in some respect is that we find the situation of mental conflict between belief and action—between our beliefs about what is good to do and what we in fact do—intolerable. So, unless we in fact sometimes do the good, we hide from ourselves its goodness.[4] Suppose, being white, I find myself with a desire to abuse, insult, and subjugate black people; but also the belief that this is a bad desire to have. The more I indulge my desire, the more indulging it becomes natural, and then the less I am willing to admit to myself that it is a bad desire to have. That is compatible with my still believing that it is a bad desire to have while refusing to admit it to myself, but it is also compatible with my having eliminated the desire. I do not think that we have the empirical evidence about which is the final state of bad humans who have so allowed their character to be corrupted that they have lost the power to choose what is good because it is good.

Which of these alternatives would a good God produce in those who have chosen a bad character? It is good, we have seen, to desire the morally good, and bad indeed to have no moral sensitivity. It is also bad to be unable freely to choose what we recognize as morally good, for our conscience to be thus incapacitated. Clearly the latter state is the worse; the former state is simply the absence of a good. It may be, however, that there is something very bad in God allowing us to lose something so valuable as our moral sensitivity; but on balance I would think that a good God in allowing us to become a prisoner of our desires would allow us to eliminate our awareness of goodness, perhaps not ever on Earth, but in the end. The medievals disputed whether it is possible for our awareness of moral goodness to be eliminated. Aquinas argued that it is not possible, but, as I interpret him, Philip the Chancellor argued that it is possible; and in this dispute I side with the latter.[5] Either way, the great moral evil of an evil character may very well occur if we have the great

[4] For fuller philosophical and empirical justification of this claim about the possibilities of corruption open to humans, see my *Responsibility and Atonement*, 173–8.

[5] See the extracts from Philip the Chancellor and Aquinas in T. C. Potts, *Conscience in Medieval Philosophy* (Cambridge University Press, 1980), 108–9 and 129–30.

good of the free choice of what character to have. But of course God would only be good in giving us this terrible choice, if he allows us some long time in which we have many (but not endless) opportunities of turning back; he must thereby ensure that our commitment to it is firm.[6] Christian doctrine has normally held that we do have the opportunity so to immunize ourselves that we are no longer able to choose to seek the good of the Beatific Vision in the Heaven of the Blessed.

Given my earlier claim that a good act is better if done contrary to temptation, it might seem open to question whether it is a good thing to seek to encourage good desires and discourage bad desires, for that—if successful—would remove the possibility of resisting temptation. However, we do not have the right to put ourselves in situations where we are likely to do wrong, and so we do not have the right to seek a temptation to do what is wrong. If the temptation to beat my wife becomes very strong after I have drunk two glasses of whisky, I do not have the right to drink two glasses of whisky. Obligations must be fulfilled first before we seek any greater good.[7] 'Lead us not into temptation' is indeed the proper Christian prayer. God, however, has the right to cause us to be tempted to do those actions (which include harming others) which God has the right to allow us to do. For if it is right for *A* (parents or the state, say) to allow *B* to do some action which *B* ought not to do, it must be right for *A* to allow *B* to be tempted to do that action, for unless *B* is tempted to do a wrong action, he will not do it, and so preventing temptation is preventing the action. And if God has the right to cause us to be tempted, *a fortiori* he has the right to allow others to cause us to be tempted. The extent of God's right to allow others to do wrong actions will be considered in Chapter 12. Yet, even though it is not right to seek temptation, it may well be appropriate to rejoice when it is foisted upon us, because of the opportunity presented to us to resist it. St James tells his readers to rejoice 'when ye fall into manifold temptations'.[8]

---

[6] This provides the answer to Scobie's concern: 'It seemed to Scobie that life was immeasurably long. Couldn't the test of man have been carried out in fewer years? Couldn't we have committed our first major sin at seven, have ruined ourselves for love or hate at ten, have clutched at redemption on a fifteen-year-old death bed?' (Graham Greene, *The Heart of the Matter* (Heinemann, 1957), 56).

[7] And if there is a God, the scope of obligation is much larger than it would otherwise be. (See my *Responsibility and Atonement*, ch. 8.)

[8] Jas. 1: 2.

Where the temptation is only a temptation to do something less good, or bad but not wrong, it could in theory on occasion be good to seek to be tempted and so to allow bad desires to continue, or even to develop them. But the probability of achieving the good of overcoming temptation would need to be weighed against the intrinsic badness of the bad desires, the probability of yielding to the temptation with the resulting bad consequences (two bad states), and—since one bad act today makes it easier to do a bad act next time—the increasing probability of forming a bad character. The circumstances would have to be very special indeed for it ever to be good to seek to be tempted even to do what is bad but not wrong.[9] Only under the most exceptional circumstances would a good agent not seek to eliminate their bad desires. A good God, seeking for agents choices of great significance, will allow them the choice of whether or not to do so.

One of the greatest of all our responsibilities in respect of ourselves is the responsibility for our own life or death. We can through negligence shorten our lives, by drinking ourselves to death, for example; or through taking care, extend them. And we have, almost all of us, the power to end life there and then—to commit suicide. I hope that my readers will forgive my dwelling for a little here and subsequently on this grim choice which is ever available; for it seems to me a very important aspect of the human condition that it is available, and its availability is an important strand in the solution to the problem of evil.

The choice between life and immediate death is one of the most significant of all the choices open to us. God has not made humans naturally immortal. We can end each other's lives. For most of us it is quite easy to end our own lives, if we so choose: by jumping off

[9] I have argued elsewhere (*Responsibility and Atonement*, 158–9; *The Christian God* (Clarendon Press, 1994), 203–7) that God, in becoming incarnate in Jesus Christ, took upon himself desires to do lesser rather than supererogatory goods. He did this in order that, by overcoming the temptations to do only the lesser goods, he might atone for our sins. However, I sometimes expressed the point misleadingly by writing that he acted with the foreseen consequence that he became subject to the desires for lesser goods; I should always have written that he intentionally subjected himself to those desires. Such an action was indeed one done under the most exceptional circumstances. Maybe too the prayer of St Ephrem (as recorded by St Peter of Damascus, in G. E. H. Palmer, P. Sherrard, and K. Ware (ed. and trans.), *Philokalia*, iii (Faber & Faber, 1984), 152) to be given temptations in order to overcome them was a prayer which concerned temptations to do lesser goods, made under exceptional circumstances! But we have no reason to suppose this.

a tall building or throwing ourselves beneath a railway train. These may be, we reasonably judge, painful ways of ending life. And for some few, the disabled, the only ways of ending life unaided are the processes of starvation which take weeks. There are (in the painfulness of the process) these and other deterrents to suicide, and we will consider them later in the chapter. And if we have any relatives or friends who love us or are dependent on us, suicide is a very wrong act. And if there is a God who gives us life, it is always a wrong, for it is throwing back a very good gift in the face of the giver. But if there is a God, he has made available to us the possibility of this wrong act; and it is a mark of his generosity that he has done so. It is, we shall see in a later chapter, part of what gives him the right to allow us to suffer for the sake of a greater good.

The Bad Involved in Responsibility for Others

But what an awful world it would be if the only good or harm we could do was to ourselves. It is of course a good for us to be able to mould the inanimate world, but clearly a much greater good is to have responsibility for other animate beings—and that serious responsibility involves again the ability to benefit or harm them, as we saw in Chapter 5. If my responsibility for you is limited to whether or not to give you some quite unexpected new piece of photographic equipment, but I cannot make you unhappy, stunt your growth, or limit your education, then I do not have a great deal of responsibility for you. For the way things go with you will not in that case be largely up to me. Other factors will determine how it is with you; I will only be able to tinker a bit, and top up your well-being. If I am to have significant responsibility for you, I have to have the alternative of hurting and maiming as well as the alternative of greatly benefiting. But if free agents are to have this responsibility, there is a high probability that others will be harmed, and that often means suffering. The more free individuals there are and the more responsibility they have, the greater the probability of more harm to many.

We cannot do good or harm to each other in many ways without humans already cooperating in the acquisition of knowledge. I cannot discover by myself many of the consequences of my own individual actions. The world is so arranged that much cooperation is needed to discover the long-term consequences of smoking etc. And it is good, for all the reasons discussed in Chapter 5, that things should be thus. What I can choose to do or not to do is to choose whether to tap into the process, and acquire the knowledge which others have produced; and also to choose whether or not to help in the process of knowledge acquisition. And so many goods and harms which we know how to bring about can only be brought about by the cooperation of many humans, sometimes over many decades.

It is good that humans have a responsibility for animals. A child who is given a hamster to care for is benefited, when it all depends on the child whether the hamster is fed and watered at night or not. The child is pleased to be trusted by parents with the hamster; and by an argument of a kind which I have used a number of times, if the child is right to be pleased, that can only be because it is a good thing that the child is trusted. More generally it is good for humans to have the responsibility for the animal kingdom. And it is good for more mature humans to have the deeper responsibility of choosing whether or not to produce children, and whether and how to educate and nourish them. Again, if there is always someone else in the background who will step in to save those children who are neglected and abused, parents will not have the serious responsibility of care. The good of serious responsibility makes almost inevitable many great moral evils.

To prevent misunderstanding at this stage, I should make clear again that I am not saying that a good God would give creatures unlimited responsibility for others; only that there is a trade-off: the more responsibility for some, the more probable harm to others; the less probable harm, the less responsibility. Nor am I saying that responsibility for children ought to rest solely with parents. There may or may not be a good case for a strong team of social workers keeping an eye on 'problem families'. The responsibility for children would in such a case still remain with humans—but with a wider group of humans being responsible for each child. Yet interference by social workers, just like interference by God, does diminish the responsibility of individual parents.

As we saw in Chapter 5, it is good that the web of responsibility should extend to parents, relations, and friends; and, further, that we should be able to make a difference to people in distant places and future times. But once again, inevitably of logical necessity, the more responsibility free agents have, the greater the probability of much moral evil. We can allow bad states to occur either by doing an action which, we foresee, will bring them about; or by neglecting to do an action which, we foresee, would stop them occurring. So many of the world's ills (e.g. recent mass starvation in Africa, foreseen by relief agencies who warned governments) seem to be in the latter category. And as human control grows, so those and more bad states which in earlier ages would have been natural evils move into the category of moral evils, because preventable by the actions, if not of those now living, of earlier generations.

We are born into a world in which the good things of life are divided unevenly—by our genes, initially. Some are born so as naturally to develop into physically strong, clever, or beautiful people; others, not so. And society so often adds to the unevenness of the distribution of the good. The physically strong, clever, and beautiful naturally (unless prevented) acquire enormous power over others. The lame need help, but the beautiful command with a smile. There is no reason why a good God should distribute the good things of life evenly. If people contribute in some sense equally to a common enterprise, there is something wrong if they do not receive an equal share in its benefits. But if our creator creates us out of nothing, and gives to some ten good things, and to others twenty good things, no one is wronged; nor has he failed to be perfectly good. He has been generous, and, more so, he has made it possible for us to be generous. For the more power someone has and the more someone else lacks it, the greater the opportunity the former has to use his power to benefit the latter and above all to increase the power of the latter. If you are strong, you can use your strength to do things for me which I cannot do for myself. If you are beautiful, you can use your beauty to make me happy. If you are clever, you can use your cleverness to devise ways of making me clever. If we all had the same number of the same good things, there would be so much less scope for helping each other.

It is good, we saw in Chapter 4, that we should desire to have whatever is good to have, and that we should desire not to have whatever is bad to have. That way our desires will be properly attuned to the world. There is something less than perfect about us if there is something good to have, especially something about which we know, and we do not want to have it. But if everyone desires what is good to have, since some good things can (of logical necessity) only be possessed by one person (as I pointed out in Chapter 7) there will be the natural evil of many frustrated desires. Power over some individual area is just such a good: if you are President, I cannot be President too. And monogamous long-term marriage to a particular individual is another such good. Because being President of the United States would be a good thing for many people, it is good that many people should desire it (though not bad if they lack the desire); and so inevitable that almost all of them should suffer from frustrated desire. And because being married monogamously for life to John is good for many women, it is good that many women should desire it; and so inevitable that almost all of them should suffer from frustrated desire. If we were so made that we only desired what we could get, our desires would not be responsive to what is good in things. So it is good in one way that we should be bored by what is uninteresting, saddened by our failures, mourn the loss of loved ones. Then our emotional nature pays proper tribute to what is good and bad in things.

One of the deepest of all our responsibilities for our fellows, as for ourselves, is the responsibility for life or death. God could have made a world in which all creatures unavoidably live for ever. But in such a world we would not have the very deep responsibility for how long others live. Our world is one in which we can do to each other the worst of wrongs, for we can deprive each other of the greatest of goods—life itself. It is always a mark of supreme trust to allow someone to have a gun. If God made this world, he made a world with many guns—many ways of depriving others of life, and many ways of allowing others to die through negligence; and therefore also a world with many ways of acting to keep others alive. This is a world with much scope for saving individuals in the short term (e.g. rescuing them from drowning), saving individuals in the longer term (paying for their medical care), and acting so as to save many future individuals (founding hospitals, and making non-polluting motor vehicles). Among the ways in which the choice of killing or saving the life of others is available to us is by our having the choice of preventing or not preventing the suicide of others. And the choice available to us here is a choice of how much responsibility we are willing to give to others. It is no doubt good to stop others acting hastily under the influence of a desire which they desire or think it good not to have; but bad to stop someone exercising an ultimate freedom whose consequences he desires, and desires to desire, and has thought through. But once again in all these ways much responsibility given to free agents will make it enormously probable that there will be much moral evil unprevented by God.

Human choices, I have emphasized, may reinforce each other and have long-term consequences; and it is good that they should. The possibility that our bad choices will cause the suffering of victims distant in time and space (which God is unlikely to prevent) gives us a yet greater responsibility in the choices we make. The suffering and deaths of the Jewish victims of the Nazi concentration camps were the result of a web of bad choices stretching back over centuries and continents. So many humans spread false rumours about Jews, developed anti-Semitic propaganda without considering counter-arguments, limited the employment and educational possibilities for Jews, confined Jews to ghettos, and so on, until Hitler was able to issue orders to exterminate Jews which had some prospect of being carried out. And the sufferings and deaths in the concentration camps have in turn caused or made possible a whole web of actions and reactions stretching forward over the centuries of sympathy for victims, helping their relatives (to set up the state of Israel), avoiding any such event ever again, etc. The possibility of the Jewish suffering and deaths at the time made possible serious heroic choices for people normally (in consequence often of their own bad choices and the choices of others) too timid to make them (e.g. to harbour the prospective victims), and for people normally too hard-hearted (again as a result of previous bad choices) to make them, e.g. for a concentration camp guard not to obey orders. And they make possible reactions of courage (e.g. by the victims), of compassion, sympathy, penitence, forgiveness, reform, avoidance of repetition, etc., by others. (On the goodness of different kinds of reaction to suffering, see the next chapter.) Of course, I am not saying that anyone other than God would have the right to allow such things to happen, without intervening to stop them. (On God's right, see Chapter 12.) And, as I am emphasizing throughout, there is obviously a limit to the moral evil which God will allow us to cause (as there is to the natural evil by which he will allow us to be afflicted), but it is not obvious where that limit lies. And note again that the suffering in the Nazi concentration camps was the result of a very large number of free bad choices over many centuries, and made possible very many future good choices.

Incentive and Deterrent Desires

If ignorance about the consequences of our actions is a good thing, in order that we may have the choice of whether or not to acquire knowledge, and ignorance by some is a good thing in order that others may have the choice of whether or not to give them knowledge, there is clearly a risk of us harming ourselves without realizing that we were going to do so. And even if to some extent we do realize the consequences of our actions and realize that they are bad, the bad desires may sweep us on to act badly in such a way that it would take a very strong and very quick act of will to stop them. We need time for serious consideration of alternatives.

In considering what a God will do when he sees creatures knowingly or unknowingly taking steps which lead to disaster, we have an obvious analogy in the case of the human parent in relation to her children. In the case of some of their actions children, especially very young children, are often quite unable to understand the consequences, even if the parent tells them (the consequences, for example, of running into the road after a ball or not taking medicine). And in the case of other actions, although a child may understand the consequences, his will may be weak: he may not clean his teeth or do his homework, through sloth. What does the good parent do in these situations? The parent provides incentives and deterrents. In the case of the very young who cannot understand the consequences of their actions, the parent ties the child's action to consequences which he can understand. She may provide an immediate deterrent by tying the action to a corporal punishment: 'If you run into the road, I will beat you.' Or an immediate incentive by tying the unwelcome medicine to a welcome food ('sugaring the pill'). With respect to how to deal with the actions of somewhat older children whose will is nevertheless very weak, the parent is inevitably torn. She is anxious for her children to grow up to have increasing freedom to choose their own lives and work out what is best for themselves. Too much interference, especially as a child grows older, would be bad. Yet, aware that the child's will is weak, the parent wishes to encourage him to do what is right, but not to force him. So here too she will to a limited extent reinforce the child's will with incentives and deterrents, but typically delayed incentives and deterrents (see Chapter 4) to a continuing course of conduct which give the child time to make a considered judgement about what to do; rewards for doing the homework regularly, more distant punishment for not cleaning teeth regularly. A good parent steers the middle course between leaving everything to the child on the one hand and on the other hand dictating what the child is to do.

Analogy suggests that a good God will behave like a good parent. He will provide immediate incentives and deterrents to do actions needed for life and growth into undamaged organisms. There are the incentive desires for food, drink, sex, and sleep; and the deterrent desires to avoid the pain of the fire, or the danger of heights or dark. And as we come to know how the world works, he provides the delayed incentives and deterrents to courses of conduct which give us a chance to choose our course of action in a more considered way. When we come to know that frequent smoking causes cancer or that considerate courting will gain sexual pleasure, we are provided with deterrents and incentives to actions good for us and others for other reasons—our survival and that of our race.

Often, however, our only way of coming to know that some course of action will lead to a lengthy frustration of desire (a pain we cannot immediately remove, an urge we cannot immediately satisfy) is by previous experience. I know that drinking more than eight pints of beer will cause a hangover, because it has done so several times before. I shall be arguing in Chapter 10 that, unless we learn that way, further good things will be lost.

The biological incentives and deterrents which lead us to eat and drink the right things and avoid the dangers of injury, heights, and the dark are reinforced by the desire to be thought well of, especially by those who love and care for us; and the desire to give pleasure and not sadness to those who love us, which leads to the very young accepting guidance to do certain things and avoid other things, when they cannot understand why it is good to do so. The latter great desire is operative to deter agents from doing so many harmful things—and that includes deterring them from suicide. The desire to live is almost always a very strong one, and the would-be suicide who thinks that there is no good in his staying alive has an initial strong counter-inclination to overcome. And some of the kinds of suicide which I mentioned earlier look pretty painful or drawn out, and that also deters. But the desire not to hurt those who love us is also a powerful influence. It is the influence of love.

The biologically useful desires which form the nursery safety barrier are not of course always strong or relevant enough to keep even babies safe. But if they were, then parents would have no responsibility. As children grow older, they can choose by yielding to strong contrary desires to overrule the biologically useful desires; to force themselves, in order to win a bet, to keep their hand in the fire, say. And, a major theme of this book is that only if agents have the power to do bad do they have significant responsibility. True, I am suggesting both that it is a good thing that agents have bad desires, and that it is a good thing that agents have good desires which provide a counter-balance, at any rate initially, to indulging those bad desires. The former are necessary for a situation of temptation at all. The latter are necessary to prevent things going awry too soon or too often, with immediately disastrous consequences. True, there are not desires to help us to avoid all disasters and seek all goods, for, if there were, there would be no incentive to find out the consequences of our actions. But the simple deterrent and incentive desires which we do have are a useful protection which a caring God would provide if he was interested in our simple pleasures and continuing life as well as in our having deep responsibility.

Our best desires may sometimes get crowded out; we ignore the long-term issues of the sort of person we choose to be in favour of putting all our energy into fulfilling other desires, good but less good; desires for instant sensory gratification, or for fame and fortune. While it is good that we shall be allowed to choose in the end whether to be the sort of person whose desires for the bad or less good are stronger than the desire to form a good character, this is a momentous choice which it is good that we should have time to make. It is therefore good that God should provide some mechanism to help us in this situation. One mechanism which he does provide is simply failure of an irrecoverable kind. Failure in an exam which cannot be taken again, or evidently final failure in a personal relationship, give us an opportunity to rethink our priorities. But we are also made so that failure of a recoverable kind (in an exam which can be taken again; or a bankruptcy from which we can be released), with the resulting frustration, pulls us up, dampens the immediacy of the drive, so that again we have time to think. We have time to choose whether to allow ourselves to be the sort of person who is dominated by those desires or gradually to make ourselves a different sort of person instead (the sort of person in which desires for fame and fortune are only strong when compatible with better desires). It is good that we shall have the choice; and that means strong desires for bad states or lesser goods. But good that the choice shall be taken deliberately over time, and hence good that too quick indulgence in desires for bad states or lesser goods be met by temporary failures. How fortunate we sometimes are when some of our moderately worthy projects fail.

To draw attention to the deterrent value of various kinds of suffering is inevitably to raise the question why the suffering still occurs when it is no longer able to deter. Among the advantages of the pain caused by fire is that it leads the sufferer to escape from the fire. But the pain still occurs when the sufferer is too weak or paralysed to escape from the fire. So we ask, would it not be better if only those able to escape suffered the pain? But if that were the case and known to be the case (and it would violate the Principle of Honesty if God did not in the end let it be known), then others would know that it mattered much less that they should help people to escape from fire and that they should prevent fire. And so the opportunities for humans to choose whether to help others and guard against their future sufferings would correspondingly diminish; just as 'it's all insured' lessens the thief's reason for not stealing: stealing won't cause real hardship. And in general if God normally helps those who cannot help themselves when others do not help, others will not take the trouble to help the helpless next time, and they will be rational not to take that trouble. For they will know that more powerful help is always available. The choices of providing or not providing significant help to others, which I considered earlier in this chapter and suggested that it was very good for us to possess, would not be available to us.

One useful kind of deterrent desire is the desire to avoid punishment which an authority has vowed (see pp. 95–6) to impose on those who commit certain acts. By making a vow, we saw earlier, the vow-taker makes it a good thing that he should do what he has vowed, when otherwise it might not be good, and might even be bad that he should do that act. The badness of the suffering involved in the imposition of punishment on someone who ignores a threat to punish whoever does a certain crime (when that threat is intended as a vow) is a necessary condition of the possibility of deterrence by vow.

Sloth and Decay

So for various reasons it is good that we have good desires and good that we have bad desires, desires which by their influence provide a situation of serious temptation. The desires are desires to affect ourselves, each other, and the world in various ways. Now we embodied humans, animals, and the inanimate world could have been such as to be fine for ever if left alone. Our bodies might have been subject to no disease, ever self-renewing; and the same might have been the case for the animals and plants on which we depend for life; and for the inanimate objects we build to help us. Plants might need no tending, animals no fattening, and washing-machines and computers, once built, might never break down. We and the animals would be reasonably content. We could make things even better or harm them in various ways—but that would require active intervention and so effort. Even if the world contained sudden death, it would contain none of the infirmities of old age. Death would come suddenly and unavoidably. Although the Book of Genesis implies that the Garden of Eden was not quite like this, it suggests that it was not far off;[10] and so we may call this the Eden world.

Now our world is not an Eden world. Every human, animal, plant, and human-made structure is subject to decay; and this decay can cause misery, if not prevented or alleviated or repaired. The ancient philosophers saw decay as the mark of the sublunary world. It is because our world is a world of decay and not an Eden world that inactivity is often bad and quite often wrong; and so sloth, the inclination to inactivity, is a desire which provides us

[10] Contrast Gen. 2: 15, which implies that even the Garden of Eden required some cultivation, with Gen. 3: 17–19, which implies that the world outside Eden needed a great deal more cultivation. I should make it clear that I am not making a claim that the story of the Garden of Eden should be read completely literally; I am simply using the convenient word 'Eden'.

often with serious and quite often with very serious choices. We need to act (not merely to stop ourselves acting) in order to keep ourselves and each other healthy, fed, sheltered, etc. Sloth is a source not merely of temptation to the lesser good of not improving things, but of temptation to do what is bad or wrong (by failing to act). For we wrong our fellows (and our own animals) if we let them slide into illness, homelessness, incapacity, and so on; and we do what is bad (and, if there is a God to whom we owe our life, what is wrong) if we let ourselves and our plant and inanimate environment degenerate. In an Eden world if we did nothing none of that would happen; activity would be required only to improve things. And if things work well anyway, it would not matter very much if we did not improve things. I should add, in order to avoid misunderstanding, that of course even in our world it is sometimes a good thing to be lazy. A *moderate* amount of satisfaction of any of all self-directed desires, including sloth, is, other things being equal, a good thing. And sloth is instrumentally useful in that its indulgence enables us to regain our strength. But indulgence beyond a moderate amount is undoubtedly a temptation, not merely to a lesser good but often to the bad or wrong. It is because houses crumble, disease gets hold of us, accidents cripple us, that it becomes bad if we do nothing about things; and frequently wrong.

In an Eden world temptations to the bad or wrong would have to be mainly in the form of temptations to interfere with the good rather than to let things go on as they were. Instead of being tempted not to do anything to prevent the spread of some disease and eventually eliminate the disease, by setting up an inoculation programme, starting a research institute, etc., the temptation would be to discover a new disease, manufacture the bacteria, and help them to spread the disease; or actively to do something, maybe good in itself, which, to our knowledge, would cause the spread of disease. But the temptation actively to spread a disease could only come from a desire to hurt, to cause suffering. And even if the temptation came in the second form (e.g. as a temptation to make others better off in some way at the cost of hurting many others), it would still come in the form of a temptation to do something active requiring effort which would have a known bad consequence. What goes for this example goes generally. In an Eden world temptation to do bad or wrong would come in the form of temptations to hurt or to do something active which would (knowingly) hurt others.

In our world, the world of decay, bad doing and wrongdoing can so often be achieved by doing nothing; and the temptation to do nothing is a temptation to do something good in itself (the satisfaction of a self-centred desire for inactivity). And in fact the temptation to which we are *all* ultimately subject is sloth. We may lose our appetite and our sex drive; but whoever we are, either we are satisfying a desire to do nothing; or, if we are actively doing something, in the end we desire to stop. Sooner or later we all feel tired. We need not have been made like this at all. We could have been made so that we never felt tired, but fell asleep suddenly when our bodies needed to recharge. Or we could have been made so that our bodies never did need recharging; there might be certain actions we could do if we chose, and others which we could never do—and we could not achieve any more by pushing ourselves harder. But in fact we are not made like this. In the end we all start to feel tired, and we have to push ourselves to continue.

In consequence of all this, in our world of decay, we have open to us both the actions of negligently allowing something bad to happen and the actions of actively causing something bad in itself or causally connected therewith (all of which actions may be wrong ones). It is good that we should have the opportunity of very serious choice (in our actions towards others) without having to desire to hurt, i.e. to hate our fellows (or animals or the inanimate environment), which is a horrible thing, or even to do anything active (anything which required energy) which will hurt them; only to love ourselves too much. Causing people to suffer is a far worse thing than letting people suffer. And yet it is good that we should have the opportunity to do wrong. Being subject to sloth puts us in that situation where we can do wrong without actively causing it. But it is also good that some of us sometimes have the temptation actively to cause wrong, for by resisting that temptation we make more difference to the world for good, redirecting its inbuilt tendency. Our world, being a world of decay, provides abundant opportunity for wrongdoing merely through sloth. But it is also a world where we are subject to some bad desires actively to cause what is bad. But blessed be God for putting us in a world of decay, where so many of our temptations are temptations to idleness.

Conclusion

So, to conclude this chapter, like free will itself, responsibility can come in degrees. We could affect only ourselves, or make great differences to many others, including future generations. It is intrinsically good (good for us) that we shall have much responsibility, and make significant choices between many good and bad alternatives. To have a serious choice of doing the bad we must have a desire for what is bad. The desire may be a desire for something normally good, but under the circumstances of the choice bad. It is, however, good that the serious choices should include the choice of doing nothing. It is intrinsically bad (bad for us) that the bad consequences come about through our choice. But the more freedom and responsibility we have, of logical necessity the more and more significant are the bad consequences which will result (unprevented by God) from our bad choices; and so the more probable it is that many such will result. Every slight addition to our freedom and responsibility increases slightly the probability of sadness and pain; every slight diminution of the probability of sadness and pain resulting from human actions diminishes slightly our freedom and responsibility.

9

Natural Evil and the Scope for Response

And as [Jesus] passed by, he saw a man blind from his birth. And the disciples asked him, saying, Rabbi, who did sin, this man, or his parents, that he should be born blind? Jesus answered, Neither did this man sin, nor his parents: but that the works of God should be made manifest in him. We must work the works of him that sent me, while it is day: the night cometh, when no man can work. When I am in the world, I am the light of the world. When he had thus spoken, he spat on the ground, and made clay of the spittle, and anointed his eyes with the clay, and said unto him, Go, wash in the pool of Siloam (which is by interpretation, Sent). He went away therefore and washed, and came seeing.

(John 9: 1–7)

Human Response—in Feeling and Action

My main concern in Chapters 7 and 8 has been to show that the great good of very serious human free will and responsibility cannot be provided without (the very great probability of) much moral evil. In the next three chapters I shall be concerned with natural evil (i.e. the bad states not brought about or allowed to occur by humans), and I shall seek to show how it makes possible many of the good states which I described in Part II.[1] I shall be arguing in this chapter that natural evil extends enormously the range of good desires which agents have and may cultivate; and the actions available to them and, in the case of free agents such as humans, the range of actions which they can freely choose.

---

[1] 'Moral evil (*malum culpae*) God in no way wills . . . but the evil of natural defect (or the evil of punishment) he does will by willing some good to which such evil is attached' (St Thomas Aquinas, *Summa Theologiae*, Ia. 19. 9).

A particular natural evil such as pain makes possible felt compassion—one's sorrow, concern, and desire to help the sufferer. It is good that if pain exists, compassion exists, whether or not it can lead to action. It is good that one feel compassion for the suffering of those with whom one is involved (for spouse, children, parents, friends), but also for those with whom one is not involved, in distant lands and at distant times. But of course, the objector will say, even if pain is better for the response of compassion, better still that there be no pain at all. Now obviously it would be crazy for God to multiply pains in order to multiply compassion. But I suggest that a world with some pain and some compassion is at least as good as a world with no pain. For it is good to have a deep concern for others; and the concern can be a deep and serious one only if things are bad with the sufferer. One cannot worry about someone's condition unless there is something bad or likely to be bad about it. If things always went well with someone, there would be no scope for anyone's deep concern.

It is good that the range of our compassion should be wide—extending far in time and space. Good for those who suffered long ago that they are not forgotten; good for us to react with love to distant creatures about whom we know little. One of the great benefits of television has been to tell us about the tragedies and triumphs of peoples distant in space, so that they too can be within the beam of our concern, even if we can do nothing about them. And it is not beyond the powers of science to provide us with similarly detailed information about the triumphs and tragedies of peoples long ago.

The sorrow of one in a distant land who really cares for the starving in Ethiopia or the blinded in India is compassion for a fellow creature, even though the latter does not feel it; and the world is better for there being such concern. And although it is good if the sufferer is aware of compassion shown to him, there is peculiar merit in an act of compassion which cannot be returned, just as there is peculiar merit in acts of generosity which cannot even be recognized as such by the recipient, let alone acknowledged.

I wrote in Chapter 4 also about the goodness of the persistent desire which persists though temporarily frustrated. It is good for animals to long for the return of the lost mate, or offspring. It is a proper response to what is lost. And again, though it would be crazy for God to multiply losses to secure the good of persistent desire, it is nevertheless good that we should each be able sometimes to manifest serious longing, which is the response of emotions to important things.

The supreme tribute of our desires to loss is grief, and though it could never be enough of a good that we should evince grief to justify the permanent loss of a loved one, it is nevertheless a small good which, together with other good states made possible by that loss on which I have already commented and others to which we will come in due course, might make the loss overall justifiable. Bad states often serve many good purposes, none of which by itself may give God enough reason for allowing the bad state to occur but together they may do so.

What is known as the 'higher-order-goods defence' draws to our attention the good of performing certain sorts of good action, namely those done in the face of bad states, and of having the opportunity freely to choose to do such actions. The structure of this 'higher-order-goods' defence is as follows. A particular natural evil, such as physical pain, gives to the sufferer a choice: whether to endure it with patience, or whether to bemoan his lot. His friend can choose whether to show sympathy towards the sufferer, or whether to be callous. The pain makes possible these choices, which would not otherwise exist. There is no guarantee that the actions directed towards the pain will be good ones, but the pain gives agents the opportunity to perform good actions. The good or bad actions which we perform in the face of natural evil themselves provide opportunities for further choice, of good or evil stances toward the former actions. If I am patient with my suffering, you can choose whether to encourage or laugh at my patience; if I bemoan my lot, you can teach me by word and example what a good thing patience is. If you show sympathy, I have then the opportunity to show gratitude for the sympathy; or to be so self-involved that I ignore it. If you are callous, I can choose whether to ignore this or to resent it for life. And so on.[2] There are different special values in doing the different good actions. Courage is doing good

---

[2] Aquinas sees the central point of the higher-order-goods defence: 'Many goods are present in things which would not occur unless there were evils' (*Summa contra Gentiles*, 3. 71. 6). He gives the examples of patience in the face of persecution and justice in the face of wrongdoing—which are clear examples, in the spirit of the present chapter, of evils logically necessary for goods. But his example of 'in the order of nature, there would not be the generation of one thing unless there were the corruption of another' raises the question what good is served by the order of nature being so structured, an answer to which I sought to provide at the end of Ch. 8.

actions when it is harder than normal. An agent evinces his most substantial commitment to the good when he does such actions when it is hardest, when he gets no encouragement from the success of other plans, and things are happening to him which he does not desire. He makes such a commitment when he shows courage of a certain sort. And it is good that others should be involved with people at their most naked making the hard choices, for the others then show sympathy when it is hardest (because there is nothing about the appearance or success of the sufferer to make him attractive) and when it is most needed, doing what they can for him in all ways, including helping him to make the right choices. Help is most significant when it is most needed and it is most needed when its recipient is suffering and deprived. We are also involved with a sufferer at his lowest when we merely feel compassion, but we are more involved when we actively help to do something about the situation, and do not merely have the appropriate feelings. And in cases of both kinds, the sufferer often has the good of feeling and seeing the concern of others for him when he is unattractive and unsuccessful. 'Sorrow shared is sorrow halved', says the proverb, and it is only doing the sums in so far as they affect the original sufferer who knows of the compassion. If we add the benefit (not altogether an enjoyed benefit) to the sympathizer, the sums may well sometimes come out level.

But could not the absence of a good (of an ability to walk, say, or the ability to talk French) give to the victim equal opportunity: whether to endure it with patience, or whether to bemoan his lot; and to friends, whether to show sympathy or whether to be callous? To answer this question, it is important to recall (see p. 68) why pain is a bad state and so, if uncaused by humans (and not negligently allowed to occur by them), a natural evil. Such pain is a natural evil because it is a sensation strongly disliked. Any state of affairs believed to hold, not caused (or negligently allowed to occur) by humans, disliked as strongly, would be just as bad. Some people dislike their disabilities just as much as they dislike pain; they so dislike their inability to walk that they will undertake a programme to conquer it which involves their 'overcoming the pain barrier'. True, it would be unusual for anyone to dislike anything quite as much as some of the pains caused by disease or accident (and to call those pains 'intense' just is to say how much they are disliked). And for that reason, pain normally provides more opportunity for

evincing patience rather than self-pity, despite contrary temptation, than does anything else. But any state of affairs (believed to
hold) disliked as much would be equally bad and so provide as
much opportunity. And the choice between being sympathetic
rather than callous matters more then than it does if the suffering is
less. If the absence of the good is not disliked nearly as much as the
sensations caused by disease and accident, then of course it is still
very good to show courage in seeking to remove that absence, but
the courage is not in the face of such strong dislike for the existing
state of affairs.

The mutual involvement for which suffering provides opportunity is an involvement which more than one other can have with the
sufferer. Suffering provides the opportunity for chosen cooperation
in mutual involvement. That is especially so with respect to
the good of cure and prevention. Pain often needs more than one
doctor to cure it; it needs a team of nurses and chemists. And the prevention of pain often needs the cooperative research of generations
of research workers, backed by the money provided by taxes for
which political parties have fought in elections, or which charity
workers have gathered in collecting boxes over many years. And the
frustration of desire which is mental distress at deprivation of some
kind provides further opportunity of a different and deeper kind for
chosen cooperative effort: cooperative political and charitable effort
to help the exiled, the disadvantaged minorities, the victims of child
abuse, divorce, murder, or theft—systems of judges and lawyers,
social workers and counsellors. And with respect to cooperative
effort, as with respect to individual effort, there is good in involvement with people at their most naked, for the same reasons.
Whatever it is good that we do, it is good that others help us to do,
even if sometimes it is also good that we have available the even
harder choice of showing courage on our own. The bad state of pain
(or other suffering) is the grit which makes possible the growth of the
pearl. Once again of course there clearly comes a point where additional pain is a worse state than the good possibilities for courage and
sympathy which it allows. But it does not follow from that that some
pain is not on balance a good thing for this reason.

Showing sympathy and courage are good actions which may be
done in the face of the simple natural evils of pain and other suffering. Other good actions such as making reparation and forgiving
are done in the face of moral evils. But, in these latter cases, how-

ever the sums add up (whether the good of reparation and forgiveness ever outweighs the bad of the wrongdoing), it cannot provide justification for the agent's wrongdoing; for wrongdoing would not be wrongdoing if the agent was justified in so acting for the sake of a greater good.[3] And clearly sometimes there is wrongdoing. But that does leave open the possibility that though the agent ought not to have done the wrong, a balance of good resulted from his doing so. There are, too, good actions of certain kinds which can only be done in the face of good actions of various kinds, such as showing gratitude, showing respect (e.g. in recognition of achievement), and reward; and the possibility of these responses to actions which may themselves be responses to pain and suffering (e.g. showing gratitude to doctors who have worked hard to relieve pain) provides further reason for permitting the pain and suffering.

There are, however, two kinds of reason why, it may be suggested, the choice of showing courage, sympathy, etc. might be made available without the existence of natural evil. First, for most of these choices, apparent suffering, not real suffering, is all that is necessary to provide the relevant opportunity. While an agent can only be courageous in the face of his suffering if he really is suffering—for the reason that necessarily if we suffer we believe that we are suffering, and conversely—an agent can show compassion for the suffering which he believes another to be suffering, without that other actually suffering anything. But for God to bring it about generally that humans seem to be suffering when they are not really would be to practise a large-scale deception on the human race which would violate the Principle of Honesty. It would be wrong of God to create a world of unfeeling robots surrounded by a few human beings who are deceived into supposing that the robots suffer a lot, and so are moved to show sympathy and generous care when there is not the slightest need for it. The only morally permissible way in which God could give the opportunity of exercising such higher-level virtues as compassion is by actually allowing or making others suffer.

It may, however, be suggested, secondly, that adequate opportunity for the higher-level virtues would be provided by the occurrence of moral evil without any need for suffering to be caused by natural processes. You can show courage when threatened by a

---

[3] See St Paul: 'Shall we continue in sin that grace may abound? God forbid' (Rom. 6: 1–2).

gunman, as well as when threatened by cancer; and show sympathy to those likely to be killed by gunmen as well as to those likely to die of cancer. I commented at the end of the last chapter on how a world of decay gave us the opportunity actively to prevent disease and other malfunctioning, or to neglect to do so. That opportunity, which arises only in so far as we know how to reverse the decay, is an opportunity to do or avoid moral evil. My concern here is with the suffering which we do not know how to prevent and so constitutes natural evil (some but not all of which may be caused by decay; for example, the effects of earthquakes are not a matter of decay), and for the opportunities for response which it gives us. The objection is that all these opportunities could be provided by human malevolence (actively causing suffering) or negligence (allowing it to occur). Mere malevolence would not provide much opportunity for courageous response, but the possibility of negligence allows more.

Yet just imagine all the suffering of mind and body caused by the disease, earthquake, and death not immediately preventable by humans, removed at a stroke from our society. No sickness, no unavoidable diminution of powers in the aged, no birth deformities, no madness, no accidents. Then not merely would none of us have the opportunity to respond with sympathy or courage or reforming zeal etc. directly, but so much of the oppression of one group by another stimulated by such suffering would also be removed. Starvation and disease of one group have so often served as the triggers leading to their oppression of another group whose good things they sought to possess. (That is, those natural evils have so strengthened the desires of the former for food and easier living that they yielded to them despite their dim awareness that they had no right to oppress the other group.) Then so many opportunities for coping with difficult circumstances would have been removed that many of us would have such an easy life that we simply would not have much opportunity to show courage or indeed manifest much in the way of goodness at all. It needs those insidious processes of (currently) unavoidable accident and dissolution which money and strength cannot ward off for long to give us the opportunities, so easy otherwise to avoid, to become heroes. True, God could compensate for the absence of natural evil by subjecting humans to such temptation deliberately (or at any rate knowingly) to cause suffering to each other that there was again plenty of opportunity for courage. He could make us so naturally evil that we lacked much natural affection and had inbuilt urges to torture each other (or at any rate allow each other to suffer), in face of which we others could show courage and sympathy. But it is, I hope, in no way obvious that it would be better for God to replace disease by such an increase of inbuilt depravity (i.e. a system of strong desires for what is known to be bad or to cause what is bad). Rather, I would have thought, the reverse. A world in which humans (and animals) lacked much natural affection for parents, children, neighbours, etc. would be a horrible place.

So by permitting (by bringing about) the natural evil of physical pain and other suffering God provides a bad state such that allowing it, or an equally bad state, to occur makes possible and is the only morally permissible way in which he can make possible many good states.

All the actions with which I have been concerned in this chapter, of showing courage, sympathy, generosity, etc., are actions of benefiting others. But I now apply to these examples points which I made in Chapter 5. It is a great good for the agent if he can help someone who needs help. He is privileged to have the opportunity to be of use and blessed if he takes it. God does a great good for us if he gives us such opportunity. He can only do this by building a world in which natural processes ensure that by our actions we can bring benefits to others which they cannot easily secure in any other way. But there are also benefits for the one who needs help. He is also privileged to be the vehicle who presents the one who can help with the opportunity to help; he makes the life of the helper matter, by giving him a serious choice whether or not to help someone who needs help. And if help is provided, then of course the sufferer is further blessed by someone caring for him. My pain gives you the opportunity to show sympathy and help to relieve it. You are fortunate to have that opportunity. I am fortunate to be able to give it to you; and doubly fortunate if you mind and get involved with my need.

Human Response in Forming Souls

It is good, as we have noted earlier, that we should have the opportunity over time freely to form our characters, to determine the kind of people we are to be. One aspect of character is moral belief. As I argued earlier, beliefs are a passive matter: we do not choose our beliefs; they are forced upon us by our experience of the world. But what we can choose to do is seek out relevant experiences, think through their consequences for morality, and so acquire new moral beliefs (not ones which we choose in advance but whatever ones new experience forms for us).

Given the goodness of natural sympathy, a natural desire for the well-being of others and sorrow at their suffering, it is clearly good that moral growth should be advanced by experience of the suffering of others, sympathy with whom leads to deeper understanding of wherein lies their good, rather than by mere abstract thought. And that, of course, is what often happens. Those with experience of particular situations (rape, abortion, marriage breakdown, etc.) come to change their views about the morality of actions which involve these, through sympathy with those concerned. And when we have not ourselves had such experience we can freely choose to seek out those who have before coming to form a view about the moral principles involved. The suffering becomes the tool which we use for our growth of moral understanding, and so in yet another way the sufferer is of use to us in helping us so to grow. I think that moral growth could be attained other than by experience of suffering, but because of the goodness of sympathy, it is good (good for the others) that the suffering of others should be of use in this way. Also, in enabling one to detect the good, sympathy acts as a countervailing desire to pride in the correctness of one's own views. It is, however, important to note in this connection, sympathy with sufferers is not going to be enough to enable someone to form correct moral views about a situation. Abstract and disinterested thought has also its role to play in moral growth. Those who have had experience of and reflected on only a narrow range of situations may be blind to moral distinctions to which they would become sensitive by a wider knowledge of the world, and by reflection on the connections between situations. Someone who reflects only on the suffering involved for some wife in an unhappy marriage may fail to see the suffering which would be involved for the children in a divorce and the influence which such a divorce would have on others with marital difficulties; and failing to see these things would fail to see what would be wrong in a wife getting divorced. Whether humans choose to reflect on the connections between situations is a matter for their free choice.

But of course character is not just (or even largely) a matter of true moral belief; it is largely a matter of desire, of the natural inclinations we have to respond to situations. And while it is good in itself that we should have some opportunity to exercise the higher-level virtues of showing courage, sympathy, etc., it is also good that we should have the opportunity significantly over time to form our souls so that we are the sort of persons who naturally show courage, sympathy, etc. It is good that that choice itself requires hard work in order that our commitment be genuine. As I emphasized before, it is a very important contingent truth about humans (and animals) that by doing actions of a certain sort when it is difficult, we make ourselves the sort of persons who do such actions readily. So showing courage etc., which can only be done in the face of suffering, has a dual role. It is good that we show courage, and it is good that thereby we make ourselves naturally courageous. Humans only have a really good character if it is the sort of character which responds readily to suffering (in others and in oneself) in the right way. Natural evil provides the opportunity not merely to be heroic, but to make ourselves naturally heroic. Without a significant amount of natural evil, we simply would not have the opportunity to show patience and sympathy on the heroic scale required for us to form heroically good characters. It is a great good for us to be able, through free choice over time, to form such characters.

The formation of our character through our own free choices which I have emphasized to be so good a thing can only be made by choosing to do the (believed) good rather than the (believed) bad or wrong. But many, as a result of their own bad choices or the bad environment (in the formation of which the bad choices of others will have played their part), do not recognize much bad or wrong as bad or wrong. Only the starkest and most horribly wrong acts do they recognize as such. They have not yet reached but are close to the brink of total insensitivity to moral goodness. Their only hope is to be presented with stark choices—evils which even they can recognize; and a God as concerned for their salvation—i.e. their becoming good people (through their free choices)—as for the salvation of near-saints will, if compatibly with his goodness he can, provide them with such choices. That means giving them the opportunity to resist temptations to do cruel acts. He will give them the opportunity to feed the dying beggar rather than leave him to starve, to disobey orders to kill a Jew imprisoned for his race, or not to torture animals. Yet of course those choices are only available if these terrible evils will happen if the chooser refuses the right choice. And there must be, as there is, a limit to the suffering which God allows anyone to endure for the sake of such a great good as the salvation of the hard-hearted. But it remains the case that it is a great privilege for anyone to be the means of making available serious choices, even or possibly especially for the hard-hearted.

That suffering is a blessing for the sufferer in the opportunities which it provides him for heroic action and character formation is a constant theme in the spirituality of much Eastern Christianity, and especially of that compilation of the spiritual writings of the Eastern Fathers the *Philokalia*, which has, more than any other book, formed the spirituality of the Eastern Orthodoxy of the last two centuries. Take, for example, the passages which it includes from St Peter of Damascus:

> Through what are regarded as hardships we attain a state of patience, humility and hope of blessings in the age to be; and by these so-called hardships I mean such things as illness, discomfort, tribulation, weakness, unsought distress, darkness, ignorance, poverty, general misfortune, the fear of loss, dishonour, affliction, indigence, and so on. Indeed, not only in the age to be, but even in this present age these things are a source of great blessing to us.[4]

These 'gifts', as St Peter calls them, allow us (but do not compel us) to respond in the right way to them, by actions of a kind which we would not otherwise have the opportunity to do. The point of poverty is that 'one can endure it with patience and gratitude'; the point of sickness is 'so that one may earn the crown of patience'; the point of unsought loss of goods and possessions is 'so that one may deliberately seek to be saved and may be helped when incapable of shedding all one's possessions or even of giving alms'. And these gifts provide opportunities for others to respond in the right way, and a point of the opposite gifts is to enable them to do so. Wealth, writes St Peter, enables us to 'perform acts of charity'; and he comments later that 'without the poor' the rich cannot save their souls

[4] G. E. H. Palmer, P. Sherrard, and K. Ware (ed. and trans.), *Philokalia*, iii (Faber & Faber, 1984), 172–7. For an example from a work which is not included in the *Philokalia*, see St John of Damascus, *On the Orthodox Faith*, 2. 29 on the diverse goods which diverse bad states make possible.

or flee the temptations of wealth. Health enables us to 'assist those in need and undertake work worthy of God'. And so on.

To repeat myself so as to avoid any possible misunderstanding, wealth and health must be good for other reasons also, e.g. for the simple sensory pleasures they can give their possessors; otherwise there would be no point in seeking to pass them on to the poor and diseased. And of course poverty and disease are bad states, but they do serve the good purposes which St Peter states, among other good purposes; and that provides reason for a good God to give them to us for a limited period.

Animal Response

It is good that the intentional actions of serious response to natural evil which I have been describing should be available to simple creatures lacking free will. As we saw earlier, good actions may be good without being freely chosen. It is good that there be animals who show courage in the face of pain, to secure food and to find and rescue their mates and their young, and sympathetic concern for other animals. An animal life is of so much greater value for the heroism it shows. And if the animal does not freely choose the good action, it will only do the action because on balance it desires to do so; and when its desire to act is uncomplicated by conflicting desires, the good action will be spontaneous. And (even if complicated by conflicting desires), animal actions of sympathy, affection, courage, and patience are great goods.

Yet an animal cannot go on looking for a mate despite failure to find it unless the mate is lost and the animal longs for it; nor decoy predators or explore despite risk of loss of life unless there are predators, and unless there is a risk of loss of life. There will not be predators unless sometimes animals get caught. A hunt would be only a game unless it was likely to end in an animal getting caught and killed; and animals would not then be involved in a serious endeavour. And there will not be a risk of loss of life unless sometimes life is lost. Nor can an animal intentionally avoid the danger of a forest fire or guide its offspring away from one unless the danger exists objectively. And that cannot be unless some animals get caught in forest fires.

For you cannot intentionally avoid forest fires, or take trouble to rescue your offspring from forest fires, unless there exists a serious danger of getting caught in fires. The intentional action of rescuing, despite danger, simply cannot be done unless the danger exists and is believed to exist. The danger will not exist unless there is a significant natural probability of being caught in the fire; and to the extent that the world is deterministic, that involves creatures actually being caught in the fire;[5] and to the extent that the world is indeterministic, that involves an inclination of nature to produce that effect unprevented by God. (And, I shall argue in Chapter 10, the danger cannot be believed to exist by animals or—barring a crucial qualification—humans, unless the animal or human has observed creatures actually being caught in fires. Fawns are bound to get caught in forest fires sometimes if other fawns are to have the opportunity of intentionally avoiding fires, and if deer are to have the opportunities of rescuing other fawns from fires.)

True, the deterministic forces which lead to animals performing good actions sometimes lead to animals doing bad intentional actions—they may reject their offspring or wound their kin—and in this case the bad action cannot be attributed to free will. Nevertheless, such bad actions, like physical pain, provide opportunities for good actions to be done in response to them; e.g. the persistence, despite rejection, of the offspring in seeking the mother's love or the love of another animal; the courage of the wounded animal in seeking food, especially for its young, despite the wound. And so on.

It is a mistake, in my view, to regard the killing of one animal by another for food as in itself a natural evil. To be killed and eaten by another animal is as natural an end to life as would be death by other natural causes at the same age. For, given that animals do not have free will or moral concepts, the actions which they perform do not have a moral character, and so the killing of one by another is as much part of the natural order as is accident or disease. And if death by such natural causes is not as such an evil, as claimed in Chapter 6, but simply the end of a good, so too with death by predator.

---

[5] If the behaviour of tossed coins is deterministic, talk about a natural probability of a coin landing heads can only be intelligibly construed as talk about proportions of coins tossed in typical set-ups which result in heads. ('Natural probability' or 'physical probability' is probability in nature in contrast to 'epistemic probability', which is probability relative to our knowledge.) See my *An Introduction to Confirmation Theory* (Methuen, 1973), chs. 1 and 2.

Natural evil comes in only in so far as there is pain involved in the killing, or offspring who need parents are knowingly deprived of them.

So given all this, is the opponent of theodicy really right to insist that the world would be better without the challenges to and courage shown by animals? I do not think so. The world would be much the poorer without the courage of a wounded lion continuing to struggle despite its wound, the courage of the deer in escaping from the lion, the courage of the deer in decoying the lion to chase her instead of her offspring, the mourning of the bird for the lost mate. God could have made a world in which animals got nothing but thrills out of life; but their life is richer for the complexity and difficulty of the tasks they face and the hardships to which they react appropriately. The redness of nature 'in tooth and claw' is the red badge of courage. In the absence of humans intentionally caus- ing animal suffering, animals could not do these significant actions without there being natural evils to which to react. And it would not be better if the possibility of animals doing these actions was brought about by humans causing animal suffering, for humans have no right to cause animals to suffer. God alone, as we shall see in due course, has that right. And if he exercises it, he makes it pos- sible for animals to do things that matter. But, as ever, there is the price to be paid for this possibility; and if nature would not obvi- ously be better without it, it would not obviously be worse. There is something to be said for the lion lying down with the lamb.

The Extent of Animal Suffering

It is important to say something at this stage about the extent of animal suffering. Just how far down the evolutionary scale sen- tience, and so suffering, goes is something about which we must inevitably be uncertain. For the grounds for ascribing sentience to animals are the similarity of their behavioural responses to the stimuli which induce pain in ourselves, and the similarity of the organization of their brains to our brains, which are the vehicles of pain in ourselves. As we move down the evolutionary scale we come to animals less and less like ourselves in these respects; but there is no obvious place at which we should conclude that sentience begins. Since behaviour and brain states are but fallible evidence of mental states, our uncertainty on this matter is unavoidable. That said, I suggest that there are only weak grounds for attributing sentience to invertebrates (to ants and crabs and moths), for they do not have anything like our sort of brain. When conscious life began, it probably began with slight sensations; and then as it became more complicated, purposes, desires, and beliefs of the simplest kinds, and finally the more sophisticated kinds of these (such as the cat's desire for knowledge), would have emerged. The first feelings of pain in animals lacking belief must have been very slight in comparison with our pains.[6] For if at some stage there was no feeling and now with humans there is much, and all the indicators of mental life show a progressive development in intelligence, belief patterns, and other aspects of the mental life, we would expect a similar growth in the intensity and complexity of suffering. The lower mammals, I therefore suggest, suffer very much less than humans do. Further, for creatures without any beliefs, pain would be without significance; they would not be sad because they had lost offspring, nor would they believe their physical pain to be inflicted by enemies. Nor would they feel a pain as part of a lengthy period of pain; that would require memory of what had happened and knowledge of what was going to happen. On the other hand, for such creatures who feel but do not believe and so do not perform intentional actions, their pain could not be justified by any good for the suffering creature itself except the good of being of use to others, e.g. by making available opportunities for proper response to it by others, opportunities to show sympathy and to heal.[7] However long ago was the suffering of some child or animal, and even though no one at the time knew about it, we humans can find out later and be sorry. Our compassion for sentient creatures is often far too narrow; it needs to extend far over space and time. (I

---

[6] Marian Dawkins suggests that since pain would only have given organisms liable to it an evolutionary advantage if it was correlated with risk of damage to the organism and if the organism was clever enough to see how to escape from the suffering, i.e. if pain arrived on the evolutionary scene at the same time as beliefs and intentionality, it would follow that without the latter, pain would not survive for long. She argues that in consequence very good evidence of when animals suffer is provided by whether they seek energetically to avoid some state of affairs. See her 'Minding and Mattering', in C. Blakemore and S. Greenfield (eds.), *Mindwaves* (Blackwell, 1987).

[7] 'One of the functions of pain, in species that are capable of it, is to awaken compassion' (Austin Farrer, *Love Almighty and Ills Unlimited* (Collins, 1962), 102).

come to discuss the issue whether, good though it may be for the sufferers, God would be justified in allowing some to suffer to give others such opportunities, in Chapter 12.)

Where animals do begin to have beliefs, then physical pain will be felt more and come to have a bit of the meaning which makes it so much worse for us. But that is necessary if animals are to be able to perform those intentional actions which this chapter has urged to be such a good thing. And of course as the capacity for more intense and sophisticated suffering increases, so too does the capacity for more intense and sophisticated pleasure and other good states. The higher mammals can enjoy play and courting; and they can long for things absent which they eventually find. They can be inquisitive, and rejoice in the success of their activities.

10

Natural Evil and the Possibility of Knowledge

With most of [our fathers] God was not well pleased: for they were overthrown in the wilderness. Now these things were our examples, to the intent we should not lust after evil things, as they also lusted. Neither be ye idolaters, as were some of them; as it is written, The people sat down to eat and drink, and rose up to play. Neither let us commit fornication, as some of them committed, and fell in one day three and twenty thousand. Neither let us tempt the Lord, as some of them tempted, and perished by the serpents. Neither murmur ye, as some of them murmured, and perished by the destroyer. Now these things happened unto them by way of example; and they were written for our admonition.

(1 Corinthians 10: 5–11)

The Need to Know about the Effects of our Actions, Good and Bad

For humans to have a choice between doing good and doing bad, we need to have true beliefs about the effects of our actions, for the goodness or badness of an action is so often a matter of it having good or bad effects. It is bad to kick other people because it will hurt them, good to give the starving food because that will enable them to stay alive. And so on. So if God is to give us the choice between good and bad, he must give us, or allow us to acquire, true beliefs about the effects of our actions—beliefs in which we have enough confidence to make it matter how we choose. We need a whole sheaf of strong true beliefs with respect to many different actions, about what effects will follow from them. How is God to give us these beliefs? Clearly we will have to think of our beliefs as justified₂ (see p. 59), for if we do not think them likely to be true, we will not really believe them. And so if God is to provide us with beliefs, he must, by the Principle of Honesty, provide us in general with justified₂ beliefs, for if our criteria of evidence were generally erroneous, we would have no criteria by the application of which we could discover this, and so we would be systematically deceived in innumerable ways about the world, and could not correct this.

Our justified₂ true beliefs could only rarely depend for their justification on false beliefs unless the world is organized on a systematically deceptive basis. If our true beliefs depended generally for their justification on false beliefs it is most unlikely that they would often be other than false, barring the institution of a system designed to prevent this. For example, it is most unlikely that erroneous reports of observations of the past would allow us to infer to a conclusion about the future which turned out to be true, unless reporters were programmed to give exactly those erroneous reports which allowed justified inference to true beliefs about the future. But if God created a world in which that sort of thing normally happened, that massive deception would violate the Principle of Honesty. Suppose, for example, that God created a world in which so far no one has taken heroin, yet, by making it the case that many observers erroneously report cases of taking heroin leading to death, allows us to reach a strong justified true belief that taking heroin leads to death. These observers would need to be systematically deceived if this sort of thing was to happen on a regular basis. Further, we will only have justified beliefs as a general rule (as opposed to being the result of an accident in particular cases) if there is a mechanism in place for ensuring that; that is, beliefs must be correctly 'based'. So if God is so to give us the strong true beliefs we need to make our serious choices, he must give us in general *knowledge* of the effects of our actions: knowledge, that is, in the internalist sense, with which alone I shall be concerned henceforward.[1]

[1] I first advocated the defence from the need for knowledge in 'Natural Evil', *American Philosophical Quarterly*, 15 (1979), 295–301; and developed it more fully in *The Existence of God* (rev. edn., Clarendon Press, 1991), chs. 9, 10, and 11 (see esp. ch. 11); and in 'Knowledge from Experience and the Problem of Evil', in W. J. Abraham and S. W. Holtzer (eds.), *The Rationality of Religious Belief* (Clarendon Press, 1987). It has come in for quite a bit of criticism. See David O'Connor, 'Swinburne on Natural Evil', *Religious Studies*, 19 (1983), 65–73; Eleonore Stump,

I distinguished in Chapter 1 between the necessary truths of morality, and the contingent truths which follow therefrom when factual information about the effects and circumstances of actions is added. It is (plausibly) a necessary moral truth that it is wrong to give money to beggars if they will spend it only on drugs which kill. It is a matter of fact that certain beggars will spend money only on drugs which kill. It follows that it is a contingent moral truth that it is wrong to give money to those particular beggars. Now I do not know of any good reason to suppose that experience is necessary either for the possession or for the acquisition of concepts or knowledge of necessary truths or their interconnection. Someone has a concept to the extent to which he can conceive what it would be like for it to have application, and to the extent to which he can recognize that it does apply. And someone can see what is involved in its application (i.e. know necessary truths which concern it) without ever having observed its application. Someone might be born with an ability to conceive what it would be like for something to be red or green and to recognize red and green objects, even if he has never observed such; and this ability would enable him to recognize as a necessary truth that nothing can be red and green all over. The same applies to the necessary truths of morality. Someone might know what wrong was when the world as yet contained none, and he might know which actions were wrong and which states of affairs were bad before ever they had occurred. Our moral knowledge is not acquired in this way but there is no reason why that of some human agent should not be. God could ensure that humans were given moral concepts and a deep imagination which would enable them to comprehend necessary truths about their application without their having any experience of harsh moral realities. We could know that it is good to feed anyone starving even if we knew of no one who was starving; that torturing in order to extort belief in a creed is wrong, even if no one had ever done it. However,

'Knowledge, Freedom, and the Problem of Evil', *International Journal for the Philosophy of Religion*, 14 (1983), 49–58; Paul K. Moser, 'Natural Evil and the Free Will Defence', *International Journal for the Philosophy of Religion*, 15 (1984), 49–56. In my elaboration of it here I seek to defend it against these criticisms. Those familiar with this discussion will recognize that I have amended the defence considerably in the light of these criticisms. It is no longer in the form of the need for natural evil if we are to have knowledge of the consequences of our actions; but in the form of the need for natural evil if we are to have very well-justified knowledge, and the opportunity to learn from experience and to choose to seek new knowledge.

I argued in Chapter 9 that although humans could acquire moral knowledge without experience, there was, nevertheless, a certain value in their acquiring it through experience.

My concern here is not with knowledge of necessary moral truths, but with the factual knowledge of the effects of our actions (the effects being described in non-morally loaded terms, e.g. just as pain or death) and so with the nature of our actions (e.g. as causing pain or killing) which we need in order to know the contingent moral truths, e.g. that certain particular actions are wrong (because they do have those effects). How is God to make such knowledge available to us? The argument of this chapter is that while God might be able to give moderately well-justified knowledge of the effects of our actions, good and bad, without too great a cost, he could not allow us to learn what the effects are, let alone to choose to seek such knowledge, without providing natural processes (in which humans are not involved) whereby those effects (good and bad) are produced in a regular way—or rather he could not do this without depriving us of a very considerable other benefit. Natural evil is needed to give us the choice of whether to acquire knowledge of the good and bad effects of our actions, and indeed in order to allow us to have very well-justified knowledge at all.

God could perhaps implant in us strong true beliefs about the effects of our actions; or make us such that we gradually find ourselves with more and more such beliefs as time goes by, beliefs which open up more and more possible actions for us. We could start life with beliefs that crying causes adults to feed one, and kicking the bedclothes off causes one to be cooler (and perhaps we do start life with those beliefs; however, I write 'perhaps' because it may be that when babies want food or want to be cooler, they just cry or kick without having a belief that these actions will have the desired effects). And then as we get older we could find ourselves with more and more complicated beliefs about the effects of actions. Wondering how to hurt someone, I could find myself believing strongly that kicking him, or telling others about the misdemeanours of his youth, would in different ways hurt him. I could perhaps find myself believing strongly, for no reason at all, that setting light to hydrogen will cause an explosion, and that giving money to Oxfam will relieve starvation, whereas spending it on buying books will not have this effect.

If we are to have the opportunity of doing an action of any complexity over time, we will need to have beliefs at each time as to which sub-actions in the particular circumstances of the time will contribute to the total action. In order to have the choice of sailing round the world, I will need to find myself at each stage with a true belief about which actions (tacking, going about, taking this course rather than that) will produce the sought-after result. And I will need to find myself with beliefs about the effects of my actions on others of the crew. All that could happen. I could find myself with the relevant beliefs. They might even be probabilistic beliefs—that if I pull the sail in further there is a 30 per cent chance that the boat will capsize. These beliefs, combined with the moral beliefs about which effects are good and which effects are bad, would then allow us to choose between doing good and doing bad. Beliefs need never come through experience of what we or others have done in the past or observed to happen in the natural world, or others have told us; let alone as the result of our constructing a complicated scientific theory on the basis of many observations.

Would these spontaneously arising beliefs amount to knowledge? I think that they might—just. I suggested in Chapter 4 that perhaps it is right for us to start from any beliefs (about contingent matters) with which we find ourselves; and that would include any hunches about the effects of our actions such as those mentioned above. Such beliefs would perhaps be justified; and the other conditions for knowledge (see earlier) would be satisfied. But these beliefs would not be nearly as strongly justified$_2$ and so amount as obviously to knowledge, as beliefs based on observation of what has happened in the past and extrapolation therefrom. My belief B that if I set light to hydrogen there will be an explosion is far better justified if it is not a basic belief, but justified by many beliefs to the effect that I have observed that when I have set light to hydrogen in the past (or it has accidentally caught light) there has been an explosion. That would seem to be involved in the necessary a priori standards of inductive inference (see Chapter 4) which upon reflection we realize to be correct. For instead of a particular belief connected to the state of the world at the time it concerns (the future) by an indirect causal chain, we would have many beliefs about past states of the world connected to them by direct causal chains, from which our a priori standards allow us to make a strongly justified inference to the future.

An intermediate position is possible. *B* might not be justified by my beliefs about the past explosions which I have observed, but simply by (true and justified) beliefs to the effect that I have always found in the past that my basic beliefs about effects of my actions have subsequently proved true. But if I have always done actions with effects of a certain kind—e.g. actions whose short-term effects concern only myself, or the physical well-being of those close to me, or actions such that I have basic beliefs only about their good effects—there will remain a doubt about whether my basic beliefs about the effects of actions with effects of other kinds are equally trustworthy.

If a belief that my action will have a certain effect is to be as well justified$_2$ as possible, it will need to be backed up by beliefs that in the past actions of just that type have had that kind of effect; or that the immediate result which the action consists in bringing about has had that kind of effect in the past. What I mean by the latter is this. Every human action done by means of the body consists in bringing about some bodily movement or immediate effect in the environment, which in time has more distant effects. If I move my hand (intentional action), this consists of my bringing about the motion of my hand; if I open the door, this consists of my bringing about the door being open. The latter events—the hand moving or the door being open—I shall call results of my actions of moving my hand or opening the door; they are events which could be produced by non-intentional causes. My belief that if I light hydrogen it will explode will for its strongest justification depend on beliefs that in the past when I (or others) have lit hydrogen it has exploded; or our beliefs that in the past when hydrogen has caught light accidentally it has exploded. By the Principle of Honesty, such justifying beliefs must in general be true.

So if my beliefs about some contemplated action having a bad effect are to be as well justified$_2$ as possible, this will in general require there having been similar actions, or events not produced intentionally, producing similar bad effects in the past, which I can observe (or others can tell me about) and I can take account of. Given that it is good that our actions shall be guided by our beliefs, it is good that we should have beliefs as well justified as possible. For in so far as there is a justified doubt about which effects our actions will have, we can evade the moral force of a choice between good and bad on the ground that it is not certain which effects our actions will have. The less certain the effects, the less serious the choice. If there is a doubt about whether smoking causes cancer, it is less evidently a bad thing to smoke. To be well justified our beliefs need to be backed up by experience. It may not be a necessary truth that all knowledge (of matter of contingent fact) comes from experience of similar matters, but it is a necessary truth that it is better justified and so will give a firmer basis for action if it does.

But yes, perhaps, with this rather important qualification, we could simply find ourselves with knowledge of the effects of our actions, well enough justified to provide a basis for considerable moral choice of which effects to cause. As described it would not be a knowledge based on any understanding of how the world worked: I could just find myself with the knowledge that to make this arm movement after this leg movement would enable me to sail round the world; but I would not know how wind and tide and sail interact to make this possible. I could find myself with knowledge about such matters also. Yet such knowledge would not be knowledge which I acquired by learning, let alone knowledge that I chose to have and was prepared to sacrifice much to get. Knowledge would be ours unchosen.

Although I have done my best to describe this situation as one where humans would have something amounting to knowledge (even if not knowledge as well justified as possible), it is difficult for me to avoid the feeling that my best is not good enough. Could mental attitudes of mine really be described even as beliefs, let alone knowledge, about the geography and history and science of the world if they did not result from experience, argument, challenge, falsification? The mental attitudes which guided my behaviour in the absence of such empirical backing seem more like instincts or hunches. Is that quality of reason which we value so much in humans really present at all in this situation? If it is not, the need for natural evil will be even stronger than I am representing.

What, however, we could not do in this supposed situation of innate knowledge is to learn from experience, to discern by observing its unintended consequences that some action of ours caused good or bad of some new kind and so to learn that by doing a similar action we could cause good or bad. Above all, we could not choose to seek new knowledge by thinking, searching, and asking— knowledge of what we can do and can bring about by our actions, as well as theoretical knowledge of the structure of the world.

We saw in Chapter 4 that the greatness of human (and to a lesser extent, animal) reason consists not only in having knowledge, but in acquiring it and changing one's beliefs in the light of evidence. And we saw in Chapter 5 that it is a great good for humans that we should have the free choice of whether to exercise our reason in finding out deep theoretical truths about the universe—how big it is, how old it is, what it is made of, whether God sustains it, and so on—as well as important factual truths about the human race and those close to us. And it is good also that we should have the choice of whether or not to extend our power over others and the world; and extending that power involves acquiring knowledge of which present actions will lead to humans being killed or fed, being educated or depressed, going to Mars or living beneath the ocean. Not to have the choice of extending our knowledge of such matters is not to have the choice of helping or harming people in new ways; and to refuse to exercise the former choice is not merely to refuse to acquire the power to help or harm, but to risk helping or harming through the consequences of our actions of which we are still unaware. Free choice without knowledge of effects is empty, and a significant kind of free choice is the choice of seeking knowledge of how to bring about different effects.

Learning Involves the Operation of Natural Processes Producing Good and Bad

Creatures who are to learn how to produce some distant effect must have a limited repertoire of basic actions that they can do at will; and learning will consist of discovering that some basic actions done in certain circumstances will have certain effects. Thereby we learn to produce those effects. We saw in Chapter 5 how having such a limited repertoire is part of embodiment: I can move my hands at will, but produce more distant effects only by moving my limbs in circumstances where those motions will have more distant effects. If God is to allow me to choose to acquire knowledge of how to travel to Mars or to kill millions of people, he must allow me to learn which immediate states of affairs (which could be results of my bodily movements) will lead to those effects. He must allow me to learn in which circumstances will the depression of a button lead to a rocket going to Mars, and in which circumstances will it lead to nuclear explosions which will kill millions of people.

Much acquisition of knowledge comes from being told by others, that is from testimony. But a belief of mine acquired by testimony will only amount to knowledge if my informant or someone from whom he acquired his belief via a chain of informants had a belief amounting to knowledge, whose strong justification was of a different kind. And if the chain of testimony is too long, the justification which it produces for the resulting beliefs will be very much less. The human race as a whole must learn in a different way.

All knowledge of the future is knowledge either of what natural processes will bring about or of what agents will bring about intentionally (or both, if intentions are moulded by natural processes, or if they mould those processes). Someone may infer to a future event either by regarding what will happen as to be produced by a natural process or as to be produced intentionally. So knowledge that my action A, which consists in bringing about some result C, will have a further consequence E, will be knowledge either that natural processes dictate that C brings about E, or knowledge that some other agent on observing C will bring about E intentionally. Knowledge that putting cyanide in a man's drink will kill him is knowledge of a natural process—that cyanide kills; and knowledge that you will visit me today when you have promised to visit me is knowledge of intentional agency.

If God is to give to humans a range of actions with consequences bad and good, he must ensure that human actions have these consequences, either as a result of a natural process which he implants in the world, or as a result of his direct intentional action. And if the human agent is to learn about those consequences, he must learn about them either by discerning the natural process or by discovering God's intention. God could allow me to learn the consequences of my action by allowing me to ask him what he will bring about if I do the action. I might ask him, 'How can I kill John?' And then I might hear in my ear or see on the screen the English words 'If you shoot John, he will die'. But if I regard my actions as having the consequences they do in virtue of some other agent intentionally making the actions have those consequences, I must regard that agent as in control of my life; and not merely my life, but, since he determines the effect of my actions on others, as in control of their lives too. I must regard him as in control of the Universe, at least locally. And I must regard him as perfectly good. For his local free-dom of operation to determine what happens is (to all appearances) absolute, and so therefore is his local knowledge of what will hap-pen. And so, as the simplest hypothesis, I must regard him as knowledgeable also in other fields, including morality, and free in other fields; and so as knowing the good, and, not being distracted by temptation from pursuing it, as perfectly good. Under those circumstances I could indeed discover the consequences of my actions, and know whether they are ones which I believe good or ones which I believe bad. But I would regard my every movement as overseen by an all-knowing and perfectly good being, i.e. a God. And this would be no mere balance-of-probability belief. It would be an evident belief which guided every action of mine. That—I shall be arguing in the next chapter; and I must ask the reader to take this result on trust until then—would make the choice between good and bad impossible, given that we have certain good desires.

So, to preserve our serious choice between good and bad, God must implant in nature a system of natural causal processes and let us learn what they are. I understand by a natural process one in which a cause of a given kind produces an effect of another kind in a regular way either with natural necessity or with natural probabil-ity. Natural processes are predictable processes; and if they are to be of any use to humans for prediction, the regularities must be of a simple recognizable kind. The a priori principles of what is evidence for what outlined in Chapter 4 have the consequence that the strongest evidence for the claim that Cs bring about Es will come from past observations of Cs being followed by Es in varied condi-tions. If in the past mustard seeds being put in the ground and watered has always been followed by the appearance of mustard seedlings, then very probably the implanting and watering of mus-tard seeds causes the appearance of mustard seedlings. So the basic way in which God can allow us to acquire knowledge of natural processes, that Cs cause Es, is by providing us many instances of the successions involved under different conditions. He will implant in the world many instances of Cs being followed by Es under differ-ent conditions; and allow us to reach our knowledge by reflecting on these observations, or—making it a choice which involves more effort by us—allow us to search for and eventually find such evi-dence. Once we have this knowledge of causal succession, then we know that if we produce a C as an immediate effect of a bodily movement, thereby we cause an E. Observing many mustard seed–seedling successions, we come to know that the way to produce mustard seedlings is to sow mustard seeds. We can make this kind of inference without automatically needing to suppose that God causes the system of natural processes (although, I believe and have argued elsewhere, the operation of natural processes does in fact provide an important part of a cumulative case for belief in God). And this of course is the way in which we do come to learn about the effects of our actions, and see any beliefs about this we already have as strongly justified.

We (i.e. humans in general) learn that eating toadstools causes stomach pain by seeing people eat toadstools and then suffer pain. We learn that alcohol makes people unsteady drivers by seeing people have many drinks and then drive unsteadily, and so on. And we choose whether to acquire such knowledge, by choosing to search for and find observational evidence from which we infer such causal processes. These observations open up a range of possible actions, good and bad, which would not otherwise be available. Once we learn that eating toadstools causes stomach pain, we then have open to us the opportunity to cause others to suffer stomach pain (by feeding them with toadstools), to allow others (e.g. children) to be exposed to the risk of stomach pains (by allowing them to gather toadstools without warning them of the possible effects), or to prevent others from incurring this risk. These opportunities would not have been available without the knowledge; observation of natural processes producing pain provides that knowledge. We know that rabies causes a terrible death. With this knowledge we have the possibility of preventing such death (e.g. by controlling the entry of pet animals into Britain), or of negligently allowing it to occur or even of deliberately causing it. Only with the knowledge of the effects of rabies are such possibilities open to us. That knowledge is provided by observations of various people suffering subsequently to being bitten by dogs and other animals with rabies in various circumstances. Or, again, how are humans to have the opportunity to stop future generations contracting asbestosis, except through knowledge of what causes asbestosis? We can choose to obtain that knowledge through laborious study of records which show that persons in contact with blue asbestos many years ago have died from asbestosis thirty years later.

Our study of nature may reveal processes with which we cannot interfere, but whose further consequences we may learn to avoid by learning where and when they will occur. We may come to learn when comets will appear, volcanoes erupt, or earthquakes strike, without (yet) being able to initiate or prevent these; but whose further consequences we may be able to influence. Knowledge of when and where earthquakes are likely to occur gives us the opportunity deliberately to cause, negligently to risk, or, alternatively, intentionally to prevent suffering and death caused by earthquakes, e.g. by taking the risk of building on areas subject to earthquake, or by making the effort to mobilize the human race to avoid in future the consequences of a major earthquake.

The claim that a particular future C will cause an E will be justified by past observations, paradigmatically of past Cs being followed by Es. Our a priori inductive criteria reveal that such a claim is better justified if it is based on many recent purported observations of Cs in many different circumstances being followed invariably by Es. Observations remote in time may have been misrecorded or have occurred under circumstances different in some way from those holding in the present which affects the causal sequence in some crucial way. The more observations there are in different circumstances, the better the evidence that the sequence of Cs being followed by Es is a genuine causal sequence, not a mere occasional regularity. The observations might concern, not Cs and Es, but many very different sequences which provide substantial but indirect evidence for a general scientific theory of which it is a remote consequence that a C will be followed by an E. But the less similar is the evidence to the kind of phenomena predicted, (because of the greater probability of alternative explanations of the evidence) the greater the doubt must be whether the sophisticated scientific theory really works for Cs and Es; and that will require to be checked out by looking at phenomena very similar to those predicted. Our knowledge of the future consequences of our actions is better justified in so far as it comes from many recent observations in similar circumstances.

So sure knowledge that if I take frequent large doses of heroin I shall die must come from observations of frequent heroin intake being followed by death. And many recent observations under different conditions provide the surest knowledge possible. There could be a complicated scientific theory of which it was a remote consequence that heroin would have this effect. The theory would be confirmed by it being a simple theory which yielded true predictions of the consequences of taking other, chemically similar drugs, perhaps tested sometimes on animals rather than humans. The remoteness of the theory, and its never having been tested with respect to heroin on humans, would, however, make its prediction about the effect of heroin on me much less well evidenced. And that some drug causes pain is hardly likely to be even remotely evidenced, except via observation of other drugs causing pain or other unpleasant sensations (so different are sensations from other things). Pain there must be which is observed if we are to have knowledge of when our actions will cause pain.

The events by far the most important for the moral significance of actions which bring them about are mental events, i.e. experiences of sentient beings. As noted earlier in this book, actions are paradigmatically good in so far as they promote pleasurable and knowledge-deepening and friendship-deepening experiences; bad in so far as they promote pain, ignorance, and poverty of imagination and understanding. Most sure knowledge of the experience to be caused by some natural process is to be had through having experiences oneself of what followed from past occurrences of the process. One knows best just what it feels like to be burnt by having been burnt oneself in the past. But the public behaviour of others also produces strong evidence about their experiences. And if we have actually observed others being burnt, we shall know quite a lot about what it feels like to be burnt. A person's knowledge is, however, less securely based if the observations which support a theory are not their own, but ones known only through the testimony of others; and that, of course, is the most usual case. My justification for believing that heroin causes death is that everyone says that observers report (via television programmes and newspapers) that many who have taken large doses of heroin have died quickly thereafter. This evidence, though good evidence, is always open to the possibility of lying or exaggeration; or, where description of experiences is involved, lack of adequate vocabulary for the purpose.

So I conclude this complicated discussion thus: if God is to allow us to acquire knowledge by learning from experience and above all to allow us to choose whether to acquire knowledge at all or even to allow us to have very well-justified knowledge of the consequences

of our actions—knowledge which we need if we are to have a free
and efficacious choice between good and bad—he needs to provide
natural evils occurring in regular ways in consequence of natural
processes. Or rather, he needs to do this if he is not to give us too
evident an awareness of his presence.

Knowledge Provided by Animal Suffering

The suffering which provides knowledge is not confined to
humans. The higher animals acquire knowledge by normal induc-
tion, knowledge of where to obtain food, drink, and fellowship; and
also knowledge of the causes of pain, loss of health, and loss of life.
Seeing the suffering, disease, and death of others in certain circumstances, they learn to avoid those circumstances. And not
merely do they observe and infer passively, but many animals
actively seek knowledge: they look for food, spy out the land for
predators, put their feet gingerly on possibly unsafe surfaces, etc.
The lower animals of course avoid many situations and do many
actions instinctively; but in those cases they cannot be said to be
doing the action or avoiding the situation through very well-
justified knowledge of its consequences. We have noted that acting
in the light of such knowledge is a good thing even if the agent does
not have free will; and so too, I suggest, is actively searching for
knowledge.

As I argued in Chapter 9, it is a great good that animals are not
mere digestion machines with pleasurable sensations attached to
the digestive process; but that they struggle to get food, save themselves and their offspring from predators and natural disasters, seek
mates over days, and so on. But they can only do these things with
some knowledge of the consequences of their actions, and they
could only acquire this by learning and seeking (as opposed to
being born with it) and it could only amount to very well-justified
knowledge, if it is derived from experience of the actions of others,
of the unintended effects of their own actions, and of the effects of
natural processes. Languageless animals could not acquire knowledge by being told (by God or anyone else). They can acquire
knowledge only by learning from experience. Other animals must
suffer if some animals are to learn to avoid suffering for themselves

and their offspring. If deer are to learn how to help prevent their offspring from being caught in fires, some fawns have to be caught in fires for the deer to see what happens. If gazelle are to learn to avoid being killed by tigers, they have at least to have been mauled themselves or seen others mauled. Otherwise it will all reasonably seem a game. There will not be any difference between playing 'tig' with tigers and playing 'tig' with other gazelles. And then animals will be deprived of the possibility of serious and heroic actions.

The suffering of animals provides us, as well as themselves, with much knowledge; though since they are only somewhat, not totally, like ourselves, the knowledge which the suffering provides is a less sure guide to what we would suffer in certain circumstances than would be the suffering of humans; but still it is quite a good guide. Indeed, a great deal of our knowledge of the disasters for humans which would follow some actions comes from study of the actual disasters which have befallen animals. The bad states which have naturally befallen animals provide a huge reservoir of information for humans to acquire knowledge of the choices open to them, a reservoir which we have often tapped: seeing the fate of sheep, humans have learnt of the presence of dangerous tigers; seeing the cows sink into a bog, they have learnt not to cross that bog, and so on. (And alas humans have for a long time chosen to increase their knowledge of the effects of actions by deliberately doing things to animals which might cause them to suffer. They have discovered the effects of drugs or surgery or unusual circumstances on humans by deliberately subjecting animals to those drugs or surgery or circumstances. Before putting humans into space, we put animals into space and saw what happened to them. Now I certainly do not think that humans had the right to do many such things. My only point here is to illustrate the claim that animal suffering, however caused, often provides valuable knowledge for humans.)

And as regards *very* long-term consequences of changes of circumstances, environment, or climate, the story of animal evolution provides our main information. Human history so far is too short to provide knowledge of the very long-term consequences of our actions; and yet we are doing things which may have a considerable effect on the constitution of the atmosphere (e.g. on whether there is still an ozone layer), on the balance of nature (e.g. on whether there are many vertebrates on Earth other than humans), and on the climate. And we may discover how to make some very big changes to the Earth and its surroundings, e.g. alter the Earth's magnetic field, drive the Earth nearer to the sun or further away from it. And so on. We need information about the long-term effects of all these actions. There is a lot of information to be gleaned from pre-hominid history on all these matters, for climate, magnetic field, and balance of nature have changed often over the past 300 million years and if we learn more about their effects on animals we shall avoid many disasters ourselves. But those effects must include suffering, in virtue of the similarities of animals to ourselves. If there were not these similarities, the information would not show what would happen to us. To take but one more and very strong example: biologists are beginning to acquire the power to cause much good or ill by inducing various genetic mutations. Human history does not provide the data which will give them any knowledge of the consequences of their actions. Their surest knowledge of those consequences will come from a study of the evolutionary history of the consequences in animals of various naturally occurring mutations.

In addition to these detailed bits of information, the story of pre-human nature 'red in tooth and claw' already provides one very general bit of information crucially relevant to our possible choices. For suppose that animals had come into existence at the same time as humans, and always in situations where humans could save them from any suffering. Naturally it would then seem a well-confirmed theory that (either through act of God or nature) suffering never happens to animals except such as humans can prevent. So we would seem not to have the opportunity to do actions which would cause suffering to present-day animals let alone later generations of animals of a subsequently unpreventable kind, or the opportunity to prevent such suffering. We simply would not (and rightly would not) seriously consider the possibility that some of our actions might have enormous and subsequently unpreventable long-term bad consequences. As evidence of this claim of mine, I point out that hardly anybody ever did consider such matters before the nineteenth century. It is difficult to get back into a pre-Darwinian way of thought, but if you do, you do not (and rightly do not) take seriously the possibility of our actions having long-term effects on nature. The story of evolution tells us that the causation or prevention of long-term suffering is indeed within our power; such suffering can happen because it has happened. The story of

pre-human evolution reveals to humans just how much the subsequent fate of animals and humans is in our hands—for it will
depend on the environment which we form for them, and their
genes, which we may cause to mutate.

We may not know exactly when and where the past natural evils
occurred, but the mere knowledge that suffering of a certain type
occurred to certain kinds of creatures under certain conditions provides us with very good reason to avoid actions which may produce
those conditions. Indeed all past evils of which we know provide
knowledge of past events, and, more strikingly, since all natural
evils occur as a result of largely predictable natural processes (there
are no kinds of natural evil which occur in a totally random way),
all such knowledge helps to build up knowledge of the natural
processes which we can utilize to produce or prevent future evils.
All past and present human and animal natural evils of which we
know thus contribute to the widening of human choice when we
learn about them. And (except at an undesirable cost) we could not
learn, and especially choose to learn, without them.

11

The Evils of Sin and Agnosticism

Now the serpent was more subtle than any beast of the field which the Lord God had made. And he said unto the woman, Yea, hath God said, Ye shall not eat of any tree of the garden? And the woman said unto the serpent, Of the fruit of the trees of the garden we may eat: but of the fruit of the tree which is in the midst of the garden, God hath said, Ye shall not eat of it, neither shall ye touch it, lest ye die. And the serpent said unto the woman, Ye shall not surely die: for God doth know that in the day ye eat thereof, then your eyes shall be opened, and ye shall be as God, knowing good and evil. And when the woman saw that the tree was good for food, and that it was a delight to the eyes, and that the tree was to be desired to make one wise, she took of the fruit thereof, and did eat; and she gave also unto her husband with her, and he did eat. And the eyes of them both were opened, and they knew that they were naked; and they sewed fig leaves together, and made themselves aprons. And they heard the voice of the Lord God walking in the garden in the cool of the day: and the man and his wife hid themselves from the presence of the Lord God amongst the trees of the garden.

(Genesis 3: 1–8)

So far I have been considering evils, moral and natural, which are bad states, whether or not there is a God. In this chapter I pass to consider three states which occur or are bad only if there is a God: sin, punishment by God for sin, and agnosticism. Sin, which is failure to perform our obligations to God, would not exist if there were no God; and neither would punishment for sin. Agnosticism is bad only if there is a God to be known about. If there is a God, then in containing these states, the world is a worse place than it would otherwise be; but, I shall be arguing, these very states which make it worse make possible good states which could not otherwise occur.

The Value of the Possibility of Sin

We saw in Chapter 6 that the existence of God makes an enormous difference to the moral quality of all intentional actions. There are more obligatory and good actions, and more wrong and bad actions, than there would otherwise be. All human acts of wronging others are acts of wronging God, that is sins. So too is any total failure to worship and praise God and tell others about him. And failure to please God in many other ways, including the pursuit of our vocation, becomes bad. And so, above all, does failure to seek the wonderful well-being (for ourselves and others) of the Beatific Vision. Failure by the agnostic to attempt to find out whether or not there is a God is in any case (whether or not there is in fact a God) also a moral evil. The reason why this is so is that whether there is a God or not makes such a difference to what is our duty and what is good beyond duty to do; and it is good to put some effort into finding out what our duties are, and it is good to find out what is good, beyond what duty requires.[1] But if there is a God, then failure to investigate whether there is a God to whom duties are owed is not just the absence of a good but a wrong, because there is now someone wronged by the failure—God.

The possibility of the occurrence (unprevented by God) of all this further moral evil has, however, the consequence that we have far deeper responsibilities than we would otherwise have. We can give our lives to finding out whether there is a God, and to worshipping and serving him if we find out that there is, or we can not bother. Our choices affect our own destiny after this life and influence the destinies of others (for their destinies depend on their characters, which we can help to form for good or refuse to do so). And in making all such choices we become responsible for loving or hurting God. God, I argued in Chapter 6, will seek to be loved by those of his creatures who are capable of understanding what he is like. While it is good that the love should involve a desire for God, it is good that it should also involve freely chosen good actions of loving response to God. Love, I argued in Chapter 5, involves doing and seeking to do things with and for the beloved. Doing and seeking to do things for God involves fulfilling our duties and doing

[1] On all this, see again my *Responsibility and Atonement* (Clarendon Press, 1989), ch. 8.

and seeking to do supererogatorily good acts, including seeking to worship and interact with him. It is good that the free choice of whether to make such a loving response to God should be a serious one: that we love God, not as robots programmed to do so, but as free agents who have chosen to do so because they have seen how good God is and resisted the temptation to pursue lesser goods. Hence without the possibility of moral evil resulting, not merely will humans be deprived of the great good of a free choice between good and bad as such, they will be deprived of the possibility of loving God in a very full way. God has every reason to provide for humans the possibility of such love for himself. But, if someone is to have the opportunity to choose (despite contrary temptation) whether to give you his love, he must also have the opportunity to hurt you instead. Hurting God means sinning. Vincent Brümmer describes well the situation in which God must put himself if he is to give us that sort of opportunity to love him:

In creating human persons in order to love them, God necessarily assumes vulnerability in relation to them. In fact, in this relation, he becomes even more vulnerable than we do, since he cannot count on the steadfastness of our love the way we can count on his steadfastness . . . If God did not grant us the ability to sin and cause affliction to him and to one another, we would not have the kind of free and autonomous existence necessary to enter into a relation of love with God and with one another . . . Far from contradicting the value which the free will defence places upon the freedom and responsibility of human persons, the idea of a loving God necessarily entails it.[2]

Although with the existence of God moral evil is worse by far than it would be otherwise, it serves the further supremely good purpose of making possible a certain sort of very full love of God.

---

[2] Vincent Brümmer, 'Moral Sensibility and the Free Will Defence', *Neue Zeitschrift für systematische Theologie und Religionsphilosophie*, 29 (1987), 86–100: 97. The passage continues: 'In this way we can see that the free will defence is based on the love of God rather than on the supposed intrinsic value of human freedom and responsibility.' I have of course argued that human freedom and responsibility do have great intrinsic value, but I agree with Brümmer that they have this very great further value as well. See also Brümmer's valuable full development of the idea of love involving vulnerability to rejection in his *The Model of Love* (Cambridge University Press, 1993), esp. pt. IV.

Punishment—Here and Hereafter

The Christian tradition has taught that God sometimes punishes wrongdoers for their actions by causing them to suffer in this world—and so that some of this world's bad states are punishment for sin—and always punishes wrongdoers who do not repent (or do not repent adequately) in the next world, either for a time or permanently.

Wronging someone gives them (or someone else, such as the state, acting on their behalf) the right to deprive the wrongdoer of some good that they would otherwise have had, or to impose on them some bad state which would not otherwise be theirs.[3] That is their punishment. If you steal from me my watch, I have the right to take it back, and to take more in return for the difficulty of getting it back and the trauma of loss. And if you cannot pay in kind, I surely may choose in what form I take the compensation: I may deprive you of liberty, force you to work, force you to have unpleasant experiences, up to some reasonable amount (in proportion to the harm you have caused me). If you deprive my wife of life, I have the right (on her behalf), I suggest, to deprive you of your life. But rights are not duties, and I do no one any wrong if I do not impose an equivalent punishment or any punishment at all; and it is sometimes bad and more often not good for wrongdoers (or others on their behalf) to impose punishment. In particular the imposition of pain or deprivation of life (from one who wishes to continue to live) is in itself a bad thing, and there needs to be some good which it serves if it is to be good for the authority to impose it (although it has the right to do so). For human imposers of punishment (parents and the state) there are often good utilitarian reasons for carrying out the punishment (or some part of it): the traditional three reasons of prevention, deterrence, and reform. And all these reasons are also reasons why it would be good for God sometimes to punish sinners on Earth.

God could punish me in some way which prevented me from sinning in that way again (he could cripple me so that I could no longer pursue victims from whom I planned to steal); and preventing me from indulging the desire to pursue and steal inevitably involves

[3] On justifications of punishment, see, more fully, *Responsibility and Atonement*, ch. 6.

the suffering of frustrated desire. Such prevention of sinning is a good, although it is coupled with the deprivation of the good of wide choice of action. Seeing me suffer harm can also deter others—God could allow others to see what happened to me when I sinned (e.g. that the state imprisoned me). And earthly suffering is a spur to reform sinners against God for the same reason as it is a spur to reform those whose wrongdoing is of a more secular kind (for the reasons described on pp. 153–6). And God can provide these spurs to deter and reform without making his own involvement in providing them too obvious (with a disadvantage which I shall describe later in this chapter).

The Christian tradition has also claimed that there is punishment after this life. It has affirmed fairly universally (until the last two centuries, when a contrary minority position developed) that there is everlasting punishment for impenitent sinners. And the Catholic and Orthodox branches of that tradition have held that there is also temporary punishment for the inadequately penitent. Punishment of the former kind is punishment in 'Hell'; punishment of the latter kind the Catholic tradition has called punishment in 'Purgatory'. The tradition has been that the everlasting punishment consists of two parts: the *poena damni*, the penalty of the loss of God, the really heavy punishment; and also a *poena sensus*, a suffering of some sort represented pictorially as the 'flames of Hell'. There is, I think, no reason to take the 'flames' too literally—the point is that there is suffering.

As regards the *poena damni*, I argued in Chapter 6 that our acts so mould our characters that firm and continued wrong acts and lack of any regret for them will get us into the condition of incorrigibly rejecting the good.[4] It will only be a bad thing that those in that condition should be deprived of the Beatific Vision if they still desire to have it. I pointed out in Chapter 8 that one account of the state of the incorrigibly bad is that they have lost any desire for the good; and so for them the *poena damni* will be in no way a bad thing. But if there remains in the incorrigibly bad some residual desire for the good (and so, to the extent to which they know wherein it consists, for the Beatific Vision), clearly it is a bad thing if it is not satisfied. The trouble is that the incorrigibly bad have, through

---

[4] Aquinas wrote: 'There would be no everlasting punishment of the souls of the damned if they were able to change their will for a better will' (*Summa contra Gentiles*, 4. 93. 2).

their own considered choice over time, allowed themselves to develop stronger unalterable desires for states of affairs incompatible with the desire for the good. They desire not to be penitent for their wrongdoing, not to be generous with their lives, and to dwell on their own imagined greatness rather than worship God. A good God, I argued earlier, will respect a considered choice of destiny. If their residual desire for the good remains through the choice of the incorrigibly bad humans, God will respect that too; and the bad state that their desire for the good is unsatisfied will be the known consequence of their own considered choice.

If, however, it was logically necessary that any human (or at any rate any human who once acquired such a desire) must continue to have a residual desire for the good as long as he exists, then the only way in which God could eliminate the bad state of it not being satisfied would be by eliminating the bad themselves; and maybe that is what God would do with the incorrigibly bad—but surely only if that is what, after long consideration, they strongly desire. Either way, whether or not the incorrigibly bad still have a residual desire for the good, *poena damni* will not serve any purposes of prevention or reform, but if it is known to or suspected by others that that may be the fate of those who sin continually, it can certainly deter those others.

It is good that God should provide humans with deterrents to sin, for the reason stated in Chapter 8. Humans are weak. They need to be encouraged to do objectively good acts; and to start with, that may involve providing reasons for doing such acts additional to the reason of their intrinsic goodness, tying the performance of such acts to lower-grade self-centred rewards and punishments. To gain such rewards and avoid such punishment are of course good reasons for acting, but there are better reasons. Once the human begins to get into the habit of doing the good acts, doing them for the better reason becomes a serious possibility and threats are less needed. All parents and other educators encourage good behaviour by threats and rewards as a preliminary to children learning to do good for its own sake. And it would be good for God to do the same.[5] (Why make us so weak in the first place that we need threats

[5] 'Men are of three kinds: slaves, hirelings or sons. Slaves do not love the good, but refrain from evil out of fear of punishment; this . . . is a good thing, but not fully in accord with God's will. Hirelings love what is good and hate what is evil, out of hope of reward. But sons, being perfect, refrain from evil, not out of fear of punishment, butbecause they hate evil violently; and they do what is good, not because they

and rewards? To allow us, as I argued in Chapters 7 and 8, by our own choices to form our characters, and to allow others to help us to do so. That can only happen if we do not have a firm character to start with.)

Now the deterrence could be provided either by showing what happens to others (showing others being punished), or by a vow to impose punishment which the hearers believe would be fulfilled. As we noted, humans can be deterred from doing actions of some kind by seeing others punished (or at any rate suffering) on Earth when they do actions of that kind. But there is obvious advantage in a mode of helping to deter some which does not involve the actual punishment of others, and hence the advantage of the second method of deterrence. So God has reason to vow to punish in the next life (temporarily or permanently) those who sin in this life. Most major theistic religions, including Christianity, have taught that God does so vow. We saw in Chapter 5 that when an authority vows to punish those who do certain acts, in order to deter them from so acting, it is good that it should execute that punishment if the acts are done. And when the punishment consists simply in the loss of the Beatific Vision, which it is not good that those who have corrupted themselves beyond correction should have anyway, there is a point in God vowing publicly so to punish them—to be weighed against a major consideration to be adduced later in this chapter.

But why a further punishment (*poena sensus*) as well? That surely is a bad thing. But the threat of *poena sensus* will (because of the strong desire to avoid it, which is (see Chapter 4) the essential part of suffering) be a more powerful deterrent to the hard-hearted who have little love for God, than the threat of *poeni damni*. The former threat may—and through the centuries so often has—started the hard-hearted on the road to sanctity. And there is some good, apart

hope for reward, but because they consider it their duty. They love dispassion because it imitates God and leads Him to dwell in them; through it they refrain from all evil, even if no punishment threatens them' (St Peter of Damascus, 'That Stillness is of Great Benefit', in G. E. H. Palmer, P. Sherrard, and K. Ware (ed. and trans.), *Philokalia*, iii (Faber & Faber, 1984), 168.

'Fear of punishment hereafter and the suffering it engenders are beneficial to all who are starting out on the spiritual way. Whoever imagines that he can make a start without such suffering and fear . . . thinks he can build in the air without any foundations at all' (St Symeon the New Theologian, 'One Hundred and Fifty-Three Practical and Theological Texts', in G. E. H. Palmer, P. Sherrard, and K. Ware (ed. and trans.), *Philokalia*, iv (Faber & Faber, 1995), 37–8.

from the fulfilment of a vow, in allowing *poena sensus* to occur. For those who reject the good will probably be left with substantial desires for what is wrong, not merely for the bad. They will want to deceive and hurt others. But while there is good in allowing them sometimes to satisfy those desires before their evil character is formed (i.e. when there is some possibility that they will resist those desires), it would be bad and indeed wrong of God to allow them to satisfy their desires everlastingly. Yet God would violate the Principle of Honesty if he allowed them permanently to believe that their desires were being satisfied when they were not. So inevitably if such people continue to exist, they will have frustrated desires (even if those desires do not include a residual desire for the good). That suffering can hurt quite as much as pain which has merely physical causes. Maybe again it would be best if God simply eliminated such people; and if that is what they firmly desire, maybe he will do so. Yet if they go on existing with the character they have firmly chosen to have, they will suffer. And surely God would not choose to cause them not to exist, against their wishes.

Maybe some of those who have firmly rejected the good are left only with desires for what is bad, including everlasting enjoyment of the trivial (quite out of proportion to its worth) but not for what is wrong. The mere having of bad desires, satisfied or not, is a bad state for their possessor; and constitutes itself a punishment but not suffering.[6] And maybe God will allow such desires to be fulfilled. Such creatures could live for ever without *poena sensus* in the sense of suffering (George Bernard Shaw's vision of Hell in *Man and Superman* is a life of people following trivial pursuits for ever). It is not at all obvious, however, that the desire for everlasting 'well-being' of someone whose idea of well-being was limited to very trivial goods is a desire for well-being and so one which God would not leave frustrated. A desire for chocolate tomorrow is a good desire, but a desire for nothing but chocolate for ever seems to be a desire so out of proportion to the worth of what is desired as to be a bad desire which it would not be good for God to satisfy. However that may be, for those with wrong desires fixed incorrigibly there will inevitably be suffering. Yet the Christian tradition has been far from unanimous over the kinds and lengths of punish-

---

[6] Jeremiah saw it as an appropriate punishment for the wicked that they should 'serve other gods day and night' (Jer. 16: 13), i.e. ones less worthy of service.

ment of the bad;[7] and I side with some of its more moderate exponents in holding (in effect) that God would not impose permanent intense suffering on wrongdoers who do not desire to go on existing.

What of temporary punishment for the inadequately penitent? The inadequacy of their penitence shows a mixture of desires good and bad. Penitence involves a resolution to reform, and that can only be made by someone who has some desire to reform or sees it as a good to reform. But if the penitence is half-hearted, the penitent has allowed other desires to influence him. Such a person has not firmly chosen what character he shall have; and for reasons yet to be discussed the overwhelming presence of God would inhibit such free choice of character. Hence the need for a further temporary *poena damni* to give the opportunity for reform. (Maybe, as in the Catholic version, Purgatory is so arranged that its 'inhabitants' cannot, in virtue of the good desires they have formed or kept intact on Earth, ever finally lose the Vision of God. In that case their choice will be simply between staying put or finally and firmly choosing the good.) This intermediate state might involve suffering, for the same reason as the permanent state, through the frustration of wrong desires. The punishment of the intermediate state would serve the purposes not only of deterrence (if others on Earth know of it) and prevention (of satisfaction of wrong desires), but above all of reform; i.e. it would provide the opportunity for the sinner to choose to reform.

The Religious Value of Worldly Failure

I argued in Chapter 8 that it is good that there should be desires which provide natural incentives to do good actions and deterrents from doing bad ones—temporarily, when we are ignorant or lazy or start to go wrong. A good God, like a good parent, would not let us make a mess of our lives without providing temporary encouragement to do good and discouragement from doing bad. My concern there was mainly with the biologically produced desires to do

[7] For a fuller account of the differences in this respect in the tradition, and justification for my siding with the more moderate part of it, see *Responsibility and Atonement*, ch. 12.

actions for our mundane well-being. But it is good also for God to provide (whether or not in the form of a punishment here or here-after) temporary spurs and deterrents in regard to the action of seeking God, and to the other God-directed actions of worship, petition, and evangelism which it is good that we pursue. If we neglect such actions because we yield to mundane desires for food and drink, fame and fortune, it is good that these should be frustrated (temporarily); and that means suffering. The existence of God has the consequence that frustration of desire provides an opportunity to develop better the desires whose fulfilment lies outside this world. You can resist that opportunity by indulging in such worldly pleasures as remain open to you or by self-pity. But if past pleasures yield pain, that at any rate gives you an opportunity to rethink your goals. The Israelites were 'bitten', says the Wisdom of Solomon addressing God, 'to put them in remembrance of thine oracles'.[8] And as Eleonore Stump has written, echoing so many others: 'Natural evil—the pain of disease, the intermittent and unpredictable destruction of natural disasters, the decay of old age, the imminence of death—takes away a person's satisfaction with himself. It tends to humble him, show him his frailty, make him reflect on the transience of temporal goods, and turn his affections towards other-worldly things, away from the things of this world.'[9]

True, I am suggesting both that it is good that people have strong desires for worldly well-being (food, drink, health, success in work and love, a happy domestic life, and so on) and also that it is good that such desires are sometimes unsatisfied, so that we suffer in consequence. The satisfaction of the former desires is good. But we can let them become too important to us. Peter of Blois wrote:

You could say that tribulations are unnecessary to induce this remembrance of him, for God by conferring benefits gives us sufficient warning, as Augustine says, that God's kindnesses are nothing other than reminders that we should proceed to him. So it should be enough for God to convey warnings by conferring kindnesses, for such warnings befit God more than those delivered with canings. To this a possible reply is that though kindnesses recall you to acknowledge him, on occasion an uncontrolled love for

---

[8] Wisd. 16: 11.

[9] Eleonore Stump, 'The Problem of Evil', *Faith and Philosophy*, 2 (1985), 392–423: 409. See also C. S. Lewis, *The Problem of Pain* (Fontana Books, 1957), ch. 6. Pain 'shatters the illusion that all is well' and then 'the illusion that what we have, whether good or bad in itself, is our own and enough for us' (p. 83).

those very kindnesses holds us fast, and the Creator, the highest unchange-able God who bestows eternal blessings, is then forgotten.[10]

If we are to have a serious choice of Heaven-seeking, we must have, to start with, mundane desires stronger and Heaven-seeking desires weaker than in proportion to their worth. But if we yield too much to worldly desires, it is then good that we are encouraged to pull ourselves out of submission to the former by some of them proving unsatisfiable. Failure in love or work lets us rethink our priorities. It is not necessary that we learn Heaven-seeking by suf-fering; but there is a good, if we fail to learn it by any other route, that this final spur be available.

The Value of Agnosticism

We saw in Chapter 6 that if there is a God, among bad states is the fact that (even on Earth) so many who long for God have no vision of God (not even a limited one), doubt his existence, and often believe that he does not exist. I call this non-awareness of God, in all its various forms, agnosticism. If there are good arguments for the existence of God (as I think that there are), then some human ignorance of God may be moral evil. Humans may not have both-ered to consider these arguments seriously, may not have told each other about them, and may have refused to allow themselves to feel the force of the arguments because in consequence they would see the obligation to lead a different sort of life. The same goes if there is an experience of God to be had for those who, having heard some preacher tell them what God is like, begin to pray to him. Humans may not have bothered to preach the Gospel message or respond to it. And above all, it would be a moral evil if someone had an ex-perience of God and then tried to persuade themselves that it did not occur.

In a situation where a belief which is in some way unwelcome is only of moderate strength, there will, I noted earlier, always be the temptation to self-deception, to get ourselves not to believe by

[10] *Commentary on the Book of Job.* He sets out 'Twelve Advantages of Tribulation' (PL 207.989). English translation in J. Walsh and P. G. Walsh (eds.), *Divine Providence and Human Suffering* (Michael Glazier, 1985), 141–62: 149.

irrational means. If there is some doubt about whether there is a God, although on balance evidence or experience suggests that there is, we may choose (subconsciously) to set about deceiving ourselves into supposing that the evidence is misleading or the apparent awareness of God illusory. But self-deception is never easy. We cannot just choose there and then to believe things or not to believe things (see p. 55). It takes time and effort to force oneself to believe something contrary to the way the evidence seems to point. And the more something stares you in the face, the harder it is to persuade yourself that it is not really there. No doubt some theists become atheists by this route (as no doubt some atheists become theists, or theists or atheists keep themselves theistic or atheistic also by self-deception). But clearly not all human ignorance of God is due to refusal to teach or preach, or to listen to teaching or preaching, or to self-deception. Some are unmoved by preaching and in all honesty cannot see the force of such arguments as they have heard.[11] Some who have prayed have not come to have any awareness at all of God's presence. So much agnosticism is a natural evil.

If there is a God who is our loving creator, why does he not make his presence far better known in the world? Fathers who absent themselves too much from their children are rightly judged less than adequately loving. God's failure to make himself known is surely, an objector will say,[12] in view of God's supposed perfect goodness, evidence against his existence.

My answer to this objection is that there is, similar to the incompatibility between the good of a free choice between good and bad and the good of a spontaneous inclination to do good, an incompatibility between the great good of my having a deep awareness of the

[11] One cause of human ignorance of God is the belief of so many that moral and natural evil conclusively disprove or at least render improbable the existence of God. And so theodicy needs to explain why (if this is not so) God should allow many humans to think that it is. This chapter thus seeks to provide an explanation of why this book (among innumerable other means of presenting theodicy) needs to be written.

[12] This objection has recently been presented very thoroughly in a book devoted solely to the present topic: *Divine Hiddenness and Human Reason*, by John Schellenberg (Cornell University Press, 1993). Schellenberg's positive claim is that a perfectly good God would provide 'probabilifying evidence' (p. 35) of his existence (whether by experience of God or the availability of public objective argument) for all capable of being aware of God, 'at all times' (p. 25); and that since we do not all always have such evidence, there is no God. This chapter constitutes my answer to Schellenberg's fine book.

presence of God, and other good states of myself and others. The first of these latter is just the libertarian free choice between good and bad which I have been considering in earlier chapters. This awareness is incompatible with such a choice, given that I have either a strong desire to be liked by good persons (and especially any on whom I depend for my existence), stronger than any contrary bad inclination; or a strong desire for my own future well-being combined with a strong belief that it is quite likely that a God would not provide a good afterlife for bad people.

Before coming to detailed argument to show these incompatibilities, I draw attention to a general point. Two desires for different goals, or a desire for some goal and a moral belief about the goodness of some action, will only be in conflict with each other, only prescribe different actions in a given situation, given beliefs about how to secure the goals. My belief that I ought not to lie will only be in conflict with my desire for money if I believe that by telling some lie, I can acquire money. If I believe that my lie will be discovered to be such and not lead to my enrichment, there will be no conflict. Or again, my desire to eat will only be in conflict with my desire to be thin if I believe that eating will make me fat. If the belief which introduces a conflict between a desire and a moral belief about the goodness of some action is not very strong, if it is only a balance-of-probability belief, then the influence of the desire upon my choice will be correspondingly weak. My desire for money or love or knowledge may be strong; but if my belief that the only route known to me is only somewhat more likely than not to achieve my goal, the influence of the desire on my conduct will be correspondingly reduced.

I begin by considering the effect of the desire to be liked, which, as we saw in Chapter 4, it is good for any person to have. It is a good for me to like (i.e. to have the desire or inclination) to be liked, to like to be thought well of by others, and to have them seek my company and respect my opinions and achievements. To like and to like to be liked are essential elements of friendship. And, as we saw in Chapter 6, friendship with the good, and above all with the perfectly good perfectly wise all-powerful source of my existence, would be an enormous good. There would be something deeply wrong with someone who did not mind whether such a God liked him much or not. And yet how could such a God like him very much if he did and was inclined to do wrong actions? For God loves the good and hates evil, and while he may still love us because he has made us and we still have some potential for doing good, he will not love us for our wrong actions.

Now if I acquire a deep awareness of the presence of God, I will then become deeply aware that if I do bad, and especially wrong actions, the all-good creator will strongly disapprove. Hence if I have the proper desire to be liked, I will have a strong inclination not to do wrong; and unless that is overborne by some even stronger desire to do wrong, there will be a balance of desire against choosing wrong and so no overall temptation to resist reason. I will inevitably do the good.

The desire to be liked may be of various strengths, as may the desire to do wrong, and the belief that there is a God. But if the good desire is stronger than the bad one and I have a deep awareness of the presence of God (i.e. such that God's existence is not open to question), then the balance of inclination will be to the good and there will be no free choice between good and wrong. We will be in the situation of the child in the nursery who knows that mother is looking in at the door, and for whom, in view of the child's desire for mother's approval, the temptation to wrongdoing is simply overborne. We need 'epistemic distance' in order to have free choice between good and evil.

The only way in which a strong awareness of the presence of God will leave open the possibility of free choice between good and evil will be if the desire for divine approval is weaker than the desire to do wrong. If God makes us naturally malicious enough, keen to hurt and deceive others with no natural affection for them, then the choice may remain open. If our desire to hurt others is strong enough, we will have a serious temptation to yield to the desire even if we believe that God is watching us, so long as we care only moderately about what he thinks about us. If we feel a very strong desire to hit our brother, the belief that mother is looking in at the nursery door will be insufficient to ensure our good behaviour, unless we want to please mother fairly strongly.[13] But of course just as it is good that we desire the love of God, so it is bad if we are naturally malicious and lack natural affection. Yet it is not logically possible

---

[13] And maybe the situation of Satan, if he was strongly aware of the presence of God and yet wished to rule the world, was like that when he was first created by God: he was subject to such a strong passion of pride and such a weak desire for divine approval that the possibility remained open that he would yield to pride.

that God give us both a strong awareness of his presence and a free choice between good and evil at the same time as giving us a strong desire for his love and some natural affection for our fellows. These latter are great goods, and so again the logical straitjacket. God can only give us certain goods if he does not give us others.

God could give us a much more moderate awareness of his presence, ambiguous experiences but ones best interpreted as experiences of God, or arguments to show that on a slight balance of probability there is a God. Then a strong desire for his love will, despite its strength, be less influential on our conduct. For it will only be on balance probable that we will satisfy that desire by acting in the right way, whereas it may be much more nearly certain that we will satisfy our bad desires (e.g. to hurt) by some route (e.g. by hitting the hated one). If there is a doubt whether mother is looking in at the nursery door, we may get away with hurting our brother without displeasing her.

Yet even given only a moderate belief that there is a God, the possibility of a free choice between right and wrong will only exist given a certain ratio of strength between the desire to please God and the desire to do wrong. Even if the influence of the former is modified by doubt about the existence of God, the former cannot be too much stronger than the latter if there is to be that balance of desire for wrong action over right which alone makes possible the very serious free choice between right and wrong. Even God cannot give us that choice if he gives us fairly strong natural desires for good (including the desire to be liked by the good) and shows us, even only on a balance of probability, that he exists. But the more uncertainty there is about the existence of God, the more it is possible for us to be naturally good people who still have a free choice between right and wrong.

This point is strengthened when we take into account the other relevant desire—the desire for our own future well-being, another desire which it is very good that we should have (as I noted in Chapter 4). If we have no belief that God will allocate a fate to us in the afterlife dependent on the way we live in this life, then of course that desire will not interact with the belief that there is a God to affect our conduct. But a belief that if there is a God he will give us future well-being only if we act well (even if not a very strong belief) will influence the desire for our future well-being so that it combines with the desire to be liked by God to produce a greater balance of desire in favour of the good. Our malicious desires will need to be stronger, or our desire for our future well-being weaker, or our belief that there is a God even weaker, if there is to be that balance of desire in favour of bad requisite for serious free choice. If any God there may be does allocate fates in the afterlife dependent on the way we live in this one, then it is good that we should believe this. And then, other things being equal, the belief that there is indeed a God will deprive us of that serious choice between good and bad—unless God gives us weak desires for the good and strong desires for the bad. Again, we have the logical straitjacket; if God gives us some good things, he cannot give us other good things.

The belief that there is a God inevitably gives some degree of probability to the belief that there is for all who desire their own future well-being some life after death. For God will regard it as a good thing that there be no unsatisfied desires. But, as I have commented earlier, humans by their choices over life gradually mould their character. Those who do bad and wrong persistently lose their sensitivity to the good; and so form an incorrigibly bad character. Such people would cease to desire their future well-being (in my objective sense of 'well-being'), and so for the reasons given earlier in this chapter there would seem little good in keeping them in existence. They might desire to continue to exist, but their other desires being for the bad, they will eventually be frustrated, and so for the reasons given earlier in this chapter there would seem little good in keeping such people alive; and, if God did keep them alive, frustration of desire would make them unhappy. I conclude that anyone who believes that there is a God and reflects on the fact that bad acts destroy character will realize that they risk their eternal well-being by performing them.

While a priori considerations about what God might be expected to do with the bad in the afterlife are only of moderate force, virtually all the major religions which believe that God has revealed truths believe, as we have seen, that he has revealed that those who have done wrong will be punished in the afterlife. Any reason for believing that there is a God is some reason to believe that he would tell humans (who so obviously need guidance)[14] wherein consists human good, and so is some reason for believing that what is the

[14] On this, see my *Revelation* (Clarendon Press, 1992), ch. 5.

common content of virtually all theistic religions is true. So on both a priori and a posteriori grounds, any reflective person will conclude that the more reason there is for believing that there is a God, the more reason there is for believing that if we continually do wrong, we shall not have a good afterlife. The desire for our own future well-being will thus make it far easier for us to choose the good. The more God manifestly encourages us to do good, the less free choice we have of whether to do it.

It will be possible to combine a moderately strong belief that there is a God, with bad desires and some significant desires to please God and to have a good future, and also a free will to choose between good and bad, when the choice is quick and instinctive and not deliberate, and the bad not so obviously bad. As I noted in Chapter 6, libertarian free will is less in control in such a situation; and hence venial but not mortal sin is possible. That, I suspect, was the situation of St Paul when he wrote 'the evil which I would not, that I practice'.[15] But it is good that we shall have the big serious choices between the good and the wrong, which we can take seriously and deliberately after reflection. As I have argued, a generous God might well seek to give us the opportunity to reject all that he stands for, i.e. to commit mortal sin. And of course doing mildly bad acts which we know are bad makes it easier to do serious bad acts. Persistent venial sin opens up the possibility of mortal sin, a danger of which St Paul was well aware: 'I buffet my body and bring it into bondage: lest by any means, after that I have preached to others, I should myself be rejected.'[16] But St Paul is not, as he writes, in the position of being able to reject God and the good for which he stands; and it would be very wrong if he allowed himself to get into that position. But someone who finds himself in that position (not through his own choice) does have the advantage of being able to make the very serious choices which St Paul cannot make.

In summary of the argument so far: the greater our conviction of the existence of God, if we have one or other of two very good desires (the desire to be liked by the good, and the desire for our future well-being), the less it will be open to us to make serious choices, including the choice of our ultimate future.

There are significant biblical passages which bring out the important role of ignorance of God in making possible serious, and

---

[15] Rom. 7: 19.   [16] 1 Cor. 9: 27.

especially very serious, free choice; and they include the Bible's account of that famous first very serious free choice cited at the beginning of this chapter. The serpent persuaded Eve to take the apple on the grounds that 'God' was weak, i.e. not God: for those who eat the apple would be as powerful as God—something which Adam still believed after eating the apple, because he supposed that by hiding himself he could escape God. And the more general point that serious human choices are often made with inadequate knowledge of their divine implications is also very much a New Testament one. In the parable of the sheep and the goats at the Last Judgement, as related by St Matthew,[17] the good are rewarded for feeding the hungry, visiting the sick, etc., in ignorance that the beneficiary of their acts was God himself. ('In so far as ye did it unto one of these my brethren, even these least, ye did it unto me,' said the king.) And the bad are punished for their failures to act in similar ignorance. Their amazement at the punishment ('when saw we thee an hungred?' etc.) implies that if they had known who the potential beneficiary was, they would have fed him. Ignorance of God is a precondition here for the sheep making different choices from the goats. 'Whatever you are doing, remember that God sees all your thoughts, and then you will never sin,' wrote St Isaiah the Solitary.[18]

The belief that there is a God does not merely (given other good things) deprive us of a certain sort of free choice; it deprives us also of the possibility of doing various different actions, and so of the choice of so doing—whether free or not, contrary to strong or weak temptation. The first of these is being able to find out for ourselves whether or not there is a God. If, as I have been arguing throughout, doing things for ourselves, i.e. intentional action which endeavours to make a significant difference to our condition and that of others, is a good thing, to have a free choice of whether to bother to try to find out whether there is a God will be a great good. And a greater good will be to find the answer. All that follows from the supreme good of knowledge of the ultimate truth about the Universe and so of whether there is a God. But to seek, let alone to find, knowledge, we need ignorance to start with. And in this situation of ignorance there will be the possibility of seeking and

---

[17] Matt. 25: 31–46.
[18] 'On Guarding the Intellect', in G. E. H. Palmer, P. Sherrard, and K. Ware (ed. and trans.), *Philokalia*, i (Faber & Faber, 1979), 28.

obtaining not merely theoretical knowledge but the deep friendship with God which is such a good thing.

Joseph Butler emphasized the value of investigation in discovering the content of revelation and of uncertainty about it:

> If a prince desire to exercise or in any sense prove, the understanding or loyalty of a servant, he would not always give his orders in such a plain manner . . . Ignorance and doubt afford scope for probation in all senses . . . Men's moral probation may also be, whether they will take due care to inform themselves by impartial consideration, and afterwards whether they will act as the case requires upon the evidence which they have, however doubtful.[19]

Any goal which is good for humans to pursue is, I argued in Chapter 5, especially good if they pursue it cooperatively. In the pursuit of this very great good, the knowledge of God, it is good that humans cooperate, cooperate in investigation when none have found the great good; and when some have found it and others have not, that those who have found should try to help those who have not, to find it. What a good thing it is that those who know should be able to teach those who do not—in all matters, but above all in this most important of matters![20] Cooperative inquiry into the existence (and nature and activity) of God will not only take the form of 'centres for the philosophy of religion' (though it will include that). It will also take the form of parish discussion groups, and prayer meetings, for seeing something about God is not confined to the learned, and requires asking his help (if he is there). And teaching the ignorant always involves a lot of publicity to persuade them that they need to learn and that certain teachers are the best people to teach them. Hence the goodness of evangelism. But of course cooperative inquiry into a matter over time presupposes a general previous ignorance in the population until that time. Only those who do not want to learn can be persuaded to do so, and only the ignorant can be evangelized. If God is to give us the great good of helping each other to find him, he must make a lot of us ignorant of him over a long period. And, given the way generations inevitably depend largely on previous generations for their know-

[19] J. Butler, *The Analogy of Religion*, pt. II, ch. 6 (George Bell, 1902), 272–3.
[20] The ignorance on the part of the Jews of God's activity in Christ which evoked St Paul's desire and evangelistic effort to bring all to Christ led to that most generous of all his expressions: 'I could wish that I myself were anathema from Christ for my brethren's sake, my kinsmen according to the flesh' (Rom. 9: 3).

ledge (and what a good thing it is that parents are of such use!), that means that there must be generations and cultures ignorant of God, if the human race are to be of immense use to each other in this way.[21]

The Advantages of Human Death

I argued earlier that the belief that there is a God inevitably gives some degree of probability to the belief that there is (at least for the good) life after death, and that that makes it easier for us to do good; temptations to do bad are not so acute, and so we do not have the opportunity to stand up for the good so heroically. While this is so with respect to all good and bad actions, it is also the case, as I shall show below, that certain kinds of heroic and wicked action become unavailable to us to the extent to which we believe that there is life after death.

It will be useful at this stage to summarize the advantages (some of which I have mentioned earlier) of a world in which humans live a short, finite life, culminating in a natural death, but which they can cause to happen earlier (by killing each other or themselves); and then point out that in two respects these advantages are lessened to the extent that humans believe that death is not the end. I wrote earlier that death is only a bad thing to the extent to which it involves frustration of desire—i.e. the desire to live; and while not all humans always desire to go on living under their this-worldly conditions of existence, they almost all wish to go on living under some conditions of existence. Hence if death was really the end, it would be a bad thing for this reason as well as, of course, in so far as it involves the grief of others. But the fact of death does confer on us great advantages.

The first advantage of death is that it allows agents to do or to refrain from doing to each other a certain harm (of a qualitatively different kind to other harms)—to deprive of existence. In this respect humans would be like God, able to destroy. And God would indeed have trusted humans enormously in giving them this power.

The second advantage of mortality is to give us the possibility of

---

[21] See Additional Note 7.

supreme self-sacrifice and courage in the face of absolute disaster. The ultimate sacrifice is the sacrifice of oneself, and that would not be possible in a world without death. ('Greater love hath no man than this, that a man lay down his life for his friends,' said Christ.[22]) If we are immortal, supreme generosity is impossible. So too is cheerfulness and patience in the face of absolute disaster. For in a world without death the alternatives would always involve continuance of life and presumably too therefore the possibility that others would rescue one from one's misfortunes. There will be no absolute disaster to be faced with cheerfulness and patience.

Thirdly, a world with natural death is a world in which an agent's own contribution has a significance to it because it is irreversible by the agent. If I spend all my seventy years doing harm, there is no time left for me to undo it. But if I live for ever, then whatever harm I do, I can always undo it. It is good that what people do should matter, and their actions matter more if they have only a limited time in which to reverse them.

Fourthly, a world with birth but without natural death would be a world in which the young would never have a free hand. And birth is an evident good. It is good that some should have the responsibility for the existence and growth to maturity of others. Yet without death those others would always be inhibited by the experience and influence of the aged—given the obvious goodness that, if the aged do live for ever, they continue to possess old knowledge, acquire new knowledge, and are respected for their knowledge.

The greatest value of death, however, seems to me to lie in a fifth consideration, which is in a way opposite to my second one. I wrote earlier of the great value which lies in agents having the power to harm each other. Only agents who can do this have real responsibility. Yet it may seem, despite the arguments which I gave earlier, unfair that agents should be too much subject to other agents. Clearly for the sake of the potential sufferer, there must be *a* limit to the suffering which one agent can inflict on another. It would, I believe we would all judge, be morally wrong for a very powerful being to give *limitless* power to one agent to hurt another. Giving to agents the power to kill is giving vast power of a qualitatively different kind from other power: but it involves the end of experience.

[22] John 15: 13.

It is very different from a power to produce endless suffering. Clearly the parent analogy suggests that it would be morally wrong to give limitless power to cause suffering. A parent, believing that an elder son ought to have responsibility, may give him power for good or ill over the younger son. But a good parent will intervene eventually if the younger son suffers too much—for the sake of the younger son. A God who did not put a limit to the amount of suffering which a creature can suffer (for any good cause, including that of the responsibility of agents) would not be a good God. There need to be limits to the intensity of suffering and to the period of suffering. A natural death after a certain small finite number of years provides the limit to the period of suffering; and I shall claim in Chapter 12 that God does not have the right to entrust humans to the care of other humans who may hurt them for more than a short finite period.

Now the Christian tradition teaches that although death is not the end, it does involve God removing humans from the web of causes and responsibilities provided by life on this Earth. The fourth and fifth and (to an extent) the third advantages of death are therefore preserved. The young on Earth are no longer inhibited by the old, nor can any one human continue to harm another over the gulf provided by death. Our removal from this Earth takes us away from being able to undo harm done to things and other humans on Earth, but we may be able to undo the harm done by our actions towards God. But the first and second advantages are somewhat lessened. To kill another is to deprive him or her of life—on this Earth with its web of causes and responsibilities—but not of existence; it is rather to force the one killed (unprepared) into the nearer presence of God. That is indeed a significant action, but not as significant as depriving someone of existence for ever. And in consequence, self-sacrifice and cheerfulness in the face of death do not have quite the absolute character they would otherwise possess.

Yet while our responsibilities (what we can effect by our choices) will be less than they are, if in fact God gives us a life after death, to the extent to which we believe that this will not happen, the seriousness of our choices will be unimpeded. Ignorance of whether death is the end means that our choices of whether to kill another or sacrifice ourself become very serious indeed, for we suspect that they will involve deprivation of existence for ever; and the temptation to avoid self-sacrifice becomes enormous. I see a close and rational connection between the deep unwillingness today of Western nations to send troops to fight for justice in distant lands, and the decline in the West of religious faith. Death is a grimmer thing than it used to be.

The Incarnation and the Atonement

These are two doctrines which are above all the hallmark of Christianity, which each have the consequence that our sin which is so evil makes possible a very great good.

The doctrine of the Atonement is that the life and death of Christ on the cross was an atonement for our sins. We owe God much, who has so generously given us our lives; and if we waste those lives or use them to do wrong, we must apologize and offer reparation: to fail to do so would be to fail to take our wrongdoing seriously. But we are in no position to make reparation to God, since we owe him so much anyway. So God made available to us a life which he lived himself in Christ, which we can offer back to God as reparation; in baptism and the Eucharist and other church ceremonies we can plead in atonement for our sins, the sacrifice of Christ's life and death.[23]

Now the atoning life and death of God in Christ were marvellous things; the goodness of generous service was a major theme of my Part II, and that God himself should live such a life so that we can take our wrongdoing against him seriously is wonderful indeed. It cannot, however, be a good thing that we do wrong, simply in order that God may make an atonement and forgive us. For wrongdoing would not be wrongdoing (and so could not be atoned for) if it were good that it be done. If wrongdoing were overall a good thing, the answer to St Paul's question 'shall we continue in sin, that grace may abound?' would be 'Yes' instead of 'God forbid'.[24] Still, the difference which it makes is this: while the possibility of its misuse provides a reason for God not to create creatures with significant

---

[23] This is a very brief account of what seems to me the most plausible way of spelling out the doctrine of the Atonement. But further spelling-out is clearly needed. (For that, see my *Responsibility and Atonement*, esp. ch. 10.) The point of this section, however, that the life and death of Christ, in atoning for our sins, lessens the force of the reason which God had for not creating creatures with significant freedom, remains also on most other accounts of the Atonement.

[24] Rom. 6: 1–2.

freedom, the possibility of such compensation for misuse reduces, if not balances, the force of that reason. There is great truth, though maybe not as much as the writer of the Exultet supposed, in 'O Felix Culpa, quae talem ac tantum meruit habere redemptorem.'[25] That he was willing to make such an atoning sacrifice meant that God had more justification than he would have otherwise for taking the risk of allowing us to do wrong.

The doctrine of the Incarnation (that God was incarnate in Christ) has its relevance to human suffering, quite apart from its role in atonement. For the argument of this book is that it would have been good for God to subject humans to much that is bad, especially suffering, for the sake of great goods, and I have been seeking to show what these goods are and how suffering is needed for their attainment. We humans sometimes rightly subject our own children to suffering for the sake of some greater good (to themselves or others), e.g. make them eat a plain diet or take some special exercise for the sake of their health, or make them attend a 'difficult' neighbourhood school for the sake of good community relations. Under these circumstances we often judge it a good thing to evince and show solidarity with our children by putting ourselves in somewhat the same situation—e.g. share their diet or their exercise, or become involved in the parent–teacher organization of the neighbourhood school—even if (as in the diet example) there is no other good served by our doing so. It lessens somewhat the badness of having suffering imposed upon us that he who imposed it suffers with us, especially, but not only, if we know about it and can thus derive encouragement from it. (I write 'not only' for the same reason as I have made a similar comment in connection with similar examples. If we are glad when we learn about something, that can only be because we judge that what we learn about is something good anyway, whether or not we learn about it.) The sharing of my suffering by my friend if that suffering is for a good cause, and my friend suffers with me because he seeks to express solidarity and support, is a good which compensates in part for the suffering. It makes, I suggest, the badness of the whole less than it would be if I alone suffered. If God shares the pain and other suffering to which he subjects us for the sake of greater goods, that indeed reduces the badness of the suffering.

[25] This is the comment of the Exultet, the hymn of the Catholic Easter Eve liturgy, on the sin of Adam: 'O happy fault which merited a redeemer so great and of such a kind.'

Conclusion to Part III

In Part II I listed many good states of affairs which God in his goodness would seek to provide in a world which he created. In Part III I have shown that so many of these good states could not be provided by God without his providing certain bad states or the possibility of certain bad states which he would not prevent, at the same time.

The evils, moral and natural, which I have considered in Part III are, as far as I can see, all the ones there are, and of each one of them it is the case that by allowing it to occur God makes possible a good which he could not make possible without allowing it (or an equally bad state) to occur. Every moral evil in the world is such that God allowing it to occur makes possible (given the assumption that humans have free will) the great good of a particular choice between good and bad. Every bad desire facilitates such a choice. Every false belief makes possible the great good of investigation, especially cooperative investigation, and the great good of some of us helping others towards the truth. Every pain makes possible a courageous response (in all except animals caused to respond badly, and humans who do not yet realize what is the good response), and normally the goods of compassion and sympathetic action. And those animal pains to which animals are caused to respond badly, and those human pains to which humans respond with self-pity in ignorance of what a good thing a courageous response would be, still provide many opportunities and much knowledge for others. We can respond to the self-pitying humans by helping them to do better; their failure is our opportunity. And all animal pain gives knowledge and opportunity for compassion to animals and humans if they know of it. If the fawn caught by the fire in the thicket does not suffer, other deer will not so readily have the opportunity of intentionally avoiding fire, he will not provide knowledge for other animals of how to avoid such tragedies, other deer and humans centuries later will not be able to show compassion for his suffering, etc. (And if God gave to angels a free will which allowed them to influence how the world was organized in respect to animal pleasure and pain, then the possibility of animals suffering, unprevented by God, was a necessary condition of their choices making a difference.)

Why not let fawns suffer only if they are seen to suffer and we know about their suffering, can show compassion for them, and can rescue them? But then from our observations of fawns suffering, either humans and deer draw the correct conclusion—that fawns never suffer unless they can be seen to do so and can be rescued; or they draw the wrong conclusion—that fawns do suffer when others do not know about it. In the former case we would then rightly conclude that we need not worry about the possibility that some fawn will suffer for long in a fire which no one has taken any trouble to prevent or avoid. And then a whole range of very serious choices will be closed to humans, and a whole range of protective actions will be closed to deer (steering fawns away from possible fires from which those caught cannot escape etc.). In the latter case God would violate the Principle of Honesty, and let deer and humans show great compassion for fawns who never suffered; and take steps to prevent suffering which would never otherwise have occurred. And that would involve God practising a massive and uncorrectable deception on his creatures. I conclude that the suffering of fawns not readily rescuable is necessary for the great good of humans and deer helping fawns, without God violating the Principle of Honesty. And we can have compassion too for these anonymous but not completely unknown sufferers. As for the suffering of which we do not know at all: if we really do not know of it (not merely do not know exactly when and where particular suffering occurred, but do not know that there was any such thing as suffering of a certain kind), then we have no reason to suppose that it occurred and no reason to take it into account in our theodicy. None of these goods could be provided without the cited bad state unless God were to engage in massive deception: unless he let us believe that others are suffering when really they are not, in order to give us the opportunity to show sympathy, and so on—a very bad state indeed.

Each bad state or possible bad state removed takes away *one* actual good. Each small addition to the number of actual or possible bad states makes a small addition to the number of actual or possible good states. A reader might suggest that no good would be served by his suffering a headache today, but he would be mistaken: it serves as a deterrent—to studying too much, at the expense of doing other things; as an opportunity—for patience, not grumbling, etc.; as a source of information for the future, to guard him against too much study in future, to provide information for his doctor to develop a theory about the cause of the headaches more securely based than would be a theory with one less datum to support it. And so on. Of course removal of one bad state or the possibility of one bad state will not remove much good, any more than the removal of one grain of sand will make much difference to the fact that you still have a heap of sand. But the removal of one grain of sand will make a bit of difference, and so will the removal of one bad state.

The crucial issues are whether all of the good states made possible by the bad states actually occur (in particular, do we have free will so that our choices between good and bad are serious free choices?), whether a God has the right to allow humans and animals to suffer in these ways for the sake of a good that that makes possible, and whether the good is a great enough good for that purpose. I have argued that it is obvious that many of the good states (e.g. compassion) occur; and that Christian revelation gives grounds for supposing that the other good states occur and it is perfectly compatible with all else we know about the world to suppose that they do. To the issues of God's rights and whether the goods are good enough, I turn in the final part.

IV
Completing the Theodicy

12

God's Right

O man, who art thou that repliest against God? Shall the thing
formed say to him that formed it, why didst thou make me
thus?

(Romans 9: 20)

I have argued in Part III with respect to all the evils, moral and natural, which occur on Earth, that if God allows them to occur,
thereby—on the assumption that certain theological doctrines, and
especially the doctrine of human free will and doctrine of life after
death, are true—he makes possible various good states described in
Part II, which would not otherwise be possible and does all else he
can to ensure their occurrence. It remains to be shown, first, that it
is morally permissible for God to bring about these bad states for
the sake of good states which they make possible, i.e. that he has the
right to do so; and, secondly, that the expected value of allowing the
bad states to occur is positive, i.e. roughly that the goods which
they make possible are at least a tiny bit better than the bad states
necessary for them are bad. I shall argue the former in this chapter,
and the latter in the final chapter.

Talk of a 'right' can raise hackles. It suggests agents not concerned to be loving and generous, but insisting on their rights. I
must emphasize that I am using 'a right' in the sense that someone
has a right to do an action, if and only if it is morally permissible for
them to do it, that is they do no wrong, i.e. do no one else a wrong
by doing it. God has a right to do something if and only if he does
no wrong to anyone else by doing it.

The Rights and Duties of Carers

God is our creator. He gives us life and so many good things; and we are utterly dependent on him from moment to moment, for he keeps operative from moment to moment the laws of nature which keep us in existence and provide for us all those good things. We are God's creatures. God's relation to us is thus like that of human parents to their children, not mere biological parents but parents who give their children nourishment and education from their earliest years. As (to a limited extent, but more so than any other human) the source of being of the child, parents have certain duties towards the child. To have brought a rational being into the world gives one a considerable duty, to give her a good life. In so far as the duty is fulfilled, the parent has certain rights with respect to the child—a right to determine how she shall flourish (e.g. where she will live and be educated); and also a right to certain lesser benefits from the child in return (e.g. limited obedience while she is young but no longer an infant). Since God is so much more the source of our being than our human parents (who can only give us what they give us because God keeps them in existence and keeps operative the laws of nature which enable them to benefit us), he must, by analogy, have far greater duties and rights than they do.

Such duties of caring for others may be possessed by others than a creator or semi-creator. Grown children have a duty to care for aged parents (in consequence of the parents' previous care for them); and from that duty arise certain rights; in particular, rights to determine how the parent is benefited (e.g. that the parent will have to move house nearer to the son or daughter, in order that the latter may be able to care without too much difficulty). Most of us are dependent to some lesser extent at various times on other persons and authorities, such as teachers and the state, the latter having certain duties with respect to us, giving rise to certain rights over us. The greater the duty to care, the greater (if the duty is fulfilled) the consequent rights.

The English language has a word for those who are the object of such rights and duties: dependants. Young children are dependants of their parents, the incompetent aged are dependants of their middle-aged children; and all of us are God's dependants. But English seems to have no general word for the ones on whom dependants depend. I shall use the word 'carer' in this defined sense (not quite the same as its normal sense) for those who have a duty of care for others and rights deriving from their duty. Carers may often entrust decisions about dependants to agents whom they regard as having the proper expertise to make them, e.g. doctors.

The principles which should guide human carers and their agents in making decisions about the future of babies and young children, the senile and the mentally incompetent when they are in no position to do this for themselves have been the subject of a considerable literature in recent years. There is a full philosophically orientated survey of the issues and viewpoints in Allen Buchanan and Don Brock's book *Deciding for Others*.[1] The principles which begin to emerge here provide useful analogies for the principles which should guide God in his relations towards his creatures.

Buchanan and Brock acknowledge that in general of course people have a right to determine their own future—subject, I would add, to positive obligations to others or negative obligations not to harm others in various ways. But to the extent to which they are incompetent, the good of self-determination has to be weighed against other goods. To be competent, claim Buchanan and Brock, an individual needs to understand the alternatives and their consequences and to have a minimally consistent and stable set of values. Patients, for example, being presented with a choice between no treatment for some disease and one or two alternative treatments, need to understand the cost of the treatment, the possible dangers, the likely outcomes, and to have a view about which outcome they want and how much they want it—and a view which they do not change hourly. Buchanan and Brock also hint, though do not say explicitly, that patients need to have values which are not obviously erroneous. They write of 'mental illness' 'distorting' a person's 'aims and values'.[2] But it is an ethical judgement that illness has distorted, as opposed to merely changed, a person's values, and implies that incompetence may involve moral blindness. And that view is, I suggest, the correct one. We are incompetent to some significant extent if we fail to understand the moral significance of alternative actions. Autistic children who have no sense of right and wrong are to that extent incompetent.

---

[1] (Cambridge University Press, 1989).   [2] Ibid. 32.

Buchanan and Brock acknowledge that competence is a matter of degree—individuals may be more or less competent—and varies with the kind of task for which the competence is being assessed. Competence is also, they acknowledge, relative to importance of choice: if a choice is reversible (e.g. a choice to attend a certain school, or take a course of medication) before its consequences are fully realized, a less high level of competence in assessing consequences seems to be required. But if the choice is between one operation which may prove fatal and no operation, then a higher level of competence seems appropriate. Given his less than full competence, Buchanan and Brock hold, the good of the dependant's self-determination (to the extent to which he is competent) has to be weighed against his well-being, as determined in other ways; he may be unable to choose at all or may need to be protected from the harmful consequences of his choice. Carers or their agents will need to make choices on behalf of dependants.

There are three criteria which have been proposed for determining these choices of carers. If the dependant was formerly competent, then the first factor to be taken into account is any choice he made then, namely an 'advance directive' that, should he become incompetent, so-and-so should be done. Secondly, carers should try to form a judgement about how the dependant would have chosen if he had been competent. This 'substituted judgement' criterion raises problems about how the counterfactual ('if he had been competent') is to be interpreted. But the basic idea seems to be that you suppose the dependant to be the same in his basic moral views (i.e. his views about the overall goodness of states of affairs) and the extent to which he acts on those views, but to be properly informed about the natural (i.e. non-moral) facts of the situation (what are his life prospects under different treatments etc.) and to argue rationally (i.e. in accordance with objectively correct deductive or inductive procedures) from those premises. But even this clarification allows for spelling out in different ways, e.g. 'the same' may be read (for one formerly competent) as 'the same as he was (when competent)' or 'the same as he would have been now (if competent now)'.

Buchanan and Brock point out that the (American) law puts a restriction on the application of this criterion.[3] Carers may not

---

[3] *Deciding for Others*, 117–18.

choose on behalf of an incompetent dependant to be so generous as
to serve the interests of others at the expense of the incompetent's
own 'basic interest', i.e. to be so generous as to deprive the incompetent of basic necessities, even if (they judge that) the incompetent
would have been thus generous, if he had been competent. The reason Buchanan and Brock give for this restriction is an epistemic
one: the difficulty of judging how the dependant would have acted,
and so the risk of abuse by carers and their agents, unless the law
incorporates an absolute prohibition. This reason for the law incor-
porating such a restriction would not of course provide a reason for
an omniscient and perfectly good carer not to apply the 'substituted
judgement' criterion in all its fullness. But I suggest that there is a
further reason for the restriction: unselfish decisions (i.e. ones
which lessen an individual's own well-being from what it would
otherwise be) are not ones which others are entitled to take on
behalf of someone else; they can only be made by him.

The third criterion which Buchanan and Brock discuss for reaching decisions about the future of dependants is that of what is
objectively in the individual's best interest, i.e. promotes best what
is objectively the individual's own well-being. (Of course there may
be disagreement to be resolved at that stage about what does promote the individual's well-being. And much of this book is concerned with the issue of what our well-being does consist in.) There
is a certain not too unnatural interpretation of the second criterion
on which it collapses into the third. If we consider how the individual would have chosen if he was properly informed about the
moral as well as the natural facts of the situation, argued rationally,
and behaved rationally (i.e. was guided by his true moral views, to
the extent to which doing so did not lessen his own well-being), and
was concerned only for his own well-being, then the second criterion collapses into the third.

I need to stress that the duty to benefit, to promote what is objectively in the individual's best interest, is a duty to benefit on balance, overall. Parents have the right to cause or allow their children
to suffer somewhat for the good of those children, or of others. I do
not have the right to cause some stranger, Joe Bloggs, to suffer for
his own good or that of Bill Snoggs, but I do have *some* right of this
kind in respect of my own children. I may cause the younger son to
suffer *somewhat* for his own good and that of his brother. The right
arises, I suggest, from the parent being the source of much good for

the child which entitles him to take some of it (or its equivalent) back if necessary (e.g. in the form of the life having bad aspects). If the child could understand, he would understand that the parent gives life, nourishment, and education, subject to possible retraction of some of the gift (as well as an obligation to perform some services in return). Parents do, for example, have a (limited) right to send their children to a neighbourhood school, for the sake of cementing relations in the community, even though the children will be somewhat unhappy at that school (by contrast with the private school to which they would otherwise go), in view of the many other good things which parents provide for children. Often such rights (of carers over dependants) arise from duties of the carer towards other dependants. I have the right to force an elder child to help a younger child cope with some difficulty when I cannot help her myself directly, in view of my duty to help the younger child.[4] Among the rights of the carer, at any rate of children and subjects of the state, is the (limited) right to obedience. Parents are entitled to tell the child to help in various ways about the house. And a right to obedience gives rise to a right to punish disobedience: clearly a limited right to take back compensation and more in whatever form the authority requires, a right which, we have seen, it is often good should be exercised. The frequent exercise of that right could in theory make the overall package of benefit provided by the carer a negative one. A severe state could take from a malefactor more than it gives him. But of course that will only arise from the malefactor's choice.

The right of a carer who provides a life overall good for the dependant to cause some harm to the dependant is, I stress, a very limited one. Clearly someone who rescues a child from poverty and starvation and gives him on the whole a good life does not have the right in return to abuse him sexually from time to time. The obvious reason why there is no such right is that any human has certain absolute rights, such as the right to choose how to use their own sexual organs, by which the carer's rights are limited. While the obvious reason seems to me obviously correct, note two important qualifications. The first is that while A may have a right to x, and so everyone including B has a duty not to deprive A of x, it does not

---

[4] 'Parents' obligations towards their other children, as well as their own legitimate self-interests can conflict with doing what maximises the child's well-being, and sometimes may take precedence over it' (*Deciding for Others*, 236).

follow that everyone else has a duty to interfere to stop *B* depriving
A of *x*. Good though it may often undoubtedly be that we interfere
in distant lands to stop abuses, it does not follow that we always
have a duty to do so. And for many limited abuses of human rights
in one country, people in other countries have considered not
merely that they have no duty, but that they have no right, to interfere. While some parental abusing of children clearly does impose
a duty on neighbours to interfere, more limited abusing does not
impose a duty on people in distant lands to interfere. Exactly where
the line is to be drawn on which abuse gives whom a duty to interfere is, as are all line-drawing matters, a tricky matter, but we can—
most of us—agree on some clear cases each side of the line. The
second qualification is that the carer's rights to cause harm or to
allow others to cause harm to the dependant are greater if doing so
is the means of a greater good to (the dependant herself or) someone else. So often why people have no duty to interfere to prevent
limited abuses (e.g. to children) is because by not interfering they
will in the end make the parents and their children happier.

God's Decisions about the Unborn

What does our analysis of the duties and rights of human carers
suggest about the criteria which ought to guide God in his surrogate decision-making?

While the dependence of human children on their parents
decreases with the passage of time, human dependence on God
remains total. But human competence to make decisions does
increase with time. God has to make decisions on behalf of humans
(and animals) over a whole range of stages of their development,
but I analyse only two decision situations: the situation before there
are any humans (and animals), and the situation when a given
human on whose behalf a decision may need to be made is as fully
competent as ever a human becomes. I shall suggest answers for
these situations; clearly intermediate situations will call for intermediate answers. Let us begin with the all-important situation, the
first one. God has to decide to bodies of which kinds governed by
which laws of nature to join souls. Shall he make bodies which will
give to their owners only thrills of pleasure, or ones which will also

give pains, and under which circumstances? This decision about
our future I have pictured as being taken early in time, but clearly
one can think of it as being taken at each moment before each
human (or animal) comes into existence, or, alternatively, time-
lessly. Since those on whose behalf this decision is taken do not yet
exist, they are totally incompetent. God has a choice of what sort of
people to make and in what kinds of situation to put them. There is
no scope here for the 'advanced directive' criterion, nor for the
'suspended judgement' criterion, except in the sense in which it
collapses into the objective criterion. For there are as yet no persons
with moral outlooks and patterns of behaviour; there is therefore no
meaning in talk about how (in the more natural sense) such persons
would have chosen if they had been able to choose. Only the objective criterion has application. God must choose to give each of us a
life which is objectively in our best interest. There is not, I suspect,
such a thing as a maximally good life which God could give to anyone: whatever life you describe, there could be a better. But it must
be overall a good life.[5]

God who is so much more the source of our being than are our
parents has even greater duties than they do in respect of us, for he
has to choose the laws of nature under which we live—not merely
on what affordable food we shall be fed or by which accessible education we shall be educated. Consequently, his rights to choose how
we are to be benefited cover so much wider an area. But it must
remain the case that God must not cause harm to us which is
uncompensated by benefit to us. Just what that amounts to in detail
is, like all moral issues involving quantities of good and harm, difficult to state in terms of any helpful formula but easier to illustrate
by example. But the crucial point is that God must not over time

---

[5] Two recent theistic philosophers of religion who have made this point are
Eleonore Stump and William Alston. 'Undeserved suffering which is uncompensated seems clearly unjust; but so does suffering compensated only by benefits to
someone other than the sufferer' (Eleonore Stump, 'Providence and the Problem of
Evil', in T. P. Flint (ed.), *Christian Philosophy* (University of Notre Dame Press,
1990), 66). 'Any plan that God would implement will include provision for each of
us having a life that is, on balance a good thing' (William Alston, 'The Inductive
Argument from Evil and the Human Cognitive Condition', repr. in D. Howard-
Snyder (ed.), *The Evidential Argument from Evil* (Indiana University Press, 1996),
111). But his sentence continues, 'and one in which the person reaches the point of
being able to *see* that his life as a whole is a good for him' (my italics). I do not
endorse this further clause. One reason why I do not is that it seems to rule out God
giving life to animals who never do come to see that their life is a good for them.

take back as much as he has given. He must remain on balance a
benefactor. The overall goodness of the package—the good states
outweighing the bad—may arise from the presence in it of any or all
of the good states listed in Part II. The package is likely to consist
not merely of many ordinary desires and their fulfilment, but also
of opportunities to make significant choices of good and bad, and
above all of ways of being of use.

Note, however, that the qualification which I endorsed that
carers cannot take on behalf of a dependant unselfish decisions, in
the sense of ones which lessen a dependant's well-being from what
it would otherwise be, has no application where the carer is God
considering what sort of creatures to create. For 'what it would otherwise be' means what it would have been in virtue of acts of other
agents (animate or inanimate). But before God creates us with a
certain kind of life, there are no other agents who determine our
well-being. Note also that it follows from my earlier arguments that
God's right to allow some other free agent to cause harm to us is
likely to be greater than his right to cause that harm directly. (He
can allow wicked men to do things to us that mere inanimate
processes will not cause.) And it also follows that this right is
greater if our harm is the necessary means to some good to the sufferer or others. It will inevitably be the case that God will only
cause harm for the sake of good, as I argued in Chapter 1.

A parent does not always know for certain the effect of his actions
on the child, e.g. what will be the effect of entrusting the child to a
normally reliable childminder, or even what it is likely will be those
effects, through not knowing some aspect of the childminder's
character. But a parent has the subjective right to entrust the child
if he justifiably believes that the childminder will look after the
child well. Given that, his subjective goodness will not be affected
by the fact that the childminder does not in fact look after the child
well. But, we saw in Chapter 1, the perfect goodness of an omniscient being requires him doing no objectively bad actions, and so
only acts which he has an objective right to do. But the objectively
bad or wrong action whose badness derives from its consequences
derives this not from its actual effects but from the probable consequences detectable by a being who knows everything about the
state of the world before the action is done. Hence, although doing
no objectively bad action, on the assumption that God's knowledge
of the future is limited by the libertarian free will which he gives to

humans, even God cannot know in advance for certain the actual amount of harm one individual will suffer at the hands of another in a given situation. But since God is also omnipotent, he is able to ensure that no one remains in such a situation for longer than he (God) chooses; and is able, if he so chooses, to compensate the sufferer in other ways as and when he chooses. So God can ensure that everyone has more good than bad over the period of their existence. There must also be, I suggest, other limits to the amount of bad that God has the right to allow one creature to endure, not through their own choice: limits of intensity and length of bad state, including suffering.

If there is a God, he has ensured that there is a limit to the amount any human (or animal) can suffer on Earth (or endure by way of other bad states), not through their own choice. The primary limit is provided by the safety barrier of death. God only allows humans to suffer at each other's hands or by natural processes for periods of up to eighty years or thereabouts. If the bad, in particular the suffering, endured by any individual during that period outweighs the good, God does have the power to compensate that individual in an afterlife. The primary point of a good afterlife in the Christian tradition is, as we have seen (in Chapters 6 and 11), that people shall enjoy the Vision of God in Heaven. But, as we have noted, the Christian tradition has allowed for other kinds of good afterlife, namely Limbo. And the parable of Dives and Lazarus represents the good situation of Lazarus in the afterlife not as reward, or where he naturally fits because of his goodness, but as compensation for a bad life on Earth.[6]

Still, plausibly, there are limits to the extent to which God ought to allow us to be harmed on Earth even if there is eventual compensation in the world to come. Analogy with human parents would suggest that it would be wrong to take too much from the child before giving much to it. And the New Testament parallels and teaching about life after death, other than the story of Dives and Lazarus, are concerned more with its role as reward and punishment, or with people living the lives for which their character fits them, than with its role as providing compensation. We shall come in the last chapter to these delicate issues of just how much bad is

---

[6] Luke 16: 19–31. See v. 25: 'Abraham said [to Dives], Son, remember that thou in thy lifetime receivedst thy good things, and Lazarus in like manner evil things: but now here he is comforted, and thou art in anguish.'

too much, given the overall good for the individual and others which results. Meanwhile, however, we must bear in mind, with regard to suffering, that, because suffering is often a benefit for the sufferer in the opportunities for heroic action and soul formation which it gives him, and because suffering is often the means by which the sufferer is of use to others, the net negative weight of the suffering is not nearly as great as it would otherwise be. Often it is on balance a benefit for the sufferer, as the writers of the *Philokalia* among others have seen so well (see Chapter 9). But even if the suffering is on balance bad for the sufferer, nevertheless our creator, if he has given us many other good things, has the right to use us to a limited extent for the sake of some good to others. Kant was surely correct to emphasize that one must treat individuals as moral ends in themselves and not use them for the good of others. But the latter phrase must be interpreted as 'on balance'. It is, I suggest, permissible to use someone for the good of others if on balance you are their benefactor, and if they were in no position to make the choice for themselves.

God's Decisions about Adult Humans

We have seen that to the extent to which a dependant is not competent to make decisions for herself, the carer must make decisions on her behalf; and the principle by which the carer must be guided is simply that of benefit: he must ensure an overall balance of good (subject to any further qualification on the amount of bad involved in the overall package).

But if dependants begin to become competent to make decisions for themselves (as animals never do), dependants acquire an increasing right to determine which gifts they receive and which gifts (although objectively beneficial) they do not receive. The rights of the carer become curtailed. The dependence of human children on their parents, especially in our times their financial dependence, continues to a very limited extent long after children acquire significant competence to make decisions for themselves. Although continuing dependence gives parents continuing rights (and duties), clearly those rights (and duties) become less as children become more competent to make their own decisions. To have brought into the world a free moral agent, such as a progressively more competent human being, severely limits the decisions one can take for him.

So now consider God's choice in respect of the well-being of adult humans such as ourselves as competent as humans typically are. We remain as totally dependent on God as ever we were for our existence and the conditions thereof. In virtue of the fact that we are currently making (relatively) competent choices, the 'advanced directive' and 'suspended judgement' criteria again have no application; only the objective criterion ought to guide God's surrogate decision-making. But my arguments suggest that the right of carers to make decisions on behalf of dependants gets very much less when, even though still dependent, the dependants become competent. Ought we not to be able to decide whether we are to live in a web of interrelations in which our life is sometimes of use to others? Even if on balance our life is good, if it is not what we choose, we have some right to reject it: a limited right in view of our continued status as dependants (and our lack of perfect competence). That is surely so, and God must respect that right. And I hope my readers will forgive my alluding again to the grim truth that we do all, when we become adult, unless prevented by other humans, have the natural possibility of not continuing to live the sort of life which God makes available to us. We can all commit suicide. If we do not like our hand of cards, we can hand it back. Babies, animals, and young children may not be able to commit suicide; but of course they are not competent to decide whether to do so.

True, as I wrote earlier, we are all under a moral obligation not to commit suicide. We may be under such an obligation to parents and children and others who love us not to commit suicide. Such obligations exist either as a result of our own choice (we have chosen to have children) or as a result of factors outside our control (we have not chosen our parents). God cannot remove these obligations except by killing off those who love us or by making them love us no longer. Yet it seems implausible to suppose that a perfectly good God would do either of these things in order to remove our obligation not to commit suicide. And anyway those who are obliged not to commit suicide because they are loved are fortunate—to be loved. So many of those who decide to commit suicide decide to do so because no one loves them. And, secondly, we are under an obligation to God himself not to commit suicide. On the assumption that God ensures that the gift of life is on balance objectively a good gift, no human ought to throw it back in the face of the giver. God is under no obligation to remove that obligation, for logical reasons; for B cannot be under an obligation to A if A is obliged to let B off the obligation if B requests; for B's obligation then amounts to nothing. Nor would it be good for God to let us off our obligation not to perform what would be objectively a bad act. I conclude that a perfectly good God would not remove any of our moral obligations not to commit suicide. But we do have the power, if we so choose, to commit suicide (wrong though it would be), unless, that is, others prevent us.

Ought not God to have kept from humans the power to stop other humans committing suicide? But that would have kept from humans the power to frustrate other humans (for a while) in doing themselves ultimate harm. Having this power is a great good for the former humans. Since what the would-be suicide is about to do is a great wrong (to his creator and many others), and since the lengthening of life can be at most for a few years, and the would-be suicide might well change his mind about his decision later, I cannot see that God wrongs the would-be suicide if he does not stop others interfering in this way. For we humans recognize that we have the right to allow some humans to stop others from committing suicide for limited periods. And, as always, God's rights are greater in quantitative terms than ours, and may reasonably be supposed to extend to allowing some to prevent others from committing suicide for a limited number of years, i.e. until death. We note that God himself allows us (if others do not prevent it) to commit suicide very much sooner.

The conclusion of this discussion of God's right to allow humans (and animals) to suffer is that God does have this right so long as the package of life is overall a good one for each of us. Bad aspects have to be compensated by good aspects. But the results of Part II, that being of use is a great good, suggest that our normal estimates of the worth of the package which do not take that into account are likely to be wildly in error; and that most lives which seem (unless we take that into account) to be bad on balance are not really so. And note one final highly important point about being of use. If the world was created by God with all the providential purposes which this book has been setting out when we are of use in forwarding these we are of use to God himself. Puny humans and even punier animals are given a role to play in his plans by the all-good source of all things. Being of use is indeed a privilege. Yet if there are any lives which nevertheless are on balance bad, God would be under an obligation to provide life after death for the individuals concerned in which they could be compensated for the bad states of this life, so that in this life and the next their lives overall would be good.

One of the most frequent ways in which people express their protest against the world's ills is by saying that what happens to them or to someone else is not 'fair'. Lying behind this remark is often the feeling that God would only be justified in causing some ill as a punishment for wrongdoing. This feeling springs from a very narrow vision of which states are good and which are bad. Life, even a life which includes much bad, is in itself a great good; and the bad provides the opportunity for choice and being of use. The good things and the bad things of life are indeed distributed unevenly (see p. 149); to each is given a different package of various things, good and bad, to be used in different ways. Thus God treats us as individuals, each with her own vocation. This would only be 'unfair' if the bad states were too bad or not ultimately compensated.

13

Weighing Good against Bad

Remember the words of the Lord Jesus, how he himself said,
it is more blessed to give than to receive.

(Acts 20: 35)

I reckon that the sufferings of this present time are not worthy
to be compared with the glory which shall be revealed to us-
ward.

(Romans 8: 18)

I argued in Chapter 1 that to produce a theodicy for a certain bad
state E one would have to show that

   (*a*) God has the right to allow E to occur.
   (*b*) Allowing E (or a state as bad or worse) to occur is the only
       morally permissible way in which God can bring about a
       logically necessary condition of a good G.
   (*c*) God does everything else logically possible to bring about G.
   (*d*) The expected value of allowing E, given (*c*), is positive.

I claimed that in order justifiably to believe that there is a God,
despite the existence of bad states, one needs to have a theodicy for
the various kinds of bad states which there are. Or rather that one
needs this in the absence of very strong evidence for the existence
of God, or a record of discovering with respect to a succession of
kinds of bad states that one could in the end always find a theodicy
for each one considered. Because this book is an examination of the
philosophical issues raised by Christian theism, as opposed to theism generally, I have added to the central Christian claim that there
is a God various other Christian doctrines (such as the occurrence
of and conditions of life after death), and I have been examining
how the whole package faces the difficulty that God allows so many
awful things to happen.

I argued at the end of Part III that condition (*b*) is formally satisfied for each of the world's bad states. Each one is such that allowing it or an equally bad state to occur is the only morally permissible way in which God can make possible the occurrence of some one of the good states described in Part II. Given our theological assumptions, the good states which the bad states make possible are realized. Or, to be more precise, where the good states are such that it is logically possible that God bring them about, they are realized; where this is not logically possible (e.g. where the good is some agent freely doing some action), then God does all else needed (besides allowing the bad state) which is logically possible for him to do to facilitate the occurrence of the good state. If the good state is my freely choosing the good rather than the bad, God does his part in giving me free will. So condition (*c*) is also formally satisfied, for each bad state, as the reader can check by running through the bad states listed in Part III and the ways there described in which they make possible the good.

It is often the case, especially given our theological assumptions, that bad states make possible many different good states. Some one bad state may be needed for various different goods, each together with some other bad states different in each case. It might be that the goods are none of them individually good enough to justify God bringing about a particular bad state, but all the good states together for which all the various bad states are needed are good enough to justify God allowing the bad states to occur. There is no general explanation why God allows the bad, but a range of explanations, some one or more of which have application to each bad state. So the *G*s in the above formula may include many good states; and (*c*) may involve allowing other bad states.

With respect to condition (*a*), we saw in the last chapter that God has the right to allow a bad state to occur to an individual if the life which he gives to that individual is on balance a good one—and the bad periods are not too long or too bad.[1] Given the assumption of

---

[1] In Chisholm's terminology God has the right to allow a bad state to occur to an individual only if that bad state (together with the other bad states in the life of that individual) is 'outweighed' (or more than 'balanced off') by good states in the life of that individual. In 'outweighing', there are separate good and bad states, such that it is logically possible that the one occur without the other. But in virtue of his perfect goodness God will only allow a bad state to occur if (probably) allowing the bad state forms part of a good whole, such that it is not logically possible that God could bring about the good without allowing the bad. In such a case, in Chisholm's

life after death for humans, the compensation for bad periods may for some of them come after death. Whether the bad human periods are too long or bad, and whether an animal's earthly life is on the whole good, depends then on quantitative issues. And whether condition (*d*) is satisfied is entirely a quantitative matter. So the total quantitative requirement is that the expected value of allowing any bad state to occur should be positive; and if it is negative for a particular individual there must be enough compensation for that individual in this life, or the next life. So everything turns on the balance, or, rather, given that humans may act contrary to the objective probabilities, the probable balance of good over bad, not merely as a whole, but in the life of each individual.

This issue of whether the goods are great enough to justify the bad states which make them possible is the crux of the problem of evil. I have found in discussion of these matters that my opponents are usually happy to grant me, when I bring the suggestion to their attention, that the states which I describe as 'goods' cannot be had without the corresponding bad states, and quite often happy to grant that the former states are indeed good states and even that a world is not on balance worse for containing a few of these goods in the mildest of forms together with the necessary bad states than it would otherwise be. But my opponents usually object to the scale; there are, they claim, too many, too various, and too serious bad states to justify bringing about the goods which they make possible. There would, as I wrote earlier, be something wrong with one morally if one did not have some initial sympathy with that objection. This world's ills are many and tragic, and a conception of 'goodness' which did not lead one to suppose that a good being would try to eliminate them would be a corrupt one. And the requirement that for each individual there be a probable balance of good over bad in his life if God is to be justified in creating him looks initially hard to meet.

How are we to weigh the bad states against the good states which they make possible? Any philosophical consideration of the relative merits of these good and bad states should perhaps begin with the

terminology, allowing the bad is part of a whole in which it is 'defeated' by God bringing about the good. But in this case the bad may occur to one individual, and the good to another. Very loosely, every bad must be defeated by some good; but in the life of one individual the bad needs only to be outweighed by some good. See Roderick M. Chisholm, 'The Defeat of Good and Evil', repr. in M. M. and R. M. Adams, *The Problem of Evil* (Oxford University Press, 1990).

comment of Plato, through the mouth of Socrates, in the *Gorgias*, that it is worse to do injustice than to suffer it.[2] Spurred by that to my mind profoundly correct insight, we need to test it and similar insights by reflecting at length (as well as on our actual life experiences) on innumerable very detailed thought experiments in which we have a choice of different kinds of life to live, and thereby to draw out what sort of life we regard as on balance good for us; and then also by reflecting at length on detailed thought experiments in which we to some extent play the role of God and have a limited choice of worlds to create, and have to choose the best (or equal-best) of this limited set. These thought experiments enable us to draw out our comparative judgements. Our judgements may be mistaken, but they are the ones which must guide us until more experience and reflection leads us to judgements which we regard as better. To a considerable extent much of what I have already written in this book has been by way of thought experiments suggestive of our actual judgements about the great or little value of certain good and bad states. But I must now begin to draw out some comparative results, by means of a few further thought experiments.

Let me begin by emphasizing the goodness of life itself. Suppose that, throughout your life, you have available a machine by pressing a button on which you can become unconscious during the periods of pain, mental agony, and even boredom. Pressing the button will make you unconscious for an hour or two, during which you behave as though you were conscious, and after becoming conscious again you know what happened in the meantime. If when you become conscious again, you do not like what you then find yourself experiencing, you can go on pressing the button until you find your life more to your liking. Periods eliminated will not be replaced, and so pressing the button will shorten your conscious life, for as much or as little as you choose. How many of us would press the button for long? Not many, I suggest, would press the button very often. And that brings out that most of us value simply existing as conscious beings, whatever (within limits) life throws at us. We 'value' it, in the sense that we recognize it as objectively good for us.

To bring out this point further, I hope my readers will forgive me for mentioning again the grim fact of the possibility of suicide, but now more positively. Very few humans indeed commit suicide, although almost all of them could do so quite easily. True, some of them do not do so because of obligations to others, especially I suspect often to their children. But many others do not commit suicide because they want (i.e. desire) to go on living, even when life is unexciting or painful. One reason why they so desire is that they think that—unwilling though they often are to admit it, when badly depressed—the good outweighs the bad. They must therefore think that merely going on having experiences is a good which outweighs so much bad. Life is a tremendous good in itself. The other reason why they desire to go on living is that, even if they think that at present the bad outweighs the good, they live in hope of better times. Thereby they express their belief that a life good as a whole over time would be worth having even if its present state is on balance bad.

Throughout this book I have emphasized the great goodness of having free choice, and being of use to myself and others. It would, I suggest, be very difficult to construct a satisfactory theodicy which did not rely on the doctrine of human free will. Although some of the strands which I have deployed earlier in the book do not rely on it—e.g. some animal suffering may be justified by the good of being of use, even if the use is not freely chosen—the worst states of the world are cases of suffering (not just sensory pain, but pain including shame and humiliation) which humans deliberately and maliciously inflict on other humans together with the evils of their inflicting them. Here the moral evil is so great that we need (as well, often, as other good states), in order to justify the resulting bad, the good of those humans (and of those who allow them to get into the state of having the power and inclination so to act) having a free choice of deep significance.

But free will will not suffice for theodicy; and the other great good which I have stressed is the good of being of use. All the ways in which the suffering of A is beneficial for B are also beneficial for A—because A is privileged to be of use. The fawn caught in the burning thicket is privileged to be of use to other deer; and we have seen many times that the fact that the sufferer does not realize the benefits he is conferring and the privilege of conferring them does not affect the fact of the privilege. The fawn's life is of use; it is not wasted—he has enabled others to save themselves.

We must not overestimate the intensity of animal suffering, I argued earlier. But when we come to human suffering, the following kind of thought experiment may help us to see the value of the great privilege of being of use. Suppose that you exist in another world before your birth in this one, and are given a choice as to the sort of life you are to lead. You are told that you are to have only a short life, maybe of only a few minutes, although it will be an adult life in the sense that you will have the richness of sensation and belief charac- teristic of adults. You have a choice as to the sort of life you will have. You can have either a few minutes of very considerable pleasure of the kind produced by some drug such as heroin, which you will experience by yourself and will have no effects at all in the world (e.g. no one else will know about it); or you can have a few minutes of the considerable pain of childbirth, which will lead to the existence of a new human being who would not otherwise exist. Because the latter human being will never exist unless you choose the childbirth alter- native, you are under no obligation to bring about his or her exis- tence: no one is wronged if you make the other choice, for there is no one to be wronged. (The celibate wrong no one by not procreating.) But you seek to make the choice which will make your own life the best life for you to have led. How will you choose? The choice is, I hope, obvious. You must choose the second alternative.

We can make various alterations in this example, which will all confirm this great value of being of use. The pain may be a pain which causes not the existence of a human but that a human who would otherwise be a very happy zombie becomes capable of moral choice, and desires knowledge. You do not wrong the zombie if you do not elevate his status: he has, let us suppose, no other connection with you; and, we assume, is very happy. But you seek to benefit him: to make him no longer just a recipient object, but a choosing, agonizing, knowledge-seeking agent. If you take Mill seriously, 'better to be Socrates dissatisfied, than a fool satisfied', and you want the zombie to have a good life, you will choose again the pain. It would of course be irrelevant to your choice whether its effects were near or distant in time and space—if like Christ, or perhaps the angels, or Adam, you are making a choice whose effects are far away.

Now suppose you have a God-like choice between creating our world; or a world where all pain is 10 per cent of its intensity in this world, people only suffer it for at most eight years (though they live as long as in our world), where evil desires are only 10 per cent in frequency and intensity of those in our world, and people only have

10 per cent of the choices and can only make 10 per cent of the differences which they can in this world. Otherwise the world is programmed to move along in much the way our world does. There are
obvious advantages in such a world—who would deny that? But, as
regards the kinds of good to which I have drawn attention in this
book, it would be a toy world. Things would matter in the kinds of
respect which I describe, but they would not matter very much. It
would not matter very much if we made the wrong choices, because
not very much would depend on them. If we did not feed the starving, clothe the naked, use force to establish justice, and give love to
our children, it would matter—but it would not matter like it does
in our world. For most of the starving would get food even if we did
nothing; and although some might die, they would not feel much
pain. And the naked would not be much worse off than we are on
chilly days when we have forgotten to take a coat with us. People
would behave in a fairly just way anyway without the need for
much force, and a few swings of a truncheon would intimidate the
average wrongdoer. And our children, though valuing our love if
they got it, would not mind too much if they did not get it. Is it
really so obvious that God would be less than perfectly good if he
gave us a world where things matter a lot more than that? Of course
not.

I must emphasize yet again that I am *not* saying that a world with
a lot more choice and a lot more opportunity to be of use, together
with the bad states which would be needed for that, would be better than our world. There certainly does come a point where additional bad states make things overall worse, and a point at which it
would be quite wrong of a creator to create a world with so much
bad in it. But I am suggesting that thought experiments show that
it is not clear that we have reached that point with our world. Nor,
I emphasize once again, does it follow from God having the right to
create such a world as ours that we have anything like the right that
God has to cause someone to suffer for the sake of some good for
him or others: God's right to create, cause, and allow suffering
arises from his being from moment to moment the source of our
being.

Some writers have claimed that certain sorts of good states, say
of kind x, are not comparable in goodness with other sorts of good
state, say of kind y, in that, however many prolonged states of kind
y you have, it will still be better to have one state of kind x. Noah

Lemos, in an important article[3] on the comparison of kinds of goodness, cites Parfit, Brentano, and Ross as explicit defenders of this view, and Aristotle and Mill as giving it some oblique support. Thus Ross writes: 'with respect to pleasure and virtue, it seems to me to be much more likely to be the truth that *no* amount of pleasure is equal to any amount of virtue, that in fact virtue belongs to a higher order of value, beginning at a point higher on the scale of value than pleasure ever reaches'.[4] These writers hardly have a religious axe to grind.

I share with Lemos the opinion that Ross's particular claim is implausible: an enormous amount of pleasure *would* equal a very small amount of virtue. But Lemos uses the general idea behind Ross's view to urge that the goodness of a life of connected goods which may indeed be far better for including 'pleasure, consciousness, and knowledge' would, if it was a woven-together and integrated finite life, be better than an infinite amount of pleasure. That seems to me correct, and gives more plausibility to the suggestion that a finite life of painful utility is preferable to an infinite life of low-grade kicks of pleasure, the former, say, gaining its unity from a series of hard experiences which give to others opportunities for forming their souls through choosing between good and bad. Again if before birth I had the choice between lives of these two kinds, though I doubt if (being the sort of person I am now) I would choose the former life, I can understand it being the better life. But of course I cannot choose, and God has to make the choice for me. God sometimes pays us the compliment of supposing that, if we had the choice, we would choose to be heroes.

Our culture has dulled our moral sensitivities to the goodness of free will and (especially) to the goodness of being of use (and of much else—of honesty, fidelity, the sanctity of life, truth-telling, and promise-keeping), and overestimated the goodness of mere pleasure and the badness of mere pain—and maybe not even earlier centuries have fully appreciated the former moral ultimates. Yet even if an opponent allows the formal point that there is great value for the subject in being of use and being helped, he may fail to see that that has the consequence for theodicy which I commend, because of two characteristic human vices: short-term and short-

[3] Noah M. Lemos, 'Higher Goods and the Myth of Tithonus', *Journal of Philosophy*, 90 (1993), 482–96.
[4] W. D. Ross, *The Right and the Good* (Clarendon Press, 1930), 150.

distance thinking. He tends to think of the worth of a sentient life as dependent on things that happen during that life and fairly close in space to the life. But once you grant the formal point that things outside a life, e.g. its causes and effects, make a great difference to the value of that life, it seems totally arbitrary to confine those things to ones near to the life in space and time.

To take another particularly unpleasant example: the eighteenth-century slave-trade. The white slavers captured, inhumanely transported, and sold Africans into American slavery only because over centuries they had been taught to despise black people as uneducated savages, and had been taught that there was nothing wrong in enriching yourself at the expense of the suffering of uneducated savages. Innumerable parents, preachers, and politicians had their share in creating such a culture; and they deliberately chose to ignore the moral worth and human feelings of black people; for such a culture marked a decline in human standards: it did not exist at the beginning of the Middle Ages. But God allowing this to occur made possible innumerable opportunities for very large numbers of people to contribute or not to contribute to the development of this culture; for slavers to choose to enslave or not; for plantation-owners to choose to buy slaves or not and to treat them well or ill; for ordinary white people and politicians to campaign for its abolition or not to bother, and to campaign for compensation for the victims or not to bother; and so on. There is also the great good for those who themselves suffered as slaves that their lives were not useless, their vulnerability to suffering made possible many free choices, and thereby so many steps towards the formation of good or bad character. And for the victims there remain the possibilities of compensation and reward after death.

Note that in so many such horrible cases the free choices often became available to people too hard-hearted (as a result of previous bad choices) to do normal acts of kindness (e.g. to Africans). A good God will be desperately anxious to rescue the hard-hearted before they become incorrigibly hard-hearted, and to rescue them means to help them to make choices which will put them on the road to sanctity. But (see Chapter 9), the choices for the hard-hearted who have immunized themselves to moderate amounts of suffering in others can only be ones where the wrongness of the bad choice is very evident and very great. But to repeat quickly—yet again before anyone misunderstands—only God our creator had the right to allow bad people to promote the slave-trade. Humans had the duty to fight very hard against it; and a good God would very much want them to do that. Yet I cite this example, among so many others which could be cited, to illustrate how the possibility of large-scale human suffering opens up innumerable opportunities for significant choices in earlier centuries and distant places, and how its occurrence opens up innumerable opportunities for good or bad choices of response to it in later centuries and distant places.

If we continue to reflect on many other thought experiments similar to those of this book—how we should choose between other alternatives with longer lives or different lives (incarnation as a fawn or a suffering child[5] maybe) against a background of many centuries of effect and cause and place in the web of human and animal society, we may begin to look at things a little more *sub specie aeternitatis*, and that, I suggest, will lead us to the kind of assessments of relative value which I am commending. But of course our moral judgements are subject to limited error, especially when the comparison of goods is involved. God may reveal to us moral truths, or at any rate some details of moral truths (including the comparative worth of good states) which we are not able to discover for ourselves. If we have evidence from the circumstances of the foundation of a church which proclaims a purported revelation that God has indeed given us a genuine revelation, we will need to amend our moral judgements. But it will remain a major test of whether a purported revelation is genuine that it fits with (although goes beyond) our secular knowledge—and that includes the general outlines of our knowledge of what is good and what is bad. Given that the arguments and thought experiments which I have given do suggest that free will and above all being of use are great goods, we can appeal to the Christian revelation to confirm that they and especially the latter are even greater goods than natural reason alone suggests.

The New Testament on the Value of Service

That service of others, humans and God, voluntary or involuntary—being of use to them—is a tremendous good for the server

[5] See Ivan's speech in F. Dostoevsky, *The Brothers Karamazov*, book 5, ch. 4.

seems to me something very close to the heart of the New Testament. I have already cited St Paul's report of the words of Jesus: 'it is more blessed to give than to receive'. But let us run through other passages in the New Testament which convey the same message. I begin with the words of Jesus to his disciples on what their greatness is to consist in: 'Ye know that they which are accounted to rule over the Gentiles lord it over them; and their great ones exercise authority over them. But it is not so among you: but whoever would become great among you shall be your minister: and whosoever would be first among you shall be servant of all. For verily the Son of Man came not to be ministered unto, but to minister, and to give his life a ransom for many.'[6] The passage classically connects greatness with service, and it is most plausibly seen as saying that greatness consists in service. And, analogously, while reminding his disciples that he is 'Master and Lord' and that 'a servant is not greater than his Lord', Jesus washed his disciples' feet; suggesting, though not explicitly stating, that service is part of greatness.[7] In several places the New Testament teaches that those who suffer in consequence of their choice to confess the name of Christ are fortunate to be allowed to have such a significant role in the proclamation of the Gospel. The Apostles beaten for preaching the Gospel rejoiced 'that they were counted worthy to suffer for the name'.[8] St Paul wrote to the Colossians that he 'rejoiced' in his sufferings for their sake.[9] St Paul's reward for preaching the Gospel was to preach the Gospel—without being paid for it.[10] Conversely, the sentence ($\kappa\rho\iota\sigma\iota\varsigma$) on those that did not believe 'on the name of the only begotten son of God', is, according to Jesus as St John reports him, 'that the light is come into the world, and men loved the darkness rather than the light; for their works were evil'.[11] Good and bad actions are their own reward and punishment— which is not to deny that they may obtain other rewards and punishments as well. The Gospel teaches both a present reward for doing good and a future reward; and inevitably the two get a bit mixed up in its message. A passage which tells us of both kinds of reward is the Beatitudes, as St Matthew records them in the Sermon on the Mount.[12] The blessing for 'the pure in heart', for example, is said to be a reward: 'they shall see God', which may

---

[6] Mark 10: 42–5. [7] John 13: 1–16. [8] Acts 5: 41.
[9] Col. 1: 24. [10] 1 Cor. 9: 18. [11] John 3: 19.
[12] Matt. 5: 1–12.

plausibly be thought to lie in the more distant future; whereas the
blessing for 'the peacemakers' is the reward of being 'called sons of
God', which is something which may plausibly be thought to be
available sooner. (Emerson wrote, more prosaically, that 'the only
reward of virtue is virtue';[13] but the word 'only' seems to me to put
his remark out of line with the New Testament.)

And there is a long Christian tradition that the suffering and
death of Christ, God incarnate, constituted his glory. 'He reigned
from the tree,' wrote Venantius Fortunatus (early seventh century
AD) in the well-known Passiontide hymn 'The Royal Banners forward go'. God is glorified in his suffering and death on the cross
quite independently of what might follow for him or for us. To suffer for our sake (however that is spelled out in a doctrine of the
Atonement) is his glory. But of course after suffering he entered
'into his glory'[14] of a different kind. And if the words of dereliction,
'My God, my God, why hast thou forsaken me?',[15] are to be taken
in any way seriously, Christ's moment of supreme service was a
moment at which he did not in his human mind realize that his suffering had the value it did. I suggest that if we give to being of use
by our suffering or our action, determined or free, the kind of value
which the New Testament suggests that it should have, and if we
accept the other claims of Christian revelation (e.g. about free will
and life after death), the comparative condition is met. Each life,
animal and human (given life after death for the latter), is a good
life—whether its goodness comes from pleasure or service; and
every bad state facilitates a great enough good—often in terms of
pleasure and much else good for others.

The reader will be sympathetic to the theodicy if he or she thinks
that it matters more—a lot more—that we should be good people
than that we should be happy people, though by far the best state
of all is that we should be both; and that while pleasure is a good,
generosity is a greater good; and that while pain is in itself bad,
being allowed to suffer to allow others to exercise higher-order
goods is a privilege which outweighs that bad. A loving God will
give: like a loving parent, he will make his younger children be useful; and he will allow his older children freely to choose whether to
be useful. And he will provide an abundance of opportunities for
cooperative mutual benefit both in providing tingles of first-order

[13] Essay on 'Friendship'.   [14] Luke 24: 26.   [15] Matt. 27: 46.

pleasure as well as the effort of second-order generosity. The dark spots of bad give opportunities for particular kinds of good.

The Primary Point of Life

It remains the case, however, that bad is bad, and there is a substantial price to pay for the goods of our world. God would not be less than perfectly good if he created instead a world without pain and other suffering, and so without the particular goods which they make possible. While permitting suffering for the sake of a greater good does have its point, this is the sort of thing a parent or a king dedicated to the happiness of his subjects would do only temporarily and for some subjects. It would be getting sacrifice out of proportion to let it rip uncontrolled, saying 'If it serves a good, the more the better'. I have argued previously that God has the right to allow individuals to suffer only for a limited duration. If that is so, I cannot see that he does not have the right to allow an unending stream of individuals each to suffer for a limited duration. I suggest, however, that it is a good which God, as perfectly good, would seek to ensure—that the total should be of limited duration. This exercise with animals and humans should have finite limits. Christianity at its beginning firmly taught, and later Christian teaching (Catholic, Orthodox, and Protestant) has continued to teach, that this whole world-order in which there is suffering on Earth is due to come to an end. This world-order is a very dangerous and costly experiment which its author might be expected to bring to a halt one day. Although the divine time-scale is longer than we readily grasp, the goodness of an end to the experiment remains. And of course in the last thirty years physical cosmology has come to teach that probably the world will end in a finite time, even if God does not intervene to bring it about earlier, through natural causes, either in the cold dark of a dying universe or in the Big Crunch. That it will end does not of course serve by itself to justify the experiment in the first place, but again it does mean that its bad states are limited ones.

Neither the New Testament nor subsequent Christian doctrine contain more than parts of a full-blown theodicy and hints on how to construct one—hints which I hope I am taking into my own construction. Subsequent Christian theology has usually given the central place in its theodicies to the 'free-will defence', the virtual inevitability of wrongdoing and suffering if humans are to have the great good of free and efficacious choice. I follow the tradition in this central respect. I think that some Christian tradition has overemphasized the role of the Fall (see pp. 108–10), and under-emphasized the great good of being of service. And, as I pointed out in Chapter 2, the point made most firmly of all at many places in the New Testament is the point just made about the temporary nature of anything bad which is not the result of free choice. It has been allowed to occur by God, the New Testament always emphasizes, for some good purpose (not always mentioned), temporarily. The New Testament writers saw the healing miracles of Jesus and his disciples as a sign that the good purposes served by natural evil were being fulfilled, and the natural evil was coming to an end.[16]

And for its individual inhabitants too this world is temporary. Although what humans and animals do and suffer in it is very impor-tant in itself, quite apart from its consequences, nevertheless, the Christian tradition also firmly teaches, the primary point of (at any rate, human) life in this world is the next world. The primary point of the creation of the human race is to give it the vision of God out-lined in Chapter 6. Given the availability of life after death of this kind, the bad states of frustrated desire for immortality and the vision of God, and the other bad states this world contains, need only be temporary; and will be only temporary for those humans who choose to seek this vision on this Earth. A major task for theodicy is, then, the task of justifying the vision not being given immediately, and my Chapter 11 sought to provide the theodicy for that—to show that it was good that the choice be affirmed over the course of a life, possibly through our reaction to suffering. The alternative to Heaven, Hell, is primarily damnation (the supreme penalty of *damnum*, the permanent 'loss' of the vision of God). I have argued earlier that it is good that free agents should have the choice of finally rejecting the good, and so God and all that he stands for. But that of course is not what God seeks for us. He seeks to take us to himself in Heaven, a marvellous world with a vast range of possible deep goods, but one lacking a few goods which our world contains, including the good of being able to choose to reject the good.

<hr>

[16] Luke 10: 17–18.

The great goods of Heaven, as pictured in the Christian tradition, include that deep awareness of God which, combined with even moderately good desires, logically rules out any of its inhabitants having the good of being able to choose to reject the good. This deep awareness is an awareness of the ultimate source of things, the perfectly good, loving, and beautiful God to whom the Blessed cannot but respond in worship. There are so many different ways of worship open to them. Cooperative worship is depicted as the primary activity of the Blessed in the one book of the New Testament which gives much attention to their fate. The Blessed share in the divine life of God; but they also share in the divine work of God. The citation which I give from the Book of Revelation, at the beginning of my Chapter 6, describes them as 'reigning' for ever and ever. There is no end to possible good states: there can be more creatures; they can be given more powers, more knowledge, more choices. And the Blessed can help in the work of love in forwarding these good states for themselves and others (including others still on this Earth). They could have a choice between so many alternative good actions— between equal-best actions, or, perhaps for them as not for us on Earth,[17] a choice between an infinite number of good actions, each one less good than some other action they could do. The range of free choice open to the Blessed could be enormous compared with the range of choice open to us on Earth.

A generous God might well choose to give some of us the choice of rejecting the good in a world like ours, before giving to those who accept it a wonderful world in which that possibility no longer exists.

---

[17] We saw in Ch. 5 n. 4 that a being who has power unlimited in some respect may have a choice of an infinite number of actions, each one less good than some other action. For such a being there is no best or equal best action. God is in this situation, for his power is unlimited in all respects; we humans on Earth are not in this situation, for our power is limited in all respects. But maybe God gives the Blessed unlimited power in some respect (e.g. to create as many atoms as they choose; or to paint as large a picture, or sing as long a song as they choose). For the Eastern Orthodox tradition Heaven involves 'deification'. By 'deification', as I noted earlier, the early Fathers simply meant in some way coming to share the divine life. But for St Maximus the Confessor, whose championing of this notion led to its prevalence in the Orthodox tradition, deification meant 'becoming all that God is, except for an identity in essence' (Maximus, *Book of Antiquities*, 41; PG 91: 1308). A natural way of interpreting this is to say that the Blessed are—not by nature, but by God's grace—omnipotent, omniscient, and perfectly good. The Blessed would then have powers unlimited in all respects. But for them, as for God, omnipotence would be constrained by perfect goodness, so that it would only be exercised in ways compatible with other agents doing what is good for them to do.

Additional Notes

1. [Note 1 to Chapter 1.] For a full spelling-out of what is involved in this understanding, see my *The Coherence of Theism*, rev. edn. (Clarendon Press, 1993). All theologians of the Western church from the fourth century until the fifteenth century AD, and most of them thereafter, assume or state explicitly that God is eternal in the sense that he exists outside time. On this view, to speak strictly, God does not exist now and did not exist yesterday and will not exist tomorrow; he just exists in his own timeless moment. By contrast all the biblical writers, almost all theologians of the first three centuries, some Western theologians of the last few centuries, and (without giving much attention to the issue) most Eastern Orthodox theologians of all centuries seem to assume that God is in time: he exists at all moments of time past, present, and future; God is eternal only in the sense that he exists everlastingly. For reasons given in *The Coherence of Theism* I prefer the latter view and in general assume it in this book. It makes no difference to the main argument of the present book which view is adopted, but it would affect the way in which the argument would need to be expressed at one or two places, if we took the 'timelessness' view. For example, the limit on God's omniscience, that he cannot know what is logically impossible for him to know, would not rule out his knowledge of the (to us) future actions of free agents. For no actions would be future from God's timeless perspective. That would have the consequence that the argument in the main body of Chapter 7 against the possibility of 'middle knowledge' would need to be expressed in the way presented in Additional Note 5 below.

   The Christian understanding of God is more complicated than the general Western understanding (i.e. that common to Christianity, Judaism, and Islam), in that it conceives of God as 'three persons' in one substance, and that in my view involves these being three persons, each with the cited divine properties. (See my *The Christian God* (Clarendon Press, 1994).) But since those persons always act together, that makes no difference to the issues to be discussed in this book; and so I operate herein with the simpler general Western understanding.

2. [Note 15 to Chapter 4.] The distinction between pleasure and pain, the satisfaction and non-satisfaction of desire, and a wider conception of good and bad states which include these underlies the distinction between three kinds of utilitarianism. Hedonistic utilitarianism states

that actions are good in so far as they maximize pleasure and minimize pain. Preference utilitarianism states that actions are good in so far as they maximize 'preferences', which is plausibly interpreted as maximizing the satisfaction of desires (including, but not confined to, desires to maximize pleasure and minimize pain). Ideal utilitarianism states that actions are good in so far as they maximize the states which people would choose if they had perfect information, strong will, settled preferences, etc. But that—according to how it is developed—could turn out to be no different from the doctrine which states that actions are good in so far as they maximize good states and minimize bad ones, which is the general form of consequentialism (that actions are good or bad solely in virtue of their consequences). Now clearly the goodness of its consequences makes for the goodness of an action, and the badness of its consequences makes for its badness. But I side with the anti-consequentialist in holding that other considerations are also important in determining the goodness or badness of actions; for example, lying and some forms of deception are bad, independently of any good consequences they might have. I defend this view at various places in the book.

3. [Note 3 to Chapter 5.] In thus tying believing an action to be good to having some inclination to do it, I take an internalist realist view of morality. One alternative to this is moral externalism, the view that believing an action to be morally good, just like believing an action to have any other property such as causing pain or giving pleasure, has to be combined with some desire to do an action with that property (and whether a person has such a desire is a contingent matter) before it inclines us to act. The other alternative is moral internalist anti-realism: the view that 'believing' an action to be good is simply being inclined to do it (or approve it, or act in some other way with respect to it) without holding a belief in any literal sense. Internalist realism about morality seeks to combine the positive insights of the two approaches to moral philosophy which have characterized the last fifty years. One of these is the approach of such theories as emotivism and prescriptivism: that holding a moral 'belief' is really doing something or at least being inclined to do something—express an emotion or act in some way and recommend others to do so. Internalist realism about morality accepts that an inclination to act is involved in moral 'belief'. But it also accepts the positive insight of such theories as naturalism and intuitionism that there are moral truths, and so that 'beliefs' about what is morally good or bad really are beliefs which are true or false. To deny that there are moral truths seems immensely implausible. What can be more obvious than that it really is morally good to feed the starving and morally bad to torture just for fun? But then I suggest that there would be no

intelligible content to the claim that some action is morally good unless
that claim involved the claim that there was a reason for doing the action.
And if someone believes that there is a reason for doing some action,
other things being equal that gives him some inclination to do it.

Among internalist realists about morality are Richard Price, *A
Review of the Principal Questions of Morals* (3rd edn., 1787), ed. D. D.
Raphael (Clarendon Press, 1974); and W. D. Falk, *Ought, Reasons, and
Morality* (Cornell University Press, 1986), ch. 1. For recent full dis-
cussions of rival viewpoints see D. O. Brink, *Moral Realism and the
Foundations of Ethics* (Cambridge University Press, 1989), ch. 3; and
Michael Smith, *The Moral Problem* (Blackwell, 1994).

4. [Note 13 to Chapter 7.] Plantinga thus affirms (see *God, Freedom and
Evil* (George Allen & Unwin, 1974), 65–73) (given that God's essential
omniscience includes knowledge of the truth-value of all propositions
about the future) that:

   (1) God existed at t_1, and God believed at t_1 that Jones would do X
   at t_2, and it was within Jones's power to refrain from doing X at
   t_2

entails only

   (2) It was within Jones's power [at t_2] to do something such that, if
   he had done it, then a belief that God did hold at t_1 would have
   been false

but not

   (3) It was within Jones's power at t_2 to do something that would have
   brought it about that God had a false belief at t_1.

The difference between (2) and (3) is this. (2) says only that, if Jones did
a certain action at t_2 and God's beliefs remained the same, then one of
them would be false. Plantinga accepts that, because he thinks which
action Jones does makes a difference to which beliefs God has (not just
to whether the ones he has are true). (3) claims that if Jones does a certain action, then one of God's beliefs will be false—no further qualifications. But, given my argument in the text that no action at t_2 can make
a difference to which beliefs God has at t_1, then (2) and (3) are equivalent. So (1) entails (3). God cannot have incorrigibly true beliefs today
about what creatures will do freely tomorrow.

5. [Note 14 to Chapter 7.] The argument in the text against the possibility
of God having incorrigible middle knowledge worked with the assumption that God is in time. It argued that he cannot have essential foreknowledge of actual free actions, and so *a fortiori* of the free actions
agents would do in various unrealized circumstances. If we think of
God as outside time, strictly speaking, God would not *fore*know any-

thing; for he would not exist before (or simultaneous with, or after) our actions. He would simply exist and know everything in one timeless moment. In that case Pike's argument cannot be deployed, and I see no reason why God cannot know the actions which agents will do freely at times (to us) future. Just as we are no less free for the fact that someone after our actions knows what we have done, so we would be no less free for God seeing in his timeless moment what we do.

Middle knowledge, however, would still be impossible. For if there is to be a necessary correlation between what agents do and what God believes about what agents do, it must be sustained either by the actions of agents causing God's beliefs, or by God causing the actions of agents, or by God's beliefs and the actions of agents having a common cause. But if the agents have libertarian freedom, nothing causes them to act as they do; and so the last two alternatives are ruled out. So the correlation can only be sustained by the actions of agents causing God's beliefs. But while the actual free actions of agents may cause the beliefs of a timeless God and so be compatible with his essential omniscience, what does not happen can cause nothing. The possible but non-occurrent actions of actual agents, and the possible but non-occurrent actions of never-to-be-actualized agents can cause nothing. So God cannot know incorrigibly the truth of counterfactuals of freedom; nor can there ever be a stage at which he knows incorrigibly what would happen if he were to create a certain sort of world containing free agents. God cannot have incorrigible middle knowledge, and so ever be in a position to choose to create a world in which, he knows incorrigibly, free agents will always choose the good.

I do not, however, think that any sense can be made of the supposition that God is outside time. (For argument on this, see my *The Coherence of Theism*, rev. edn. (Clarendon Press, 1993), 223–9.) It follows, given Pike's argument, that God's knowledge at any time of all that it is logically possible to know at that time does not include the future actions of free agents. On all this, see my *The Coherence of Theism*, ch. 10, and *The Christian God*, 131–4. This is certainly not a traditional view in post-biblical theology, but it does have certain roots in the Old and New Testaments; see *The Coherence of Theism*, ch. 10. A very interesting paragraph in a second- (or maybe third-)century AD theological work which discusses Plantinga's problem is *The Clementine Recognitions*, 4. 24. The author considers the objection that God ought 'not to have created those who, he foresaw, would deviate from the path of righteousness'. The author's answer is that if God 'had been afraid of the wickedness of those who were to be', he would be 'like one who could find no other way of remedy or cure, except only this, that he should refrain from his purpose of creating, lest the wickedness of those who were to be should be ascribed to him'. This implies that God's foreknowledge is not absolute and that in creating those likely to 'deviate from the path of righteousness', he acts in hope of being able to 'cure' them.

6. [Note 3 to Chapter 8.] In recent years John Hick has championed a theodicy which sees the value of suffering in its providing the opportunity for humans freely to develop their character; the Earth is a 'vale of soul-making'. See his *Evil and the God of Love* (Macmillan, 1966), pt. 4. He rightly finds a source for this in the writings of Irenaeus. But Irenaeus seems to think that God could not have made humans perfect from the beginning; humans when first created were inevitably weak and vulnerable. He writes, somewhat paradoxically, that 'it was possible for God himself to have made man perfect from the first, but man could not receive this [perfection], being as yet an infant' (*Adversus Haereses*, 4. 38. 1). I cannot see why God could not have made man perfect from the first, but I am arguing that it is good that humans have the opportunity to choose freely over a significant period whether or not to become perfect. Hick wants to claim that in the end we shall all through our own free choices become perfect: 'it seems morally (although still not logically) impossible that the infinite resourcefulness of infinite love working in unlimited time should be eternally frustrated, and the creature reject its own good, presented to it in an endless range of ways' (p. 380). Maybe. If God always refuses to take no for an answer, we shall yield in the end. Yet if God is to give someone real freedom to reject him, he must after a finite time take no for an answer. To give us the choice to reject God, but never to allow that choice to be permanently executed, is not to give us a real choice at all.

7. [Note 21 to Chapter 11.] Against this line of argument, John Schellenberg has (*Divine Hiddenness and Human Reason* (Cornell University Press, 1993), ch. 7) a number of brief points. He claims (pp. 198–9) that, given the deep responsibilities humans already have for future generations, God would not as well give us the further responsibility for ensuring that they know about God. 'A loving God', he writes (p. 199), 'would not give anyone the opportunity to put others in a position where neither explicit acceptance nor explicit rejection is possible. God, if he exists, is concerned to make it possible for each human being, at all times at which she or he exists and is capable, to be personally related to himself.' I believe that, with some exceptions, everyone has the opportunity over life to form their character for good or ill. They may not have reason to believe that there is a God. But if they have formed their character for good, they will have a natural propensity to show gratitude and respect when it is due, and so be ready to worship their creator, if they learn of his existence. They may not have that

opportunity until after death, but I see no adequate grounds for supposing that God would ensure that they have it at every moment of
time, in view of the benefits which flow from their not having it for some
time. (As for the 'some exceptions', clearly the afterlife is needed, either
for them to form their character finally or to allow God to impose upon
those who have not formed a character at all a good one.)

If missionary work is a good thing, then, Schellenberg claims (p.
196), missionaries could still have a role in dealing with culpable non-
belief: those who have deceived themselves into believing that there is
no God, without there being any non-culpable believers. So they could.
But if missionary work is a good thing, it would be a pity if it required
wrongdoing to set it off. Schellenberg also suggests (p. 179) that the
goodness of intellectual inquiry into divine matters could be satisfied by
not making any revelation too clear (not making it too clear where and
how God has acted in history, what he has told us about himself and
about ourselves, and how we ought to behave), while leaving his presence fairly evident. But of course these two are clearly connected: if we
already know that there is a God, then it is much more reasonable to
suppose that God would intervene in history, and we require much less
by way of evidence that he has done so. Anyway, it is doubt about God's
existence which leads to most of the temptations to wrongdoing as such
having the force they do—by the previous argument. If we know there
is a God, there is not too much temptation not to find out what in detail
he has told us in revelation about how we should act. Failure to do so is
apt to indicate doubt about whether he really minds about how we act,
i.e. about whether he is perfectly good, i.e. about whether 'God' really
is God.

Index

Lightning Source UK Ltd.
Milton Keynes UK
UKOW04f2345270315

248669UK00001B/12/P

4968016